ERIC DOLPHY:

A Musical Biography and Discography

Eric Dolphy at First International Jazz Festival, Washington, D.C., 31 May–3 June 1962. (Photo by Joe Alper, courtesy Jackie Gibson Alper.)

ERIC DOLPHY:

A Musical Biography and Discography

Revised Edition

by Vladimir Simosko
and Barry Tepperman

A DA CAPO PAPERBACK

ISBN 0-306-80524-3

This Da Capo Press paperback edition of *Eric Dolphy:
A Musical Biography and Discography* is a revised
republication of the first edition published in Washington, D.C.
in 1974. It is reprinted by arrangement with the original
publisher, the Smithsonian Institution Press.

Published by Da Capo Press, Inc.
A Subsidiary of Plenum Publishing Corporation
233 Spring Street, New York, New York 10013

Contents

Foreword

The word *discography* was coined in the 1930s by Charles Delaunay of France to describe his pioneering work in researching jazz recordings, their dates and personnels. It is now commonly applied to research in recordings of all kinds of music.

Jazz discography has traditionally been a thankless pursuit, undertaken not by scholars or researchers, but by lovers of the music and collectors of its recordings, here and abroad—men whose work will surely gain them the gratitude of all future chroniclers of American culture.

It has become commonplace to point out that first serious published appreciation of the American music called jazz came from Europe. By the late 1930s, some American publishers had begun to give a sustained attention to jazz history, biography and criticism. Not so for jazz discography, however—even for the kind of expanded bio-discography represented in this study. Such work has traditionally had to shift for itself, to resort to the backroom mimeograph or offset press for publication, or has had, once again, to find its way to Europe.

We hope that the present volume, published under the auspices of the Smithsonian Institution, will announce the beginning of the end of such neglect, and that other American publishers, private and public, will also begin to find room for discographical scholarship, and that those diligent and devoted men who do such research will receive a recognition long overdue them.

But as those men know well, the final tribute should go to jazz musicians. And that realization brings us to the present volume.

As Messrs. Tepperman and Simosko's study shows, Eric Dolphy was a deeply dedicated musician. He had absorbed the work of his predecessors and had had fruitful associations with several of the most advanced musicians of his time—Charles Mingus, Ornette Coleman, John Coltrane . . . Such a career as his was obviously cut off too

soon by death. And yet not too soon for Eric Dolpy to have participated in some of the most important recordings of the late 1950s and
early 1960s.

Eric Dolphy loved jazz and he loved all music. I once heard him
speak, almost in the same paragraph, of his joyful enthusiasm for the
pioneer clarinetist Jimmy Noone, of his pleasure in Gerald Wilson's
latest recording, and of his discovery of Karlheinz Stockhausen. It
was always a joy to hear him speak of music. And it was a privilege
to hear him play.

Martin Williams
Director of the Jazz Program
Division of Performing Arts
Smithsonian Institution

Preface
to the Second Edition

When Barry Tepperman and I began corresponding in the late 1960s
to collaborate on this study of the musical career and legacy of Eric
Dolphy, little was widely known of the diversity of his contributions.
Not only were many of the recordings, now generally available, then
unissued and completely obscure, but most albums which had already
been issued were out of print and difficult to obtain. Happily, the situation has been reversed, and many of his best recordings are acknow-
leged as jazz classics and relatively available. Also, considerable
previously unavailable material has been issued, if not always on
widely distributed major labels, at least on "collectors' labels" which
can be tracked down by the devotee. Several articles, at least one discography (by Uwe Reichardt, which I have examined), and liner notes
to many of the albums of reissues and new releases, further document
his career and the vitality of his legacy. We like to think our contribution may have assisted in this wider appreciation of the work of this
vital musician. The existence of a Japanese translation (Tokyo: Shobun-
Sha, 1975), a paperback reissue by Da Capo Press (1979), and the invi-
tation to submit an updated version for French translation (resulting
in the present edition), bear testimony to the interest his work attracts.
When we began, Dolphy had been dead less than five years, and his
earliest records (with Chico Hamilton) had been available less than a
decade. The intervening years since publication, the recordings which
have appeared since, and the advantages of hindsight, afford a new
perspective on his work. However, neither I nor Barry (who as a prac-
ticing medical doctor in Florida has been relatively away from music
for the last ten years) feels the need to change most of what had been
expressed.

Our clearer perception of the contributions of the then-obscure Sun
Ra, whose own Saturn label recordings could hardly be found before

the 1970s, would necessitate reevaluation of the whole avant-garde movement of the early 1960s. While Sun Ra's direct influence on John Coltrane is now widely known and his pioneering influence on the development of cross-cultural experimentation is clear, there is no direct evidence of his probable influence on Dolphy's music. Dolphy's personal spiritual quest, perhaps understated in the text as an influence on his musical orientation, his musical curiosity, and his statement that "everything" one hears is an influence, must have also led him to at least explore the enigmatic depths offered by Sun Ra in that period.

Certainly the wealth of "new" recordings on which Dolphy participated which have surfaced in the intervening years, have provided the most significant insights into Dolphy and his work. His best work with Coltrane and Mingus, and with the Third Stream movement, was more than doubled on available releases (especially the material with Coltrane). His own work, with groups he led for concerts and especially TV and radio broadcasts, also emerged in clearer definition, with many brilliant performances added to the discography (or at least "graduating" from the "private tape" category to being issued on lp's). This material only served to reinforce the impressions which were conveyed in our study. Perhaps the most significant new insight resulting from the availability of this new material under Dolphy's leadership was the consistency of his broadcast and televised presentations. His basic repertoire and approach remained unchanged from the several European broadcasts in 1961, through the Gaslight Inn broadcast a year later, to the last radio station recording in Paris a few weeks before he died. On all releases to have surfaced, his energy, vitality and (in his best moments) his transcendent profundity, also remained consistent.

Dolphy's legacy extends to his musical descendants, perhaps most significantly represented by Anthony Braxton's multi-instrumental approach coupled with the energy and power of his improvisations, and by James Newton's emergence as the premier flautist in the new music. Both of these contemporary giants seem to have developed and extended their expressive approaches in ways that might have been similar to Dolphy's if he had lived. The frequency of Dolphy-inspired bass clarinet solos is also a consistent testimony to his influence.

In 1992 a video documentary titled *Eric Dolphy: Last Date* was made by Hans Hylkema and Thierry Bruneau for Akka Volta, consisting of the typical assortment of interviews and stills, plus video clips from Dolphy's TV appearances on 19 November 1961 and with Mingus in April 1964, radically excerpted and often talked-over. While interesting and informative to a point, undoctored footage of Dolphy in performances from these and other known TV broadcasts remains generally unavailable to date. Hence, the ideal video documentary, featuring Dolphy's performances in various contexts without interruptions or voice-overs during the performances, remains to be accomplished.

Most of the revisions in the text are solely concerned with incorporating information on the previously unavailable recordings. Similarly, Tepperman's contribution, the discography, has only been altered by my inserting the new data on recordings, and the addition of timings to the performances, plus a little editorial touching up. Hopefully, more material will continue to surface, including perhaps the video footage of his several TV broadcasts, with his own groups and with Mingus, among others. Now that video profiles of major figures are becoming common, the possibility that most, if not all, the TV appearances Dolphy made may have been preserved indicates potential for a very impressive documentary. The historical and cultural value of such a project would be incalculable.

Vladimir Simosko
Winnipeg
Summer 1992

Preface

This work was begun while I was Curator of the Institute of Jazz Studies at Rutgers University, and has continued in collaboration with Barry Tepperman, who assumed primary responsibility for the annotated catalogue of his recordings. This represents the fullest listing of Eric Dolphy's music we were able to assemble, as of publication. The introductory essay on Eric Dolphy's medium attempts to evaluate his music and his position in jazz. The musical biography, with its focus on events in his musical life, is drawn from the author's correspondence with his parents, Mr. Eric Dolphy Sr. and Mrs. Sadie Dolphy, and with Richard Davis and Lillian Polen, close personal friends; and from all published information on Eric Dolphy that we could locate, including liner notes to most of the recordings on which he appears. Further remarks and acknowledgments appear in the introduction to the annotated catalogue, under the heading His Recordings.

V. S.
August 1973

Eric in Junior High School. (Photo courtesy Mr. and Mrs. Eric Dolphy Sr.)

Eric Allan Dolphy, Jr.
1928–1964

The two things I remember most about Eric Dolphy were his extraordinary humility toward his art, his fellow artists, and toward the miracle of creation—that, and his unquenchable curiosity to learn, to absorb, to grow. And in that eternal quest—like Mozart, like Keats, like Fats Navarro—he burned himself out at an early age.

For Eric belonged to that select gallery of genuises who know that the more we learn, the more there is left to learn.

He transcended the usual definitions of a classical or jazz musician, a black or white musician. His blackness certainly was never in question, yet he never flaunted his blackness, and with a rare combination of humility and pride he offered his remarkable skills and powers of expression in the service of music and humanity.

He was, in short, one of the most beautiful men that one could, in a lifetime, be privileged to meet, and I consider it a privilege to have loved him.

Gunther Schuller

Eric Dolphy was a saint—in every way, not just in his playing.

Charles Mingus

His Medium

On 27 June 1964, Eric Dolphy arrived in Berlin, Germany, for the opening of a new jazz club, The Tangent, fronting a trio led by the German pianist Karlhans Berger. Dolphy was apparently already seriously ill on his arrival, and by the evening of the club's opening was able to play only two sets before being forced to leave the bandstand. His condition had worsened the next day, and he repeatedly asked friends to take him home. He died in Berlin on 29 June. Joachim Berendt reported in *Down Beat* that doctors at the Berlin Achenbach Hospital had stated that Dolphy was a diabetic who had too much sugar in his bloodstream, and that he had suffered a circulatory collapse; the medical report from Europe attributed death to a heart attack. He was buried in Los Angeles on 9 July.

In an article in the Los Angeles Sentinel for 9 July 1964 an old friend of Eric's, Stanley G. Robinson, said: "Those of us who knew Eric believe that it was [his] driving determination, [his] zest and preoccupation with work, which eventually caught up with Eric and led to his fatal attack." The word spread quickly in the jazz world; the reaction was one of shock, of disbelief and dismay, not only over the loss of "one of the most significant and accomplished musicians associated with the new wave of jazz," but over the loss of a warm, friendly, and highly regarded person. Evaluations in tribute to his character and to his musical personality by friends and musical associates appeared in print; it is revealing to examine some of the more articulate statements. George Avakian's moving eulogy in the magazine *Jazz* is perhaps typical of the remarks about Eric's character:

... perhaps the most important thing about Eric was that he was a fine person, a gentle gentleman of a man, a person whose curiosity about everything led him into every kind of social milieu and whose warm friendliness made him welcome ... In the end, every man is seen as a human being. Brilliant musician that he was, Eric was still greater as a person. He was thoughtful, gracious, and genuinely interested in others.... He knew how to enjoy what came his way, and how to give in return.

3

Elvin Jones was quoted in the 22 August 1964 issue of *Down Beat:*

He was very conscientious and almost meticulous . . . . Although he rarely spoke about his music and what he was striving for, you could see what he was doing. He was just brimming over with ideas all the time. In fact, that was probably his biggest problem . . . he just had too much to say, and this occasionally would get in the way of his saying it.

In the same article, Gunther Schuller stated:

Eric was one of those rare musicians who loved and wanted to understand all music. His musical appetite was voracious, yet discriminating . . . . In time, his full contribution to music will be properly assessed. For now, we can only bemoan the loss of such a powerful musician, who even in his lesser moments never did anything with less than the maximum of intensity and devotion.

There is no doubt that Eric Dolphy was an important figure in jazz history at a time of transition between two stylistic streams, as well as an enormously vital creative musician with one of the most exciting and rewarding musical personalities ever recorded. It is useful, therefore, when considering the recordings left by Dolphy, to keep in mind certain aspects of the trends in jazz which influenced his work and to which it relates, and the nature of jazz as an art form—indeed, the nature of artistic expression itself.

While the motives, methods, and ideas behind art are as varied as the nature of the artistic products themselves, all art shares certain basic features. The work of art is always a compromise between what the artist had in mind, and the limits of his technique and of the medium itself. In this sense, art is both a result of the encounter between the artist and his medium, and an expression of the idea that the artist originally held. The artist is thus seen to be engaged in an intimate dialogue with himself through his art; and revealed in the work is a very personal exposure of his inner self.

It is therefore contrary to the nature of art to be closed, and the artist who attempts to control the intimacy of his work risks emasculating its content. Yet, thorough discipline is required to unify the intended expression in order to present a coherent work.

Most media used by artists allow for a certain amount of revision, yet the very process of revision can often destroy the intimacy of initial reactions and responses. Similarly, most media require a certain amount of time in which to complete the product. But with the passage of more and more time, as consideration and reflection take the place of spontaneity, the sense of immediacy in the execution can fade as detrimentally as it does with too much revision. It is interesting to note that these qualities of spontaneity and immediacy are stressed in Zen Buddhism, one of the most aesthetically oriented of philosophies. Pianist Bill Evans has written of the possible comparison between jazz improvisation and a certain form of Zen painting, in which the artist, working on parchment with brush and ink, creates in such a way that the spontaneous is stressed. Each stroke must carry with it the wealth of experience, discipline, and skill necessary to complete the expression, since the slightest hesitation, faltering of will, falseness of spirit, or uncertainty in execution will spoil the impact of the work.

Music, on the other hand, is not a static art form: it shares with dance and drama the kinetic quality of having time as one dimension of the product, so that it can be understood as an aesthetic unit in retrospect only. As with the other performing arts, timing becomes an essential consideration of the discipline and technique required of the artist. Improvisational music, moreover, requires the artist to create at the instant of impulse, with no possibility of reconsideration or revision. Attention is focused on the initial response. And jazz, unlike even the most necessarily spontaneous act in other media, can possess the additional quality of being an interactive art form, in that generally more than one individual is involved in creation at any one time.

In the jazz group, therefore, we are confronted with the instant and efficient externalization of the moment's precise feelings and ideas, expressed intact in a coordinated physical and spiritual discipline involving intimate interaction among all members of the group. It is not merely a collaboration, but a shared experience. If all participants bring to the act of creation adequate spiritual resources, and psychologically are sufficiently attuned to each other, so that they can respond and participate fully, the success and impact of the encounter is assured. This full synchronization is by no means always possible, and all too often its place may be taken by skill and taste; but this does not lessen the meaning of the act or the validity of the product— it means only that the content of the aesthetic experience is altered.

Examining the aesthetic impact of a group involves cognizance of its approach to jazz, not merely in the sense of what style it might represent—certainly the most superficial aspect of its approach—but rather in terms of the musical philosophy that guides the ensemble in determining and realizing its basic goals as a musical unit. This can range from the polished but spiritually empty artifice of slick commercialism, through the honest expressionism of an authentic artist with real involvement in the creative act and in the vitality of the music, to the brilliant, flashing inspiration of a dynamic innovator—a musical thinker at the moment of discovery.

The innovator in any art form brings to that form the vitality of new insights which can be realized only by altering the previously established manner of expression in his medium. He must be gifted enough to develop new techniques as he works, creating his own disciplines and adding his discoveries to the cultural legacy of his civilization, in an amount dependant upon his influence and impact, on the level of his own depth and vitality.

In jazz, the difficulty of the innovator's task is compounded by the necessity of interacting with other musicians who must be able to respond to his discoveries appropriately. The sideman who is musically a hedonist, or who is either too wrapped up in his own expression or too much of a polished craftsman, will not likely relate readily to the necessity of rethinking his musical orientation. The jazz establishment is as conservative as any other establishment, despite the emphasis of the art form on spontaneous personal expression.

The state of the art within which figures like Eric Dolphy, John Coltrane, Ornette Coleman, and Cecil Taylor developed their innovative stances in the late 1950s and early 1960s may be characterized with reasonable coherence, if oversimply, as "hard bop," the rather extroverted and drivingly emotional reaction to the "cool" jazz which, in the early 1950s, had developed as a restrained offshoot of the bebop revolution of the previous decade.

Bop itself was an earlier manifestation of marked and violent stylistic change within the art form of a dimension similar to the transition represented by these four men. Just as the bop revolution revealed new ways of musical thinking and resulted in the reshaping of the mainstream of stylistic expression to the extent that the musical vocabulary of a whole new generation of jazzmen was largely based on the bop innovations and the personalities of the innovators, so the aesthetic impact of the musical philosophies and innovations unveiled in the late 1950s diverted the stylistic evolution of jazz away from the various approaches within the bop format into entirely new directions of development. Exactly how these four did this, or even the exact nature of what they did accomplish, would be as difficult to define rigorously as jazz itself, or as the nature of art. Nevertheless, a few

6

insights regarding the nature of this phenomenon may be derived from even a superficial examination of the musical thinking that went on, and of the stylistic developments which grew out of this process.

Although Charlie Parker and others, in developing their styles, introduced many much more complex and sophisticated ideas for rhythmic and harmonic contours in improvisation than were present in the jazz that preceded their innovations, few practitioners of the new style managed to absorb and incorporate the full range of possibilities that bop extended. In essence, improvisation was still based on the rhythmic subdivision of the beat, and used the harmonic intervals within the chord given for that particular place in the structure of a given tune. Extension of the chord to include notes not utilized by earlier jazz styles, and of phrasing to transcend both the bar line and the melodic phrases inherent in the tune, were the two most obvious aspects of the generally greater sophistication of the new style. These features gave the soloist greater expressive freedom. The entire solo format had to be altered to fit this new concept, and the roles and techniques of the rhythm section were redefined considerably, primarily to open up the background in various ways to prevent conflict with the soloist's direction.

Fundamentally, however, the rhythm continued to be based on subdivisions of the beat, and the extension of harmonic choices still observed certain limits. In the late 1950s, the new wave of innovators took at least two major directions. One involved abandoning concern with harmony and rhythm as formal boundaries and the other involved in turn an even greater sophistication in dealing with the established forms.

While the former might be said to have been dominated by Ornette Coleman, the latter direction was explored by several musicians—most notably by Cecil Taylor, John Coltrane, and Eric Dolphy. Their concern was with the superimposition of rhythms and chords to expand the potential of improvised expression into totally new dimensions, admitting every note of the scale into tonal consideration in their improvisations, and ultimately even bypassing the chorus as a formal limitation on phrasing. This new order of complexity and sophistication in jazz improvisation was not merely a technical device: as with any innovation in art based on the valid development of existing idioms, the main purpose of the innovators was to expand their personal capacity for expression, and as with all innovators, their departure from the preexisting mode of expression consisted basically of adding to or replacing earlier practices. In this sense, Taylor, Coltrane, and Dolphy were among those who worked with existing idiom toward its fullest development, while, in some respects, Coleman simply transcended it in one elegant step.

In the early 1940s, the recording ban and the time limitations of the 78-rpm record prevented the bop innovators from being as carefully documented throughout their evolution as, in retrospect, one might have wished. Other, later innovators, such as Cecil Taylor and Ornette Coleman, were almost totally unrecorded out of the contexts of the groups they created as vehicles for their own expressions, and on record seem to appear out of a vacuum no matter how early they began recording. Even Dolphy and Coltrane, both of whom were recorded much more often and in a greater variety of contexts at various points in their careers than had Taylor or Coleman, have much of their early development shrouded by lack of exposure on record, and for neither figure can progress as soloist be measured with any definition before their very late 20s. Both reedmen, however, played in varied contexts in their first years of recording, and at about the time they first began to attract attention they were recorded more frequently than later, when their arts had matured further and they were able to place themselves in sympathetic surroundings. Dolphy managed to be recorded nearly every month, and averaged more than that by a good margin, for the two years following his first date as leader in 1960. Prior to 1960, his work had already been accessible for an additional two years from several sessions with Chico Hamilton, with whose group he had spent most of that period.

It is unfortunate for the student of Dolphy's music that his few recording dates prior to his joining Hamilton do not feature his solos extensively, and that copies of these earlier recordings are virtually unobtainable. It is difficult to imagine Dolphy developing as he did on the West Coast in the years when this would have taken place. In spite of the quality of his influences and his associates, the "West Coast sound" in jazz is usually associated with a more restrained, "cool," approach to improvisation rather than with that to be found in any of Dolphy's recordings. Though one or two other musicians developed intense, fiery approaches in that environment, in Dolphy intensity and passion reached a zenith as jagged, leaping, twisting patterns of notes pour forth in a torrent that constantly surprises the listener with unexpected directions and fantastic uses of intervals and phrasing. His hard, clear sound and distinctive attack are unique.

For this reason, his appearance with Hamilton's group was something rather startling to many listeners. The Chico Hamilton Quintet had been together for several years, having first appeared on record in 1955. Hamilton had already had a long and varied career, ranging from a school band that included Charles Mingus and Illinois Jacquet, through stints with Lionel Hampton and Count Basie, backing Lena Horne, functioning as a studio musician at Paramount, and performing notably with Gerry Mulligan's pianoless quartet on its first record date. Hamilton had recorded under his own name as early as 1953, with a trio consisting of himself, George Duvivier—who also provided much of the musical direction of the group—on bass, and guitarist Howard Roberts. Some anticipation of the later quintet was evident in the trio, perhaps partly because some other arrangements for the group had been contributed by Buddy Collette, the multi-reed man on the Quintet's first recordings.

Although the Quintet was obviously related to the West Coast stylistic trends of the early fifties, it was unique in several ways. The light, swinging West Coast sound and the sophisticated arrangements that were in vogue at the time were hallmarks of the Quintet, but these were performed by an instrumentation which, in an era of experimentation with "chamber jazz" and with woodwind instruments from chamber groups, went even further, to comprise cello, guitar, bass, drums, and a reed player doubling on saxophones, flute, and clarinet. This instrumentation permitted excursions into realms of tone colors and effects often accused of being affiliated with commercial-studio mood music, but which really had much more in common with the Third Stream movement which attempted to fuse "classical" music and jazz. While the group would frequently perform completely scored pieces, ranging from very attractive tone poems to interestingly arranged standards, there was usually a great deal of interplay with jazz and a well-contrived transition into strong jazz solos; many other selections from the Quintet's repertoire, of course, were straightforward jazz pieces, given unusual coloring by the instrumentation. To many listeners, the group was a unique and stimulating musical experience, distinguished usually by both depth and good taste. The success, both musically and commercially, of the group in the jazz world encouraged Hamilton to preserve the format as his usual working unit for about five years.

The group's conceptions and approach remained stable in spite of a number of personnel changes. Perhaps this stability in the face of change accounts for the fact that the most consistently satisfying of the Quintet's recordings are those from the earlier dates with Collette, who was responsible for much of the musical flavor. Indeed, the most important changes were in the reeds, since theirs was the prominent voice, and a different personality in such a dominant role results in a significant alteration in group sound. For a while, Paul Horn filled the role admirably with a style basically similar to that of Collette, but without quite the blending of improvisation and ensemble style, the balance of musical personality and format, that gave the earlier edition such vitality.

The presence of so strong a personality as Eric Dolphy altered the net effect of the group's music considerably. His stronger attack and volcanic improvisations gave the Quintet an edge of excitement not present earlier. But while the virility and passion of his approach differed markedly from the more restrained approach of his predecessors, it did not clash with the basic group sound. Dolphy's ability to provide soaring flights of lyrical beauty or to blend smoothly in the ensemble voicings proved a contrast to his flashing solo work that lent an additional vitality to the unit's performances.

In his long article on Dolphy's career (in the January 1966 *Jazz Monthly*), Jack Cooke defines the basic elements of Eric's style as "fragmentation, decoration, and a very direct emotionalism." Elaborating on this statement, he makes the point that "the random selection of phrases, the use of fragmented melody and what is often a shifting emotional foundation have given to his best solos a highly ornate quality that both complements and offsets the direct and powerful impact of the central ideas."

The careful listener would object, however, to the unqualified use of the term "random," or to the later implication that Dolphy's solos are not logical. In fact, the seemingly random and fragmented aspects of the immediate impression of a solo by Dolphy result from a highly sophisticated sense of timing which does not conform to the expected patterns of jazz phrasing. In spite of the groundwork in this direction laid by such individuals as Thelonious Monk and Sonny Rollins, Dolphy's work took most listeners completely by surprise. Most of Dolphy's recorded solos are in fact highly logical and coherent, and he was far less likely to fall into true free association than are many of his followers. In a statement made in 1960 about his conceptions, Dolphy said, "I think of my playing as tonal. I play notes that would not ordinarily be said to be in a given key, but I hear them as proper.

I don't think I 'leave the changes' as the expression goes; every note I play has some reference to the chords of the piece."

The "shifting emotional foundation" is an apt description of the nature of many recorded examples of his work, and is one of the reasons that his music is so impressive. Movement from one feeling to another is often apparently random and fragmented, yet in fact is as logical and coherent as his phrasing. This richness of content and complexity of expression is delivered with an enthusiasm and a passion that is nearly overwhelming. The overall impression is that of exuberance and of joy in life, often stemming from the astonishing ease with which he delivers the most complex technical passages. On the rare occasions when he fails to reach some astronomically high note, or unintentionally stutters or squawks, it sounds like the result of too much trying to tumble out at once, and the failure frequently adds to the impact of the phrase in the context of the solo as a unit.

Cooke's comment on ornamentation is not totally ungrounded; indeed, as he wrote of Dolphy: "His music uses decoration as an essential . . . his music is full of little elegances, complex note patterns used in a line to embellish the central statement rather than to advance it at all." This should not be understood, however, as describing the presence of superfluity in Dolphy's music. It is clear from the context that this ornamentation is neither mere "fill" nor exhibitionism, and it would be missing the point to try to derive a dialectical appreciation of Dolphy's music by opposing ornamentation with direct emotional statement. Although it seems at times that Eric defines an idea by surrounding it with notes to give it form, this is quite different from gratuitous embellishment, and few examples of digression appear in his music. Eric Dolphy was a musician of such talent and virtuosity that he could complete his ideas without understatement. These gushing storms of solos result from the expression in their totality of all facets of the concept he is presenting. Instead of the emphasis on subtle innuendos or the precisely defined statements of most jazz artists up to that time, the careful listener will discover in Dolphy's art a unique experience in texture that may be correlated more readily to the musics of other cultures (e.g., India) than to most of the earlier heritage of jazz.

There is no doubt that Dolphy's music was widely influenced by non-jazz sources, not only in textural conception, but in specific concepts of harmony and rhythm as well. Dolphy, a well-schooled musician, was certainly more than passingly familiar with the tonalities

11

being experimented with by avant-garde composers. This is amply demonstrated by his work with Gunther Schuller and with the Orchestra U.S.A. (who presented contemporary "classical" works as well as jazz and Third Stream compositions in their programs), and by his frequent attendance at concerts of all types of music. His performance at the Ojai Music Festival of Varese's *Density 21.5*, a piece exploring the sound potentials of the flute, and his naming of a composition for the remarkable Italian flautist Severino Gazzeloni (of whom *Time* wrote: "After several years of experiment, he developed [a new flute technique] that permits him to cacophonize like an electronic menagerie") are actions that testify to Dolphy's knowledge of much of the most advanced work for flute created in Western culture by the middle of the twentieth century.

Dolphy's flute work actually exhibits some very direct references to contemporary classical music. For example, the opening and closing passages of one of his most remarkable recorded flute performances, *You Don't Know What Love Is* (2 June 1964), bear strong resemblance to passages for flute in Heitor Villa-Lobos' *Bachianas Brasilieras No. 6* (1938) for flute and bassoon, and the tone and mood of the Villa-Lobos piece is echoed, perhaps only coincidentally, in Dolphy's duet with bassist Chuck Israels on *Hi-Fly* (8 September 1961). There the resemblance ends, for the *Bachianas Brasilieras* are based on the fugue form of Bach, while the form used by Dolphy in these performances is a very intricate theme-and-variations pattern. It is nevertheless quite likely that Dolphy would have been familiar with the Villa-Lobos composition.

To speculate as to whether such parallels are intentional or subliminal is of little consequence. As Dolphy stated to Robert Levin (liner notes to Prestige PR7304), "Everything affects you. Every musician I've ever heard has influenced me." And Levin comments further, "In conversations with Eric, Schoenberg is a name that will come up frequently. And he has been especially struck by the music of Africa ('the singing of the pygmies') and of India (Ravi Shankar)." As George Avakian has written, "He read books, analysed records and scores; he had recently latched on to Erik Satie, whose pungent wit entranced him."

The sounds of nature were also more or less direct influences on Dolphy's style. The singing of birds was one of the most direct. Don DeMichael quoted Dolphy at length on this point (*Down Beat*, 12 April 1962):

It somehow comes in as part of the development of what I'm doing. Sometimes I can't do it. At home (in California) I used to play, and the birds always used to whistle with me. I would stop what I was working on and play with the birds . . . . Birds have notes in between our notes—you try to imitate something they do and, like, maybe it's between F and F-sharp, and you'll have to go up or come down on the pitch . . . Indian music has something of the same quality—different scales and quarter tones.

The influence of non-Western musics, and particularly of Indian music, on the arts of Coltrane and Dolphy is widely recognized. Not only were they affected by the scales and quarter tones of the Raga structure, but also by the philosophy behind Indian classical music and the Indian concepts of performance. When Shankar toured the United States in 1957, he noted that many jazzmen attended his performances and asked questions. The results of this attention may account for the wider response to Shankar's tour in 1964; and, of course, the adoption shortly afterward of a few superficial aspects of Indian music by pop musicians brought about a great fad in the late 1960s for the music and philosophy of India. The effects of this earlier exposure were, however, anything but superficial on serious jazzmen like Dolphy, the textures of whose solos (as previously noted) indicate the influence of this encounter. Eric stated in this regard.

I've talked with Ravi Shankar and I see how we can incorporate their ideas . . . Indian music sounds to us like one minor chord; they call it a Raga or scale and they'll play on one for twenty minutes . . . it's a challenge to play a long time on just one or two chords.

Another distinctive element of Dolphy's style is his highly personal approach to the use of speech-like cadences and inflections in his improvisation. Of course, there is nothing new in this practice in jazz. The Original Dixieland Jazz Band used such effects on one of the earliest recognized recorded jazz performances, and Bubber Miley, bringing this technique to Ellington's music, began a tradition extending most notably through "Tricky Sam" Nanton and Cootie Williams. Although Eric made use of this technique to some degree on all his instruments, it is particularly effective and startling on bass clarinet, perhaps as much because the instrument was generally neglected in jazz before Dolphy revealed its potential (Herbie Mann, in the days before he turned exclusively to flute, was one of the few musicians to have worked regularly with the horn), as because of anything unique in this stylistic incorporation. Although touches of vocalization in his approach appear throughout his work, it is in his recordings with Charles Mingus that his two most intense uses of this element are to be found—*What Love* (20 October 1960), and *Epitaph I* (12 October 1962)—where extended, conversationally phrased, out-of-tempo exchanges take place between Dolphy (on bass clarinet in the first example and on alto saxophone in the second) and Mingus on bass, as highly effective suspensions within the structure of the compositions.

In many respects, Dolphy's performances with Mingus produced the most fully realized pieces of music in the careers of both men. To Mingus' compositions, Dolphy brought a depth, intensity, and versatility of approach unmatched by any other soloist to have recorded with Mingus. For Dolphy, Mingus provided a compositional framework which utilized his talents fully, and supplied the stimulus and musical freedom to allow the reedman's expressive potential to develop.

Charles Mingus could easily be considered the most important jazz composer since Ellington, by whom he was, of course, enormously influenced. Because of the eclectic nature of his compositions, drawing from gospel, early jazz styles, and contemporary classical influences, in addition to Ellington and bop, and all strongly flavored by the composer's unique personality and powerful ideas, few soloists could convincingly complement a backdrop of his creation.

Since Mingus and Dolphy had played together while Dolphy was still a high school student (Mingus was quoted in 1960 as stating, "He [Dolphy] played the style he does now in high school . . . we used to play that way with Lloyd Reese."), it is in some ways surprising that the two never met on record before 1960. Mingus had begun recording under his own name, though sporadically and for obscure labels, in 1946, and worked mainly as a bassist with, among others, such figures as Illinois Jacquet, Lionel Hampton, and Red Norvo (in the trio featuring Tal Farlow on guitar), before beginning to record his own compositions with his own groups regularly, in the mid-1950s.

It has been suggested that Mingus may have written pieces conceived as vehicles for Dolphy prior to the beginning of their long association in 1960. Mingus states in the liner notes to his recording *"Mingus at Monterey,"* that *"Orange Was the Color of Her Dress* was originally written as a three-horned thing with Eric Dolphy," and it might be held that since this piece was originally composed in the late 1950s as part of the score for the CBS television production of the play "A Song With Orange in It," this would imply that Mingus was seriously considering the saxophonist for a role in his band considerably earlier than their coming together for their tenure at the Showplace. This evidence of intention is, however, countered by the fact that a 1963 version of the same piece ("*Mingus Plays Piano*," on Impulse) is identified as a revision of part of this score. Further, the piece *Song with Orange*, also from this play, bears little resemblance as originally recorded ("*Mingus Dynasty*," 1959) to versions of *Orange was the Color of Her Dress* performed during Mingus' European tour of April 1964; this last was, indeed, a three-horn arrangement, and the statement in question may have referred specifically to this later version only. Furthermore, contact between Mingus and Dolphy prior to the latter's settling in New York seems to have been superficial, according to some who knew them, and not very extensive.

In any event, the recordings finally made by Mingus and Dolphy together during their 1960 association are among the finest selections on record by either artist. The chaotic April 1964 tour, which was apparently taped nearly everywhere the Mingus Jazz Workshop performed, produced several of the most moving versions of one of Mingus' major works, *Meditations*, owing much of their success in these performances to Dolphy's consummate artistry.

Dolphy, for his part, sounds very appropriately placed in the various Mingus units, probably more so than in any other context in his recorded career, with the possible exceptions of the groups he led himself. The saxophonist's affinity for Mingus' compositional style is indisputably a major factor here. In the majority of the other sideman contexts in which he was recorded, Dolphy was disadvantageously situated. Either the compositional frameworks were comparatively formal and inhibitory, as with Hamilton or with the Schuller and Lewis organizations, or the music was more conventional than his style warranted, as in most of the pickup or other sideman dates he made. Even with Coltrane, surely the most spiritually profound association of his career, the modal surroundings imposed limits on the kind of wildly exciting harmonic contrasts his improvisations usually entailed. In most recordings with his own groups, the compositional frameworks seem to set off his solos less impressively, even if no less appropriately, than do Mingus' compositions. After all, Dolphy's own groups and compositions represent an extension of his musical personality quite as revealing, on some levels of interpretation, as his solo work.

Most of Dolphy's recorded compositions are straightforward

themes, usually as harmonically adventurous and rhythmically angular, and often as spread out across the rhythmic foundations of the piece, as his solos themselves. However, if arranged at all, they are not overly concerned with voicings or with complex constructions. Solos are usually based on the themes in conventional bop manner, as strings of choruses over rhythmic and chordal accompaniment. Many compositions are based more or less directly on the blues, and most others follow an AABA form, even if not always thirty-two bars long. Dolphy's melodic lines are often Monk-like in character.

Several of Dolphy's themes were meant only as "heads" on which to blow. That is demonstrated by the fact that those recorded more than once were performed in a similar manner each time, regardless of session instrumentation or personnel or of the time lapse between the various versions. Changes in personnel and significant time intervals between successive recordings of a composition would seem to allow differences in interpretation to appear. But in the pieces recorded under these circumstances—*Les* and *G.W.*, both recorded twice, slightly over a year apart in 1960 and 1961; *Out There* (15 August 1960), rerecorded with changed instrumentation as *Far Cry* (21 December 1960); *Miss Ann*, for which recordings are commercially issued from 1960 and 1964; and *Mandrake* (1963), retitled *The Madrig Speaks, The Panther Walks* (1964)—thematic interpretation is quite consistent.[1]

Similarly, the various existing multiple performances of other tunes resemble each other strongly in melodic interpretation; and in three cases—the remarkable bass clarinet solo *God Bless the Child* (of which four versions are known to survive from 1961), alternate takes of tunes from commercially issued recording sessions, and repeated performances of pieces taped at concerts during the various tours Dolphy made in Europe—strong resemblances persist even in thematic development during the improvisations as well. This is not to be interpreted as suggesting that Dolphy repeated himself in any sense. Rather, he was a consistent performer who brought a strong conception to a particular piece of music. In fact, the superficial course of the solos may vary considerably without indicating any basic changes in conception; this demonstrably occurs as well in compositions other than his own.

That he was capable of composition more sophisticated than this is not well documented on the available recordings. His capacities in this regard may be estimated only by extrapolation from his most complex recorded arrangement, *Burning Spear* (1963), scored for nine pieces; from his arrangements for Coltrane's *"Africa/Brass"* album (1961); from his compositions on the remarkable *"Out to Lunch"* LP (1964); from comments by reviewer Bill Coss about his work with poetess Ree Dragonette; and from Richard Davis' report that Dolphy was at work composing a string quartet at the time of his death. From this last statement, it becomes evident that an entire dimension of Dolphy's musical life never found an outlet, at least beyond his closest circle of friends; Davis said that on his last meeting with Dolphy, they had gone over the score of this string quartet (entitled *Love Suite*) together.

While *"Africa/Brass"* and *Burning Spear* eloquently indicate the kind and quality of extended compositions Dolphy was undoubtedly capable of producing, the fact remains that his musical legacy is composed chiefly of his recorded improvisations. It is also clear from his recorded work as a sideman and from the 22 CD's and lp's issued under his own name as of this writing that this legacy defines an artist of unique versatility and enormously vital spiritual resources.[2]

The fourteen discs under his own leadership are drawn from nine recording sessions. Three of these took place neatly spaced through 1960, the year in which he appeared regularly with Mingus at the Showplace—*"Outward Bound"* (April 1), *"Out There"* (August 15), and *"Far Cry"* (December 21). It is pertinent to review the personnel for each of these sessions in brief, as the musicians' stature and roles are significant in defining Dolphy's career.

All three dates involved the brilliant drummer Roy Haynes, whose work, as documented on record since the 1940s with Charlie Parker and others, continues to grow and impress. Haynes was also present at five additional sessions on which Dolphy appeared as a sideman during the year following *"Outward Bound."* The pianist, when one was required on two of these dates, was Jaki Byard, at that time a member of the excellent Maynard Ferguson orchestra, which also included trumpeter Don Ellis, tenor saxophonist Joe Farrell, and drummer Rufus Jones. Byard later appeared with Dolphy as a member of the Charles Mingus Jazz Workshop unit which toured Europe in April 1964. The spectacular Ron Carter—on bass for *"Far Cry"* and on cello for *"Out There"*—played with Dolphy on several other sessions, ranging from an unissued Chico Hamilton set for Warner Brothers (1959) to the Gil Evans orchestra date of April 1964. Finally, we must consider the particularly extensive and vital musical relationships at the time between Dolphy and the two trumpeters involved in the three 1960 recordings, Freddie Hubbard and Booker Little. Hubbard, just short of 22 years old on the first ("*Outward Bound*") of his several dates with Dolphy, appears subsequently on Coltrane's "*Ole*," Coleman's "*Free Jazz*," and Dolphy's "*Out to Lunch*"; in addition, he used Eric as sideman on his own LP "*Body and Soul*." Booker Little and Dolphy recorded together no less than eleven times during the last year of Little's life, and worked together for a short time in an essentially cooperative quintet of their own.

This quintet was the group recorded "live" by Prestige Records at the Five Spot in New York in July 1961. Pianist Mal Waldron, who had made his reputation as accompanist for Billie Holiday in the last years of her life, and as sideman with Mingus in the late 1950s, had previously worked with Dolphy and Little in Max Roach's group. Bassist Richard Davis, who had emerged from Ahmad Jamal's and Don Shirley's groups and had been on the road with Sarah Vaughan for five years, was to become one of Dolphy's closest friends and musical associates. The quintet was completed by Ed Blackwell, who had come to prominence with Ornette Coleman, and had also participated in the "Free Jazz" date. Over a period of several years, seven albums in all have been released from three sessions in 1961—this Five Spot date, and a pair of concerts recorded two days apart with a Danish rhythm section in Copenhagen.[3]

Two further LPs, originally produced by Alan Douglas, have so far appeared from sessions taking place over five consecutive nights in the spring of 1963—"*Conversations*" (later retitled "*The Eric Dolphy Memorial Album*") and "*Iron Man*"; and a final two represent Dolphy's work in 1964, "*Out to Lunch*" and "*Last Date*," the latter also using a Scandinavian rhythm section.[4]

Therefore, fully a third of the sessions ultimately issued under Dolphy's name found him using Scandinavian sidemen. Two of the three 1960 sessions and the Five Spot recordings used conventional bop quintet format, with a few quartet tracks here and there, while the "*Out There*" date echoed the Hamilton group by using a cello and eliminating the piano. The 1963 recordings and the 1964 date for Blue Note also omitted piano, but used vibraphonist Bobby Hutcherson on most selections to produce the most fully realized pieces of music to be issued under Dolphy's name.[5]

It is clear that this line-up of trumpet, vibraphone, bass and drums behind Dolphy was no accident, and that the particular flavor emanating from the eight selections released using this instrumentation provides ample aesthetic justification for this choice. Dolphy had worked with this instrumentation previously, and is heard on record with vibraphone on his two albums with the Latin Jazz Quintet, and more notably on *"Jazz Abstractions"*; but his use of the instrument in his own groups was quite different.

By replacing the piano with the vibraphone, Dolphy more purely balanced the families of instruments in the group. Musicologists recognize four basic types of instrument: idiophones, which produce sound by being struck directly; membranophones, which produce sound by means of a struck or rubbed membrane; chordophones, which depend on the vibrations of strings; and aerophones, which produce sound directly by the vibration of air, or of a column of air, as in any wind instrument. Thus, most jazz groups feature only cymbals as an idiophonic device. Replacing the piano with vibraphone provides a tuned idiophone with harmonic potential, balancing the two families of aerophones (reeds and trumpet), chordophone (bass), and membranophones (drums) quite elegantly.

Of course, much of the success of these groups is due to the fine degree of rapport between Dolphy and Hutcherson, whom the reedman had met in California. Hutcherson had played with Charles Lloyd and others, attracting some attention on the West Coast before coming east. Dolphy had heard him in a club where he was working, and suggested that they try playing together. Dolphy was quoted as saying, "Bobby's vibes have a freer, more open sound than a piano. Pianos seem to control you, Bobby's vibes seem to open you up."

Something must also be said in this context of the near-telepathic rapport between Dolphy and Richard Davis on the duet tracks by the two, particularly those duets featuring Dolphy on bass clarinet— *Come Sunday* and *Alone Together*. Davis has stated, "He and I would often rehearse together, just the two of us," and these pieces are indisputably the high points of a close musical and personal relationship that can be traced on record back to the 1961 Five Spot recordings and forward to the Andrew Hill session shortly before Dolphy left for Europe with Mingus.

Precedents for these duets exist in *Hi Fly*, recorded with bassist Chuck Israels in 1961; in the "conversations" with Mingus mentioned earlier; and, notably, in improvised work with Scott LaFaro on the album *"Jazz Abstractions."* In addition, during the April 1964 tour a flute-bass dialogue passage formed a major part of most concert performances of *Meditations,* and at at least two concerts whole tunes were performed as duets.

Dolphy's work with John Coltrane, along with his association with Mingus, one of the most spiritually vital musical relationships of his career, is rather more poorly documented on commercial recordings than his tenure with Mingus—nearly as weakly represented as the true extent of his work with the Third Stream movement. Apart from his arrangements for brass on Coltrane's "*Africa / Brass*" album, and his performances at the augmented quintet date that produced "*Ole,*" only two titles from the Village Vanguard sets, and the limited edition pirate concert recordings from the November 1961 European tour (Historic Performance HPLP's 1 and 5), have been commercially released. It is fortunate that private tapes, from the quintet's tour and from a February 1962 radio broadcast at Birdland, which was issued on a bootleg LP in Japan, survive and circulate actively among collectors. The Historic Performance LP, HPLP-5, is more representative of the concert repetoire that Coltrane and Dolphy were offering at that time than anything released by the record companies, but achieved limited distribution and is now almost impossible to obtain. Of the commercially available material, only the two selections with Dolphy from the Village Vanguard sets give adequate definition to the enormous significance and depth of this relationship. No recordings either suspected or known to have been made later in their continuing intermittent partnership have surfaced to date. Therefore, one of the most significant musical periods of Dolphy's career is representatively preserved only because the quintet had been taped on several occasions while touring Europe in late 1961, and once further on their return to New York. So little of this group's total recorded output has ever been made readily available commercially that access to these private recordings is essential to a real comprehension of their work together.[6]

The one remaining long-term musical association at all represented on record, Dolphy's affiliation with the group of musicians involved with the Third Stream, had at its focus the aggregations led by Gunther Schuller and John Lewis. These men were early supporters of Dolphy, who had proved in his work with Chico Hamilton that he was more than capable in performing in an atmosphere of sophisticated arrangements. Dolphy was featured extensively when Schuller unveiled a new group of compositions in concert at the Circle in the Square in May 1960. Two of these compositions make up much of

Schuller's "*Jazz Abstractions*" LP (December 1960), and remain among the most successful Third Stream efforts to appear on record. Dolphy later continued to appear in concerts of this nature, and performed on several highly orchestrated recording dates with John Lewis and, later, with Orchestra U.S.A. ("*Debut,*" 1963). In 1964, he was featured with the Sextet of Orchestra U.S.A. on one side of an album of Kurt Weill compositions given jazz treatment, and made one of his rare appearances on film when he performed in Schuller's *Journey into Jazz* at one of Leonard Bernstein's Young People's Concerts, televised in March 1964 and later marketed as film and videotape by McGraw-Hill. Unfortunately, most of these recordings are less than fully successful, and frequently Dolphy is not featured at all. Only "*Jazz Abstractions*" gives good evidence of his potential role in the music.

Something more of Eric's value in these experiments may be surmised from an album recorded after his death, including pieces written in 1962 which had featured him in performance. The LP, entitled "*Dedicated To Dolphy*" (Cambridge Records CRS1820), contains two fascinating tracks, *Night Music* and *Densities I*, both by Schuller, in these instances featuring Bill Smith (on bass clarinet and clarinet, respectively) in Dolphy's role. These are quiet, chamber-like pieces, in very modern compositional style emphasizing textures and tonal colors, but the former builds to a solid improvisational climax. Although Smith performs admirably, the music obviously sounds differently, and affects the listener differently, than as if Dolphy had been the performer; without him, these are different pieces of music.[7]

Most of the records on which Dolphy performs as sideman are strongly affected by his presence if he is featured at all. Apart from the long-term working affiliations documented on record as described above, shorter-term affiliations developed in the period 1960–61 with Oliver Nelson, who used Dolphy on three similar bop-rooted sets and in his orchestra behind Eddie "Lockjaw" Davis; and with Max Roach, whose working unit had included Booker Little during the period of Dolphy's collaboration with the trumpeter. This association is documented on record by the sessions producing Abbey Lincoln's "*Straight Ahead*" (22 February 1961), Little's "*Out Front*" (March and April 1961), and Roach's own "*Percussion Bitter Sweet*" (August 1961). All three albums share a similar personnel and certain advanced concepts of composition and voicing.

Apart from these basic relationships, there are few anomalous sessions in the discography. The Ken McIntyre and Latin Jazz Quintet dates for Prestige, a date with a completely different Latin Jazz Quintet for United Artists (dates initiated by the respective companies involved), and the truly unexplained Sammy Davis Jr. recordings (early 1960) with what was essentially the Basie band of the time, are the only sessions which cannot be connected with these few basic long- or short-term associations by one or more common band members in addition to Dolphy. Thus, he usually appeared on record either as sideman with these basic groups, or on dates for other sidemen from these or his own groups, or on dates which share in common one or more sidemen with these or his own groups for recording.

His freelance life can therefore be seen not to have been quite as promiscuous as a casual glance over the discography might imply. In fact, this interrelationship of personnels in the studio may at times seem almost incestuous! Outside the recording studio he indeed seems to have played with nearly every jazz musician in sight—with the notable exception of Cecil Taylor.

There are certain apparent similarities in approach between the two men which Taylor also recognized, leading to the suspicion that a highly fruitful collaboration might potentially have taken place between them. It would have been of great historical significance if a recording of their playing together existed—certainly, of importance equal to that of the recorded performances by Dolphy with Coltrane, Mingus, and Ornette Coleman; but evidence strongly suggests that the two never met on the bandstand. In the section on Cecil Taylor in A. B. Spellman's *Four Lives in the Bebop Business*, the following almost psychic story told by Miss Jeanne Phillips is quoted:

Even a musician as great as Eric Dolphy looked forward to the time he could play with Cecil. Eric had all Cecil's records . . . and he used to say, "I think I'm learning how to play with Cecil" . . . It was the weirdest thing. Before Eric went to Europe, he told me about a dream he had had. He dreamed he was on the bandstand with Cecil . . . and he was waiting for his turn to play. He kept saying to himself, "At last, I'm going to play with Cecil." And before he could play, he fell down dead on the bandstand. This was the last time I talked to him before he went to Europe, and the next thing I heard, Eric had died . . . .

Especially after his posthumous election to the *Down Beat* Jazz Hall of Fame in 1964, much discussion and critical writing about Dolphy dealt with his potential unfulfilled at his death. Beyond doubt, when a talented artist dies early, regardless of whatever he has already achieved, a great deal more than might have come forth is lost. Death fully defines a man; potential for anything not already done no longer exists. At that point, the observer can try only to trace the fullness of the definition left behind by the artist, to discover what he did and did not do. A man, going through life, performs specific acts at specific times. The thoughts and acts of most individuals, once completed, are lost—unrecorded except for their impacts on the lives and deeds of others. When a man is an artist, however, each piece of his work captures some aspect of his personality or feelings, so that the observer may understand through this product something about its creator, and how he felt and thought at the point in time when that specific work was created. By understanding the art of another, the observer is affected and perhaps influenced by the artist, however indirectly. Each piece of work contributes to the total definition of the artist. Just as no act can be fully understood, taken by itself out of context, so an artist's single work cannot be fully appreciated away from the context of his total output, his place in history, and his particular nature and mode of existence. The logical conclusion of this line of reasoning is that full understanding is possible only through omniscience, an impractical goal. Nevertheless, for more than superficial appreciation of any work of art, a certain depth of awareness of the artist, the context, and the background of the art form is advisable. The more fully one is aware of the creator's circumstances, the more readily valuable insight into the nature of his creation may be gained.

Certain aspects of the socio-cultural environment in which Eric Dolphy lived are extremely complex issues. It would be a major undertaking to analyze exactly how he coped with the problems of being a Negro in the United States in the mid-twentieth century, or the problems of trying to remain economically solvent as a creative musician involved primarily in jazz in this culture. In the same way, it is impossible to derive precisely the motives and influences which shaped his life and art, for these are elements of a man's inner being which are seldom shared, and indeed are sometimes misunderstood by the man himself. Unless the individual in question had chosen to analyze himself or to communicate these extremely and specifically personal matters by committing them to writing, there is no way to divine them after the fact.

A distinct definition of Eric Dolphy emerges from the statements of those who knew him, from his own statements, from a survey examination of his career and legacy, and, most importantly, from the person seen through his music. He was a totally dedicated artist, one for whom music was more important than considerations of economics, race, culture, or even ego: witness how often groups performing on records released under his own name are, by his own statement, cooperatives where every man is granted an equal role in determining the direction and content of the music. The exuberant joy and total passion of his best solos are the signs of a man completely immersed, fully committed to the act of creation. Where the musical context fails him by not supporting this vital energy, he seems still to make the most of the situation, toying with the potential of what is there, to create a solo of intricate logic or, at the very least, highly interesting direction. His own comments on his approach to art confirm this impression:

To me, jazz is like part of living, like walking down the street and reacting to what you see and hear. And whatever I do react to, I can say immediately in my music.

And elsewhere—

This human thing in instrumental playing has to do with trying to get as much human warmth and feeling into my work as I can. I want to say more on my horn than I ever could in ordinary speech.

And again, elsewhere—

There's so much to learn, and so much to try and get out. I keeping hearing something else beyond what I've done. There's always been something else to strive for. The more I grow in my music, the more possibilities of new things I hear. It's like I'll never stop finding sounds I hadn't thought existed.

It was clearly this restless search for new sounds, for new ways of expressions, which led him—one might say, drove him—to studying so many different kinds of music, working with so many experimenters, trying to express these ideas on several different instruments, and expanding and thoroughly exploring the potential sounds of these instruments and of the musical formats in which he found himself. It is a measure of both his stature as an artist and of his character as a man to note that his incessant searching and probing into the secrets of his music and his instruments, and expansion of the range of expression available to a creative musician, projects, instead of the anguished torment and spiritual Angst characteristic of so many great artists working at this fundamental level of artistic exploration, a buoyant joy in living and in self-expression which—without ignoring the darker regions of the human condition or the more terrifying aspects of existence—was basically healthy and optimistic. This is especially refreshing in contrast to some lesser artists of the new wave in jazz, whose preoccupation with anguished effects amounts to the paranoid and psychotic, even grotesque, or who try to use art as a polemical vehicle and are primarily preoccupied with things political or commercial, rather than aesthetic.

Compared to the other two giants of the saxophone—John Coltrane and Ornette Coleman—sharing the center of attention at the same time in the evolution of the new style, each of whom struggled with the same problems in much the same intense way, Dolphy's art represents a third approach to the problems of growth and freedom, in terms not only of technical solutions but of aesthetic effect as well. Both Coleman and Coltrane present anguished, twisting efforts in thrashing out their personal solutions; Coleman seems to arrive at a transcendence, Coltrane at a monolithic spiritual stance. For all of Dolphy's twisting and jagged thrashing, however, he sustains the qualities of buoyancy and joy to give the impression that he dances with the energy of the cosmos, arriving ultimately and in an entirely personal way at an affirmation just as significant as that of each of his analogues.

Perhaps one of the most significant successes of the music Coltrane and Dolphy made together was that two such solutions might be presented in the fashion that they were—Coltrane standing like the proverbial mighty tree in the face of the storm from the existential abyss, while Dolphy danced and swayed like the flexible reed. It is a sad reflection on reality to observe that both were cut down in their prime.

It is possible that the impacts of Coltrane and of Coleman were felt more, and that they each became more influential in the determination of future style than Dolphy, simply because they worked for extended periods of time and were well recorded with groups of their own that became both extensions and formats for their musical personalities. Dolphy continued to spread himself over several distinct approaches to music, consistently tried to form cooperative groups when he did function as leader, and was only sporadically recorded in the contexts of his own groups.

Furthermore, it is apparent from examination of the commercially issued material on which Dolphy appears that his full potential was seldom utilized on his recordings as a sideman. He was featured as soloist on only about two-thirds of the just under three hundred selections recorded and commercially issued from the time of his initial appearances with Hamilton to his death. Almost a third of these were titles issued under his own name. Sideman dates which actually made use of his talents featured him predominantly on alto saxophone; on sessions under his own name, he made fairly equal use of his three principal solo instruments.

One senses, therefore, that his motivation to express himself on each of his various instruments is more accurately reflected on his own recordings. However, a number of the fourteen albums on which Eric Dolphy is nominally leader were not released during his lifetime. Further, reflecting on the minimal representation of his work available from the period 1962–63 (indeed, if not for his albums *"Conversations"* and *"Iron Man,"* an accurate impression of his work in those years would be impossible to come by), one can only conclude that he was very inadequately represented on records during his lifetime. Even now, his legacy is distinguished by quality rather than quantity.

Although his actual recording career spanned sixteen years, Eric Dolphy was really before a fairly wide jazz public outside Los Angeles for only about six years; and only slightly more than four years separate *"Outward Bound"* and *"Last Date,"* his first and last commercial recordings as leader. On that basis, his impact and legacy must be considered even more remarkable, and the significance of his loss may be more readily appreciated, even by those less familiar with the actual content of his work.

Yet even for a prolifically recorded musician, his recordings constitute a mere sampling of his output, and often not the best portion. The great bulk of his art is lost; to quote Dolphy (*"Last Date"*), ". . . after it's over, it's gone, into the air. You can never capture it again."

It is fortunate that at least a fair cross-section of Eric Dolphy's work, career, directions, and capabilities has been preserved in various commercial and private recordings. It is to be hoped that other examples will eventually surface, either as private recordings or as new releases from company vaults. (One wonders, for example, why seven years separate Mingus' April 1964 tour from the first wide distribution of the superb recordings his group made prior to and during this tour, or why the recordings of the Paris concerts of that time were released in Europe without being made available in the United States at first.) We can never hear enough from such a unique artistic personality, able to express such a range of human feelings, giving testimony, like all artists in all cultures, to the enduring vitality of the human spirit.

His Musical Biography

Eric Allan Dolphy Jr. was born in Los Angeles, California, on 20 June 1928, the only child of Sadie and Eric Dolphy Sr., who are of West Indian ancestry. His parents relate that by the age of two his favorite activities were listening to music and reading picture storybooks. His parents did their best to surround him with wholesome living, and both loved music, which was a favorite and frequent topic of conversation in the closely knit Dolphy household. His mother was a devoted member of the choir at the People's Independent Church of Christ, and as a small child Eric showed great joy at the anticipation of attending their rehearsals and hearing the choir's performances, which were not of the gospel variety, but included, for example, Handel's *Messiah*. He later attended Sunday school there, became a member of the choir himself, and eventually taught Sunday school at the Westminster Presbyterian Church (its pastor, the Reverend Hawes, was the father of jazz pianist Hampton Hawes), which he continued to attend whenever he was in Los Angeles in later years.

The toys of his preference were horns and drums, which he played incessantly. Eric's first elementary school was the Rosewood School. At that time in Los Angeles they started the children out in the first grade with a harmonica, and if any ability was shown, they were allowed to choose another instrument. Eric brought home the clarinet. When Eric was about eight, his family moved further to the west, and he began attending the West 36th Street School where he played in the school band. Later he went on to Foshay Junior High School, where he began studying oboe as well. A friend from this period has written:

I remember Eric as a skinny kid with a clarinet case, hurrying down West 36th Street, where he lived and where his parents still live, and having a friend tell me: "That Eric Dolphy is going to be great some day. All he does is practice and practice his clarinet."

Eric Dolphy Sr. and Eric Dolphy Jr., 1928.

Eric with his father and maternal grandmother 1933.

Eric and his pet, "Tippy." (Photos courtesy Mr. and Mrs. Eric Dolphy Sr.)

His parents have also written that although Eric enjoyed playing with his peers, and his first romantic interest was his kindergarden teacher, his first love was music, and practice meant more to him than play. His motto at a very early age was "practice makes perfect," and he continued to make substantial progress from the training he received in public school bands and from private lessons. His first teacher was Mrs. Ola Ebinger; later he studied with a Mrs. Monenieg, with Soccoro Pirolo, and eventually with Lloyd Reese and Merle Johnston. Charles Mingus was also a student of Lloyd Reese at this time, and in his autobiography *Beneath the Underdog* Mingus wrote:

[Lloyd] Reese and his wife, a classical pianist, had a conservatory . . . in Los Angeles. He was considered the greatest all-around teacher and a fine instrumentalist himself . . . . Many of the boys who later became famous studied with him and played with his big student rehearsal band on Sunday afternoons. Eric Dolphy worked his way through Reese's school by cutting the grass and hedges. He used to sit on the steps watching the band rehearsals. He was younger than the others and . . . [I] didn't know him then but years later in the East he became a mainstay in Mingus groups.

At thirteen, he achieved his first formal musical recognition when he participated in the California School Band and Orchestra Association, Southern District, Seventh Annual Band and Orchestra Festival, on 17 April 1942, and was awarded a certificate for his ability on clarinet. During this period he also performed with the Los Angeles City School Orchestra and in All-City concerts, in which participation was based on ability. While still in Foshay Junior High School, he won a two-year scholarship to study at the University of Southern California School of Music.

The first jazz musician he remembered having heard was Fats Waller, and his interest grew with exposure to Duke Ellington and Coleman Hawkins. He was quoted as stating to Martin Williams, "I used to ask myself, 'What is that?' at the things they played. I wanted to know how they did all of them." He tried to hear everyone he could, and began playing alto sax in a little Louis-Jordan-style band with his fellow students, who included Hampton Hawes. Eric even tried a little blues singing at this time. In junior high and high school he earned a little money playing gigs. This he used to pay for lessons. A friend from Los Angeles has written:

What was his first playing job? Who knows? While in junior high school, Eric was in a band led by a young black, from the eastside of town, by the name of Harry Allen. He had studied with Lester Young's father. This was important, because there was rivalry between black kids who lived on the eastside and those on the westside, and the music they played was somewhat different. On the eastside there was improvisation going on, while on the westside the kids played stock arrangements.

Bernard Roberts, probably Eric's closest friend, relates how he brought improvisation to Eric. Bernard studied with a German teacher who also taught Harry Allen. This teacher did not approve of jazz, but could recognize talent. He introduced Bernard to Harry, and they would woodshed together. This was Bernard's first introduction to improvisation. He would go back to Eric and tell him about it, and Bernard very proudly feels that he made an important contribution to Eric's musical activity, although I feel that eventually Eric (as have many musicians) would have become aware that there was much more to playing than listening to records and emulating them note for note (which was what he was doing at that time), then going down town and buying the stock arrangement. The hipper musical black kids were from the eastside, and even when Eric was in the Roy Porter band and was the lead reed man, it was Sweetpea who was noted for his improvisations.

His parents had a studio built for him behind their home so that he could rehearse his groups and practice undisturbed. This, in later years, became a location for after-hours jamming with prominent musicians when they were in town. Although he suffered the usual adolescent crushes on members of the opposite sex, and dated several girls regularly as time went on, many a date was kept waiting for a rehearsal or jam session to end.

After graduating from Dorsey High School in Los Angeles, Eric studied music at Los Angeles City College. He had also been alerted to the music of Charlie Parker. As with most young jazzmen of the 1940s and 1950s, Eric derived from Parker the major influence in shaping his style. Strong echoes of Parker are embodied in Dolphy's work, just as some traces of the shape of jazz of the future could be heard in Parker. For example, some of Parker's solos from airchecks originally issued on Le Jazz Cool seem to anticipate the elements of the style Dolphy developed as his own.

Vocalist and alto saxophonist Vi Redd, who was a college classmate and fellow band and orchestra member of Eric's from the all-city elementary school band through college, recalls:

I remember that when I had my little band and was playing someplace, Eric would come down and sit in, and we used to always kid him about playing so many choruses. If someone played four choruses, Eric would play eight. That's just the way he was: he'd work harder than anyone else.

Gerald Wilson seems to have been one of Eric's most vital musical associates throughout the earlier years of his development. Of him, Dolphy said:

Here is a man who has been making the modern sounds since the war years. He had a band in 1944 that would still be considered modern today ... He would take me around to hear all the musicians and explain things to me.

And elsewhere,

He's very encouraging and helpful to all young musicians, no matter how well he may be doing himself. He keeps everybody aroused and interested in music. It's so important because otherwise so many people would have nothing to look forward to and no hope of being able to earn their own way in music. I have recorded an arrangement he wrote eighteen years ago —it hasn't been released yet—and it sounded so fresh.

Eric definitely recorded with Gerald Wilson at some point during the mid-1950s, but no information is available. Wilson himself has stated that he has moved around so much that he can't find anything. Existing discographies fail to clarify the situation, as details on Wilson's record dates are quite hazy for that period of his career. However it is known with reasonable certainty that Eric's first featured recorded work was with Roy Porter's superb big-band of 1948–50, which included such eventual notables as Art and Addison Farmer, Jimmy Knepper, Joe Maini, and Russ Freeman. Several titles were briefly issued by Savoy, and by the little-known and poorly distributed Knockout Records, a local rhythm-and-blues label in Los Angeles. In an article in a 1970 issue of *Melody Maker*, Mark Gardner quoted Roy Porter as being quite certain that these were Eric's very first performances on record. However, out of sixteen tunes from three sessions, Eric apparently had only one feature spot with the band, on *Moods at Dusk*, which Porter termed "one of the prettiest alto solos ever recorded." Eric's contribution actually consists of a virtually unelaborated melody statement; but while there is no real improvisation, his fine tone and touch seem already recognizable, and it is of enormous interest to hear Eric in a big band context at the age of twenty.

Curiously, the alto sax solos on both sides of Savoy 944 (*Gassin' the Wig* and *Little Wig*) sound remarkably like what one would expect Eric's early work to sound like, and on the basis of aural evidence it would be very tempting to attribute them to Dolphy. They seem to bear the same relationship to Dolphy's later work as, to draw a parallel, Coltrane's solos on the 1951 broadcasts with Dizzy Gillespie have to Coltrane's later work: just as the influence of Dexter Gordon on Coltrane is much more apparent than in his later work, while traces of his mature style are already evident, so these alto solos seem to contain traces of Dolphy's mature style within a rather thoroughly Parker-influenced improvisation. Of course Eric would have been only twenty whereas Coltrane at the time of the broadcasts with Gillespie was twenty-four, so that this effect should appear even more pronounced, on the theory that the earlier one hears the development of an artist, the more evident the styles of his influences should become and the more fundamental the evidence of the mature style should appear.

While all of these tempting signs are indeed present, the fact is that on the basis of the testimonies of Roy Porter himself, confirmed by Eric's parents, *Moods at Dusk* is indeed the only feature Eric had with the band. The highly charged and adventurously imaginative alto solo on *Gassin' the Wig* and the briefer, more Parker-like spot on *Little Wig*, were by the band's regular alto sax soloist at the time, Leroy "Sweetpea" Robinson. Neither Porter nor the Dolphys were able to say what became of Leroy "Sweetpea" Robinson, and they were unable to speculate on any musical influence Robinson may have exerted on Dolphy at this time. Eric's statements to the effect that everyone he ever heard had influenced him, and the evident aural affinity of Robinson's style with what one extrapolates into an expectation of what Dolphy could have sounded like at that time, indicate at least that if such influence was not the case, there was surely some parallel development and the same aspects of their mutual model were undoubtedly absorbed.[8]

Concerning Eric's deportment while with the band and something of his role, a friend has written:

Clifford Solomon, who is the first tenorman in the Roy Porter photograph and probably one of the few survivors of that band, relates how giving Eric was with the other musicians. Eric was no doubt the best reader in the band and the one with the best technique, but he was never too busy to help anyone. If any musician needed help, it was Eric who patiently played the passage and explained. The band was riddled with young junkies, and

Leroy Robinson and Dolphy at a Savoy recording session, 1949.

The Roy Porter band, 1948; Dolphy is playing lead alto.
(Photos courtesy Mr. and Mrs. Eric Dolphy Sr.)

wine was consumed in large quantities but Eric never participated in any of this. Yet he was respected—not considered an oddball. Usually, if you don't partake with the cats, then you're almost an outcast. But somehow Eric gained respect even though he had no habit of any kind.

The Roy Porter band was indeed a vital outfit, if their few available records are any indication of the band's quality. It is unfortunate that they never received a wider exposure; one concert tour to New Orleans and Chicago ended in near disaster when an auto accident outside of El Paso seriously injured Porter and Art Farmer. One can be grateful at least that some of the band's spirit and the obvious talent of the enigmatic Leroy "Sweetpea" Robinson was captured on records.

Eric went into the Army in 1950 and was stationed at Fort Lewis, Washington, for two years. While there he is known to have performed with the Tacoma Symphony Orchestra. Later, he attended the U. S. Naval School of Music in Washington, D. C., receiving his certificate on 18 December 1952, and sitting out the Korean conflict there in the company of tenor saxophonist Walter Benton, who had joined up with Eric. (At that time, the musicians' union and the army evidently had an agreement whereby if musicians joined up together, they could play in the same band.) Following his discharge in 1953 he returned to Los Angeles, even more determined, if that is possible, to pursue music as a profession.

In 1954 he became friendly with John Coltrane, who had been with one of the bands Johnny Hodges led in his period away from Ellington, during 1953–54. Coltrane had made his professional debut in 1945 with a cocktail group, and after a stint in the Navy, during which he played in a band in Hawaii, he toured with Eddie Vinson, Dizzy Gillespie, and Earl Bostic before joining Hodges; but he was yet to win the wide recognition or the notoriety among the jazz public that was to come almost immediately after he joined Miles Davis in 1955. Years later, when Dolphy and Coltrane were performing together regularly and causing great controversy in the jazz world, Coltrane said,

Eric and I have been talking music for quite a few years, since about 1954. We've been close for quite a while. We watched music. We always talked about it, discussed what was being done down through the years, because we love music. What we're doing now was started a few years ago.

It was also in 1954 that Ornette Coleman returned to Los Angeles for his second visit. Ornette had begun as a rhythm-and-blues honker,

Eric Dolphy in uniform.

U. S. Naval School of Music, Washington, D. C., 1952; Dolphy is at extreme left.
(Photos courtesy Mr. and Mrs. Eric Dolphy Sr.)

but began to find his own voice early in his career, with the result that he was consistently fired, discouraged, and even paid not to play. Even musicians of stature were usually unable to cope with his approach to music, and his early difficulties have been well documented by Nat Hentoff in *The Jazz Life* (New York: The Dial Press, 1961), and especially by A. B. Spellman in *Four Lives in the Bebop Business*.

For Eric Dolphy, however, Ornette Coleman's was a new direction full of exciting potential. Dolphy related, in an interview with Martin Williams published in *Jazz Review* in 1960:

Ornette was playing that way in 1954. I heard about him and when I heard him play, he asked me if I liked his pieces and I said I thought they sounded good. When he said that if someone played a chord, he heard another chord on that one, I knew what he was talking about, because I had been thinking the same things.

That Dolphy did not share Coleman's problems of acceptance with other musicians is evident from the associations he held at the time. Clifford Brown, Max Roach, Harold Land, and Richie Powell were among those who used to go over to his house to play whenever they were in town; and Eric and Harold Land did a lot of woodshedding, as did Eric and Buddy Collette. Dolphy also worked around Los Angeles with groups led by Gerald Wilson, George Brown, and Buddy Collette, and he was with Eddie Beal's band in 1956–57. Beal's groups made some records about this time, but Dolphy was not on them. On the other hand, Beal and Dolphy are known to have recorded together as sidemen with other groups, but whether Dolphy was featured on these is uncertain.

Dolphy also led his own groups throughout this period, and seems to have met with notable success with at least one outfit during much of 1956; the weekly *Nite Owl Pocket Guide to Los Angeles* for Thursday, 31 May 1956, announces: "Eric Dolphy and his Men of Modern Jazz, who have been held over for 14 weeks at Club Oasis, have just re-signed a long-term contract." This was apparently a versatile group that included Norman Faye on trumpet, Wilfred Middlebrook on bass, and Arnold Palmer on drums. At the time of this announcement Fran Gaddison, formerly with Roy Milton's band, had just replaced Ernest Crawford on piano. A photograph of the group in action shows a baritone saxophone on the stand.

Lillian Polen, a close friend of Eric in this period, has written a vivid description of his character and style, describing him as—

... an extremely affable, gentle, unassuming fellow who worshipped Bird, who was very much like a playful kitten. He never walked, but loped along —a familiar gait in the black community—a warm smile, most respectful to all, apparently without any hangups.

We would talk for hours. About what? Everything. Eric's mind was like a sponge, drinking up all that he could (outside of music), and of course, we would always talk about music. Eric never spoke about himself and looking back now, I consider that strange.

Eric treated all women with respect. I cannot recall what we now would refer to as "sexism" emanating from Eric. Richie Powell's girlfriend at that time was a hooker, and badly treated by Richie; but Eric showed her the greatest respect and deference, almost as if to make up for Richie's attitude and abuse. Eric was playful and gentle with children. I remember him with Harold Land's son.

In the little house Eric's father built for him, he was a gracious host. No matter when you fell by his pad, you were welcome—all strangers welcome —without calling in advance; dealing with the usual social graces was not part of Eric's style of life, although he was raised that way. All were welcome. Some evenings I would come by and he would be engrossed in quiet conversation with Red Callender—but with Red and his reserve, one had to be cool. Then there would be Gerald Wilson, and the air would be filled with such fine gentleness—but that was Gerald. It appeared that Eric was to all what they wanted of him—raucous with those who were; he somehow knew what was expected of him.

A very important influence in Eric's life was Merle Johnston, the teacher who turned Eric on to the bass clarinet. Merle is very well known in Los Angeles. He is still teaching, although he is blind, has but one leg, is in the process of losing the other and is 75 years of age. As Merle puts it, "the three greatest musicians I turned out were Buddy Collette, Eric Dolphy and Frank Morgan."

Buddy recommended Merle to Eric, and Eric started studying with him. One day Eric informed Merle that he had seen a bass clarinet in the pawn shop and wished to purchase it. Merle went with Eric to examine it, found it to be in good condition and eventually Eric got it out of the shop. It was Merle who is responsible for Eric's tone on the clarinet. He told Eric how to cut the mouthpiece; to Merle, the tone was so important.

I would fall by the Oasis and listen to him, and my opinions seemed important to him. The questions from him were almost intense. Did he sound like Bird to me? That seemed all-pervading. He seemed happy at the Oasis—deliriously happy at just being able to play professionally. That he was the leader of the gig did not appear to impress him. He played behind the acts in the Oasis; used the baritone sax for that, but played mainly the alto with his group.

Eric with his parents (touching) and friends of the family.
(Photo courtesy Mr. and Mrs. Eric Dolphy Sr.)

Another group he led was a ten-piece band that included trombonist Lester Robinson, a close friend of his. It is likely that this band may have been a testing ground for Eric's arranging abilities.

For the most part, jobs were scarce and work sporadic. Many gigs were of the Sunday-afternoon-in-the-park type, for which the pay was small, but Eric was always happy for every opportunity to play. Occasionally it was necessary to travel as far as New Mexico for work, and on one occasion transportation was by an old car which proved unreliable. Broke and stranded, Eric phoned home and his parents wired him fifty dollars to buy food and to pay for his return home by public transportation. However, instead of returning immediately, he used the money to have the vehicle repaired so that the combo could limp back to Los Angeles together, and bought food for the whole band.

Eric's helpfulness and generosity extended to going out of his way to help friends. Vi Redd recalls an occasion on which she acquired a mouthpiece from him: "... I was playing a job in El Monte and I broke my own mouthpiece while taking my horn out of the case. I hurriedly called Eric and he came all the way out from town to bring me one I could use." Such incidents seem to have been typical of him.

Eric's career and lifestyle continued in this vein through his tenure with Eddie Beal, and it was not until joining Chico Hamilton's successful quintet early in 1958, on the recommendation of Buddy Collette, that he left Los Angeles and began to achieve more than local recognition.

Clearly, at 29 Eric was a mature and well-developed musician. George Avakian recalls that "at the first session we ever did together [April 1958; the Chico Hamilton Quintet doing Ellington tunes] ... he was a splendid musician to work with: consistent, thoroughly professional, brilliantly capable." Unfortunately only two performances from that session were issued, and these not until many years later. *In a Sentimental Mood* consists only of a melody statement, and although Eric's solo on *I'm Beginning to See the Light* does feature his improvisation, the overall performance seems to have been tampered with. Nevertheless they are the earliest recorded performances by Dolphy to achieve reasonable distribution as of this writing.

Many of the performances by Hamilton's group released on Sesac seem also to have been sharply edited. A large number of tracks consist only of very short melody statements, or contain only one brief solo sandwiched between the opening and closing ensembles, often

Performing with the Chico Hamilton Quintet. Hamilton is visible at left.

Practice session; note angle at which alto saxophone is assembled.
(Photos courtesy Mr. and Mrs. Eric Dolphy Sr.)

with the too-abrupt transition that hints at editing. Longer tracks by the Quintet, which fortunately are reasonably frequent on the Warner Bros. LPs, seem more likely to be complete performances, and are invariably more interesting and vital; these are the best representatives of the group's potential and of Eric's work in that period. One wonders if the Quintet was encouraged to play shortened versions of their tunes, or if the performances were indeed edited in order to get more material on the record. If so this is a true example of sacrificing quality for quantity. Even though this offers a broader spectrum of their arrangements, an aesthetic appreciation of a piece of music can be gained only by regarding the complete performance; an edited version presents a false impression.

Since the Quintet's performance at the Newport Jazz Festival that year was recorded for broadcast, and since parts of their appearance were filmed for the movie "Jazz on a Summer's Day," these numbers represent the earliest complete performances available of the group with Eric on reeds. *Pottsville U.S.A.* is the masterpiece of the set and features a brilliantly constructed alto solo. The very fast *I'm in Love With a Wonderful Guy* has Eric's earliest known recorded flute work. The other pieces seem completely scored, although, of course, Eric's ensemble work is prominent.

The two sessions from late October 1958, one of them with an added string section arranged and conducted by Fred Katz, made up the first LP containing Dolphy's contributions to be released. By this time Wyatt Ruther and Dennis Budimir had replaced Hal Gaylor and John Pisano in the group; this is the personnel which appears on most of the rest of the recordings made while Dolphy was with the band. The Quintet produced a number of superior performances at its several recording sessions, most notably *Modes* and *Under Paris Skies* from the October sets; several titles from the December 1958 dates which resulted in the LP *"Gongs East,"* easily the best record from this period of Dolphy's career; and the three quintet tracks from February 1959, particularly the moving *More Than You Know* and the angular *Miss Movement*, the first of Eric's compositions to be recorded. Several tone poems offer rare exposure to Eric's clarinet work in scored passages, as well.

While Eric's solos are not always as adventurous as the music he undoubtedly could have produced at this time, as is evidenced by the least restrained of his performances with the Quintet, it does not seem accurate to leave unchallenged the often-voiced opinion that his expression was restricted. Outside of the discipline implicit in the approach of the group, into which Eric was able to fit very well, there is no sense of constraint. His solos exhibit a great deal of fiery passion and the full effect of his powerful imagination, where appropriate; he is more restrained on flute or bass clarinet than on alto. Unfortunately the only real exposure of his bass clarinet is on *Gongs East*, which offers a rather conservative, Parkerish solo. From close examination, one is led to the conclusion that the differences in his solo work between performances with Hamilton and those in later contexts owe as much to his own development as to the differences in musical approach of the groups in which he worked.

Certainly, his period on the road with Hamilton was a time of learning and exposure—"hearing everyone in the country." He has said:

I listen and try to play everywhere I go. In Kansas City I heard John Jackson and lots of good saxophonists. I played with a pianist called Sleepy that they say Bird used to play with all the time. So many wonderful players . . . .

The group played often in Birdland in New York City, and at times the alternate band was the Miles Davis group which once again included John Coltrane, back from a period with Thelonious Monk. In Los Angeles they would find themselves playing to turn-away crowds. Their various engagements took them back and forth across the country many times.

Dolphy remained with Hamilton through Ed Sarkesian's Fifth Jazz for Moderns tour, which filled November 1959 with one night stands all over the country, after which Hamilton disbanded the Quintet. Ron Carter, who had joined the group on bass the preceding summer, is quoted in the 9 April 1964 *Down Beat* as saying:

I came to New York in 1959, and went with Chico Hamilton the next day. Eric Dolphy was in the band then, along with Dennis Budimir on guitar. We made a record for Warner Bros. that was so far out they never released it.

Unfortunately nothing more is known of this recording session, which probably dates from the late October "rest period" in Los Angeles prior to the November tour; it would neatly fill the ten-month gap in Dolphy's recording career following the uneven Sesac dates with Hamilton in May 1959.

Although Dolphy solos on only half of the Sesac pieces, there are high points in his thickly textured flute spot on the blues *Lady E* and in the torrential alto solos on *Fat Mouth* (another blues) and *Frou Frou*, plus what must be one of the most relaxed alto solos he ever recorded, on *Champs Elysee.*

After leaving Hamilton, Dolphy decided to settle in New York, and worked with George Tucker, the house bassist at Minton's, before joining his old friend Charles Mingus at the Showplace in Greenwich Village. Mingus opened at the Showplace late in December, and the groups he led held forth from that location for most of 1960. Although trumpeter Ted Curson has been quoted in *Down Beat* as stating: "The group was constantly changing; I expected change every night. I could say every set. The drummer, Danny Richmond, was the only person I expected to see," the fundamental group consisted of Mingus, Richmond, Curson, and Dolphy. All four men are identifiable in a painting inspired by the group's work at the Showplace, "The Mingus Quartet" by Norman Sasowsky, which appeared in the Book Review Section of the New York Times; in it Dolphy is seen to be playing the bass clarinet.

Of course, it was during this year with Mingus that Dolphy's reputation really blossomed; and he began to attract a great deal of attention and to find more outlets for his music. He did a great deal of freelancing in 1960, a habit that was consistent throughout his career, but for the first time this led to wider exposure as a sideman in the recording studios, as his reputation grew and opportunities appeared more often. Early in the year he turned up in the reed section of what was fundamentally the Basie band, accompanying Sammy Davis Jr. While Dolphy's role here was simply that of a section sideman, by 1 April 1960 he had attracted enough attention to be able to appear in the Prestige studios in Hackensack, New Jersey, for his first record date as a leader.

The title of this first album, *"Outward Bound,"* made it clear that his direction was unconventional, and the eerie greenish surrealistic cover painting by a friend of Eric's, Richard Jennings, who signed his paintings "The Prophet," enhanced the effect. (Later issues of the album replaced the painting with a photograph of Dolphy.)

Perhaps someone at the company was exercising his wit in consistently titling albums on which Dolphy appeared with similar phrases indicating the unconventional nature of the contents, for there followed eventually a series whose titles, when taken in certain order, seem to spell out the searching nature of the music: *"Looking Ahead"*

(McIntyre), *"Where?"* (Carter), *"Out There"* (Dolphy), *"Straight Ahead"* (Nelson), *"The Quest"* (Waldron), and *"Far Cry"* (Dolphy). This tendency extended even to the titles of the two albums for Blue Note on which Dolphy appeared in 1964, *"Out to Lunch"* (Dolphy) and *"Point of Departure"* (Hill), which seem to close the circle.

According to the assigned master numbers for the seven titles recorded on 1 April 1960, the first tune was *G.W.*, an original composition by Dolphy named for Gerald Wilson, and the most adventurous performance of the date. Dolphy's solos and composing on *G.W.* and *Les* are angular and dissonant, full of surprising intervals and contain, in his solos, some fantastic flurries of notes and freer phrasing than is evident in most of his work with Hamilton. However, his alto work on *245* is very basic and, except for some elements in his attack and a few turns of phrase here and there that expose his advanced conception, it is a gutsy blues piece. Although his bass clarinet solos are much more extroverted here than in the items with Hamilton that featured that instrument, they are conservative, compared to his alto work. Except for his unusual tone on the instrument and a few places where hints of his later expressionism appear in the phrasing, it is essentially Parkerish solo work. In fact it would not be unfair to say that Dolphy's playing had not changed substantially in the year since his last appearance on record, with Hamilton. The looser phrasing and slightly more adventurous solos on *G.W.* and *Les*, or the slight apparent increase in expressive use of the bass clarinet, as compared to the earlier work, may be due simply to the difference in group concept; Dolphy's own format is decidedly less formal.

The contributions of the other musicians are vital, and are responsible in very personal ways for the nature of the group context. George Tucker, Dolphy's associate several months earlier at Minton's, plays driving bass with a power in places reminiscent of Mingus; Haynes crackles away in rapport with the transitions implicit in the personal approaches of each soloist; Byard demonstrates the influences and synthesis of all modern piano styles from Bud Powell through Monk to Cecil Taylor; and Freddie Hubbard, who was Dolphy's roommate around that time for a while, offers several strong statements. All five men were playing in a very modern manner for 1960, but still almost wholly within an updated conception of bop. It is easy to understand why the record was well received critically, for it is a powerful and consistent document that exposes the personalities and depths of the artists very well.

In the light of this record alone, it is surprising to recall how often Dolphy and Ornette Coleman were linked in criticism at that time. Aside from certain superficial similarities in the effects of their techniques—most evident in the occasional flurries of notes, the shapes of certain phrases, and more rarely the nature of their attacks—there is very little resemblance in what they were doing; by that time Ornette's work had very little contact with the conception that shapes a bop performance.

Then, in mid-May 1960, Eric and Ornette appeared together in the context of Third Stream music, as part of the final program in the Jazz Profiles series held at the Circle in the Square in New York. This concert featured works by Gunther Schuller, with an orchestra consisting of Charles Treger and Joseph Schor, violins; John Garvey, viola; Joseph Tekula, cello; Robert DiDomenica, flute; Eric Dolphy, clarinet, flute, and bass clarinet; Eddie Costa, vibes; Bill Evans, piano; Barry Galbraith, guitar; Buell Neidlinger, bass; Paul Cohen and Sticks Evans, drums; and Ornette Coleman added on alto sax for *Abstraction*, a work written especially for him by Schuller. The review of the performance, by George Hoefer, which appeared in the 1 September 1960 *Down Beat*, states:

Before the end of *Abstraction* there was a frantic ensemble sound when Dolphy, playing bass clarinet, joined Coleman. Dolphy's simultaneous improvisations wove in and out of the shrill alto sounds.

This was the first performance of *Abstraction* and of two other pieces which featured Dolphy, *Variants on a Theme of Thelonious Monk (Criss Cross)* and *Variants on a Theme of John Lewis (Django)*, all of which were fortunately recorded for commercial release later that year.

On 24 and 25 May, Dolphy finally participated in recording sessions with Mingus. The occasion was atypical of their working situation, however, as it involved a larger group performing compositions by Mingus written prior to Charlie Parker's influence on his music— early works by the man who has come to be recognized as one of the greatest of jazz composers. It is difficult to imagine these pre-Bird compositions as having been in existence for up to twenty years prior to that session, for they sounded modern and fresh when they were recorded. Dolphy was featured on only one number, *Bemoanable Lady*, though he can be heard exchanging phrases and collectively improvising with Yusef Lateef (with both men on flutes) and playing an obligato to Lorraine Cousin's vocal on *Weird Nightmare,* as well as playing a very fast melody statement of *Do Nothin' 'Till You Hear From Me* on alto in that song's interpolation with *I Let a Song Go Out of My Heart.*

On *Bemoanable Lady* it becomes at once apparent that Dolphy's conception and personal expressionism are uniquely suited to Mingus' composition. In his soaring, Hodges-like phrasing of the melody, his particular attack and shaping of the notes is exaggerated in exactly the same direction as Mingus' own compositional concepts become at times his personal view of Ellington; Dolphy's freely phrased and occasionally speech-inflected solo seems the perfect improvisational approach to the piece.

This affinity, in fact, becomes more and more apparent as the recorded legacy of their work together develops; this initial record offers barely a hint of the enormous vitality of what was to follow.

Two days after these Mingus sessions were concluded, Dolphy appeared again in the studios of Prestige Records, to whom he was by then under contract, as a sideman with Oliver Nelson for the set that produced Nelson's LP *"Screamin' the Blues."* All six pieces that resulted from this session feature boppish lines and strong but fairly conventional solos, making Eric's work seem even more striking than on his own LP. Because of the stylistic approaches of the sidemen— and because Nelson's own powerhouse writing and playing were so deeply rooted in hard bop, with some occasionally overt rhythm-and-blues and gospel overtones—the experimental sound of the music can be primarily attributed to Dolphy's solos. In fact, he does play a very advanced alto solo on *The Meetin',* which is in six; a rather more adventurous bass clarinet solo than any previous effort appears on the title tune, as well.

Just a month later, Prestige teamed Eric with another young member of the avant-garde, Ken McIntyre, for McIntyre's second recording date. Dolphy and McIntyre had met several months before, when McIntyre had sat in at the Playhouse. Although their harmonic conceptions are related, and McIntyre was already using speech cadences and a peculiar laugh-like figure in his improvisations, the effects of their styles are quite different. The contrast is clearly apparent on the three tracks on which they both play alto; Dolphy is the more fiery of the two, and if either of them holds stylistic similarity to Ornette Coleman, it is McIntyre. The most successful tracks, *Head Shakin'* and *Diana* both feature McIntyre on flute; the longest pieces of the date, both are blues, the latter in six, with Dolphy playing a superb bass clarinet solo. Both men's explorations are kept within bounds by a rhythm section which played strictly conventional bop accompaniment, but this firm base actually provides an even more striking contrast for the hornmen, both individually within the context of the group, and as a basis for comparing them. This is especially the case on *Curtsy*, which features a chase between the two men on altos, and represents McIntyre's most convincing work on that horn on the record.

The cover of the 18 August 1960 issue of *Down Beat* bears a photograph of Eric Dolphy sitting on some rocks overlooking the ocean, playing his flute. The story behind this beautiful photograph by Gene Lees, then editor of the magazine, is illuminating. The events surrounding it deal with the ill-fated Newport Jazz Festival at the beginning of July. The festivities are well reported in the jazz literature. Basically, a group of musicians, spurred by feelings of ill treatment and inadequate compensation, had formed an irate coalition after much controversy and disruption (which included a plethora of distorted news stories, and beercan-throwing riots among spectators which apparently had nothing to do with the musicians' issues).

Eventually an impromptu "rival festival" was organized; this included such figures as Teddy Charles (who was with Mingus' group), Max Roach, Jo Jones, Art Taylor, Kenny Drew, Kenny Dorham, Coleman Hawkins, Yusef Lateef, Ornette Coleman, Walter Benton, Don Cherry, and Mingus himself, who organized the rival festival and used his group as an alternate to the jam sessions by the other musicians. Later, some of the members of this rival festival held a meeting and decided to form the Jazz Artists' Guild, led by Max Roach, Jo Jones, and Mingus. Several months later, several musicians who participated in this event recorded under the Guild's name an LP on which Dolphy was featured.

Dolphy had come to Newport with Mingus, and while Mingus was embroiled in the controversy Eric had slipped off to practice. Lees wrote:

I took several photographs before he saw me and broke the mood. Then we chatted a while. Eric lamented the animosity in today's world. He said he had found this secluded place among the rocks and had been coming there to practice in quiet. He said he hoped to buy an alto flute soon because of its warm, haunting tone. I left after that . . . Eric stayed on the rocks, his flute seeming to whisper to the waves, and the waves whispering back. And that's what music is all about, really.

Shortly after this eventful occasion, Mingus took some of the regulars at the Showplace to Europe to perform at the Antibes Jazz Festival held at Juan-Les-Pins, France; tapes featuring Dolphy survive from a radio broadcast of their performance on July 13. These earliest known recordings representative of the kind of music Mingus was producing with Dolphy and the others at the Showplace are vividly exciting and vital examples of the potential of the combination of musicians Mingus had assembled. The basic quartet was augmented by Booker Ervin on tenor sax and, on *I'll Remember April*, by Bud Powell, who plays a fine piano solo and also provides a firm accompaniment for the hornmen's solos. Dolphy plays alto sax on all three numbers, soloing to good effect and providing exciting lines in collective improvisations with Ervin and Curson.[9]

The Mingus group returned from Europe to reinstate themselves at the Showplace, and in August Eric continued his recording career as a leader.[10]

This recording date produced the LP *"Out There,"* which again had a fine surreal cover painting by "The Prophet" (again replaced by a photograph on reissues). The lineup echoed the Chico Hamilton period, even including Ron Carter—this time on cello. Eric's approach, however, was more freewheeling and less subtle and polished; the four compositions by him use unison melody lines with arco cello, and while the shorter and more arranged pieces were strongly reminiscent of recordings with Hamilton's group, several factors combine to give the date a more avant-garde flavor. The absence of a guitar gives the group a more open sound, especially as Dolphy and Carter for this reason soloed for the most part over bass and drums only. Because of this open feeling, the less inhibited solo work on the longer tunes tends to sound more harmonically adventurous, in relation to what had preceded this date, than it actually is. Finally, Carter's cello work demonstrates much use of quarter tones and smeared and bent notes that sound at times like sloppy attack, and intonation problems—the latter aspects especially evident in some of the melody statements. This effect caused much speculation, ranging from opinions that Carter was having trouble switching from bass to cello (opinions negated by the fact that he actually had played cello first and is a well-schooled graduate of the Eastman School of Music), to theories concerning the influence of mid-eastern and oriental musics on his style. Actually, a statement attributed to Carter indicates that in fact he was not well that day, and was having some difficulty in playing. Indeed, his strongest and clearest solo is on the first tune of the day, *Out There*; on later tunes, instead of warming up, he sounds rather more diffuse, almost faltering at times. Furthermore, other recordings with Carter on cello from around this time do not demonstrate the same techniques, and one can only conclude that many of these effects were unintentional. It was good fortune, as well as skill and conception, that enabled many of these aspects of these performances to effectively complement the music that day; this may somewhat explain why the session was released instead of remade.

Dolphy's own performances that day were excellent. *Out There*, especially, contains a fine alto solo; and again, as with the 1 April session, the first piece of the day contains the strongest and most adventurous work from all the musicians. His bass clarinet work was strongly featured on this date, and the effective Mingus tone poem, *Eclipse*, offers a rare exposure of his clarinet work, bridging his relationships with Hamilton and Mingus rather neatly by including a tone poem in a set already reminiscent of his work with Hamilton, and choosing a composition by Mingus. On the whole, this second album under Dolphy's leadership was quite an aesthetic success, and produced some startling music.

Less startling but at least as successful, the Prestige date with the Latin Jazz Quintet, recorded just four days later, offers a genuinely Latin flavor only on *Mambo Ricci*. The somewhat less Latin *Spring is Here* is probably the finest piece of the set, as the melody and Dolphy's flute are uniquely suited to the treatment offered; *Sunday Go Meetin'* provides a sense of adventurousness with Dolphy's exciting continuous obligato behind the others' solos. The remaining tracks are not strongly affected either by the presence of the conga or by the name of the group. They present two medium blues (in spite of its titles, *Blues in 6/8* does not have a hint of rhythm in six, except during the conga solo) and an attractive vehicle for bass and bass clarinet, *First Bass Line,* with the rest of the group comping gently in the background. Dolphy's alto spot on *Mambo Ricci* and his flute solo on *Sunday Go Meetin'* present some superb ideas, and he is at his most relaxed on alto on the title tune of the LP, "*Caribe.*" Pianist Gene Casey and vibraphonist Charlie Simons produce consistently good solos, but the strongest voice on the date is Eric's, both because his horn is intrinsically the strongest instrument in the group, and because his ideas and musical personality are the most forceful. However he does not take advantage of these circumstances to dominate the proceedings; he plays *with* the group, in the best sense of the phrase, yet does not sacrifice his own personal approach to playing. The same philosophy that made his records with Hamilton generally

49

successful is evident, and the resulting recordings are both interesting and satisfying.

Much the same comment may be made concerning the other Latin Jazz Quintet recording, for United Artists. Here, however, the Latin flavor predominates, and Eric plays flute either for solos or at least in melody statements on all but two pieces (*You're the Cutest One* and *I Got Rhythm*), which results in an expression of sameness throughout the LP; in addition, neither the material nor the treatment is particularly inspiring, especially relative to the other Latin Jazz Quintet's efforts. Nevertheless it is not a bad record, certainly not unworthy of Dolphy's talents, and interesting in presenting him in an unrelentingly Latin setting; the relative obscurity of this LP does not seem deserved.

In September, Eric's musical relationship with John Lewis and Gunther Schuller bore fruit in some recordings, one of which, *Afternoon in Paris*, featured Eric in a fine, relaxed alto solo that is most effective. *Night Float*, not released until 1964, did not feature Eric: his most exposed contribution on that piece was a unison melody statement with the trumpet. Another recording date at Prestige that month included Eric, but this time he was not featured at all. The occasion was an Eddie "Lockjaw" Davis date with a big band conducted by Oliver Nelson, who also contributed most of the arrangements. It is of interest to note that most of the personnel of Nelson's May 27 date were also in the band. Here, Dolphy's most exposed contribution is a scored passage for bass clarinet at the end of *Stolen Moments*.

The next record date on which Dolphy was widely featured is the Mingus session for Candid on 20 October 1960. By this time Dolphy had been a regular with Mingus' groups at the Showplace for about ten months, during which time the basic unit had evidently been the quartet featured at this session: Dolphy, Curson, Mingus, and Richmond. Although this unit cut only five tunes that day, these pieces stand as classic items in jazz history, and the original LP issues bring fantastic sums on the collector's market. Mingus attempted to simulate the atmosphere of the jazz club by introducing the group and ad-libbing verbal introductions to the tunes, an idea that produced some amusing results. The music itself is unqualifiedly superb, and attests to a high point in the careers of all concerned. In spite of there being only the two horns, bass and drums, the music sounds extremely complex and sophisticated, and Mingus succeeds in bringing out the full range of each man's expressive potential. Mingus' use of changing rhythmic patterns and of collective improvisation makes the group sound astonishingly avant-garde for the time, providing a striking contrast to mainstream jazz of the day and to the relatively conservative bop-flavored recording dates in which Dolphy had participated up to this time. *Folk Forms* is largely collective improvisation over a pattern of shifting rhythms that builds up to a terrific climax; it is the same composition as the *Folk Forms* recorded at Antibes, though without Booker Ervin the flavor is altered strikingly. *What Love* includes the famous, almost legendary, "conversation" between Dolphy on bass clarinet and Mingus on bass. On *All the Things You Could Be by Now If Sigmund Freud's Wife Was Your Mother*, Dolphy performs one of the most hard-driven, viscerally exciting solos of his career. Only *Stormy Weather*, being a bit highly charged for its meditative conception, and the insertion of topical social protest "messages" into the otherwise brilliant *Original Faubus Fables*, offer less than the startlingly consistent aesthetic achievement of these quartet recordings.

For *MDM* (initials standing for Monk, Duke, and Mingus), the quartet was augmented with other Mingus regulars. While the superimposition of melodies was not a new compositional technique for Mingus, the superimposition of three blues melodies and the string of solos which follow make this one of the more gargantuan of Mingus' recorded achievements. It also provides the unique occasion of Eric soloing on both alto sax and bass clarinet on the same number, and the opportunity to hear him trade fours with both Charles McPhereson and Booker Ervin.

During October, Mingus' group left the Showplace to go on tour; according to reports at the time, there was a rift between Mingus and the management when Mingus returned to the club after leaving his bass there overnight and found the instrument had been damaged. When his requests that the club pay damages were refused, Mingus yanked a few strings out of the house piano and left. He took his group into the Half Note, and later held forth at the Showboat in Philadelphia for part of November.

During this period Dolphy participated in recording sessions for Candid with several members of the Jazz Artists' Guild; on 1 November they recorded *'Tain't No Body's Business If I Do*, which featured searching work from vocalist Abbey Lincoln, trumpeter Benny Bailey, and Dolphy on alto. Interestingly, Jazz Artists' Guild members who recorded other tracks for the same LP in the Candid studios that day included Booker Little, Julian Priester, Max Roach, and Dolphy's old friend from the Army, Walter Benton; but Dolphy did not participate in those titles. On the 11th, the Jazz Artists' Guild members returned to the Candid studios for the recording of several more tracks, some including Dolphy, which eventually appeared on several LPs. Two of these, *Lock 'em Up* and the lovely *Vassarlean*, were with a Mingus group, but Dolphy was not featured on either one, although his bass clarinet is instrumental in providing tonal coloration on the latter piece. The other two pieces in which Dolphy participated were longer, blowing tracks, which included Jo Jones, Mingus, Jimmy Knepper, and the veteran trumpet giant Roy Eldridge. It is another measure of Dolphy's talent and of the scope of the content in his work that in such company there is neither compromise nor clash, despite the contrast of styles in their solos.[11]

By that time, Dolphy had notified Mingus of his intention of leaving the group. Later (5 January 1961), a report in *Down Beat* stated that Dolphy was not playing due to an "undisclosed accident," but there was no impairment of his facility on 20–21 December 1960, when the material for three vital albums in his career was recorded.

The first of these sessions involved the recording of several Gunther Schuller compositions originally performed at the Circle in the Square the preceding May, and produced the LP "*Jazz Abstractions*." For some reason the recorded version of *Abstraction* does not include the simultaneous improvisation between Dolphy and Coleman which George Hoefer described being performed at the original concert, but the piece remains a vehicle for Ornette Coleman. Dolphy is featured on the two items in which he participates, however, and on *Variants on a Theme of Thelonious Monk (Criss Cross)* there is a brief simultaneous improvisation with Coleman shortly after Dolphy begins his bass clarinet solo. This solo ends with some simultaneous improvisation with vibraphonist Eddie Costa, and later in the piece there is a duet between Dolphy's bass clarinet and Scott LaFaro's bass. This performance anticipates the 1963 recordings with Richard Davis and Bobby Hutcherson in the kind of interplay evident in these sections, and it is noteworthy that Dolphy and Costa worked together in a pianoless quintet that also included trumpeter Don Ellis long before the 1963 recordings. Besides providing this insight into Dolphy's later work, the record stands as one of the finest efforts of the Third Stream and of Dolphy's participation in the movement.

The next day Eric and Ornette met in the recording studios again, for Ornette's "*Free Jazz*" date. This became a highly influential record in jazz history and the first LP to be devoted to the new music. This is so in spite of Ornette's earlier recordings, because of the concept of utilizing the double quartet in collective improvisation: Ornette expanded the concept, as well as the size, of his original quartet by encouraging all participants into total freedom with respect to tonality and phrasing, and to base their improvisations only on listening and relating to the proceedings as a whole. Otherwise, there are only a few scored passages separating featured players. The musicians are featured in the sense of being prominent before and after the ensembles build a series of cacophonous edifices which develop out of this process of relating their collective improvisations to the soloist's ideas, working into and out of the scored lines. Dolphy's bass clarinet work is quite apt, especially in the collective improvisations, when its tonal color and Dolphy's use of effects are responsible for much of the excitement of the total sound. It is easy to understand why, from this record alone, this instrument gained popularity with the new wave of players. Coleman and Dolphy also engage in the same sort of conversationally-inflected dialogue that Dolphy and Mingus two months earlier had employed on record, and on the stand at the Showplace. Yet the effect here is as different as the relative effects of the collective improvising used on the respective recordings. In short, Coleman has succeeded in doing something different, significantly different even from his previous recordings, and the experiment is realized to a fuller degree than any previous effort along the same theories, from Lennie Tristano through the impressive and underrated Sun Ra to Ornette's earlier work.[12]

These sessions seem to have loosened Dolphy up considerably, for he is in very good form on his own date for Prestige later that day. The resulting LP, "*Far Cry*," not released until considerably after it was recorded, is one of the best of Eric's own records, being quite diversified and of consistently high quality. The version of *Serene* made that day was also a superb performance, but it was not issued until the 1970's. The personnel was familiar: Byard and Haynes were also on Dolphy's first record date, while Carter was on his second. Max Roach alumnus Booker Little appears on record with Dolphy for the first time, and while his playing bears resemblance to that of Hubbard, it is less aggressive and somehow pensive by comparison. Yet the record is much more uninhibited than the earlier quintet album, and Dolphy sounds particularly inspired, playing more adventurously than usual in this format, both on bass clarinet for *Mrs. Parker of K. C.* and on flute for *Ode to Charlie Parker*. His alto work sounds particularly limber, and he turns in a particularly raw and potent solo on the title tune (which, curiously, is the identical composition to the title tune on *"Out There"*). His unaccompanied alto solo on *Tenderly* is articulate and fleet, and he exhibits greater freedom than has been the case previously on *Miss Ann*, another original composition based on the blues with a two-bar tag. The quartet tracks are tight, vital performances; his bass clarinet phrasing on the head of *It's Magic* is peculiarly Sonny Rollins-like in its humor, and his flute work on Mal Waldron's lovely ballad, *Left Alone*, is exquisite. There is a vitality throughout the set, and everyone is appropriately attuned to the proceedings and responding well.

Astonishingly, after this particularly rewarding trio of sessions climaxing Eric's first year away from Hamilton, he dropped out of sight for the next two months. Perhaps the "undisclosed accident" reported in the 5 January 1961 *Down Beat* actually occurred after this series of recordings had been completed, and he was inactive during this period; or perhaps it is just that no recording dates came his way and no gigs were reported.

In any case, he next appeared on Abbey Lincoln's *"Straight Ahead"* LP for Candid, recorded 22 February 1961, a particularly unrewarding date in terms of what it has to offer of Eric's music when the potential of the context is considered. His only exposed contributions are a flute obligato behind Miss Lincoln's vocal on *When Malindy Sings*, and a continuous piccolo obligato above the proceedings on *African Lady*. The only known recording of his work on the instrument, his piccolo obligato resembles the sound of a flock of deranged canaries; but it is uniquely effective in establishing the mood of the piece. His associates on the date, excluding the conga players and tenor men, were to turn up again on several later sessions; the opportunity to record alongside Coleman Hawkins and Walter Benton, both of whom had also par-ticipated in the splinter festival at Newport the preceding summer, was not to be repeated. Hawkins' reaction to this meeting is of inter-est. In the 13 April 1961 *Down Beat*, he is quoted as saying,

You know, I've been making records with Max Roach and Eric Dolphy and them cats lately . . . . They hit this chord and all the time they got this other thing goin' down there . . . then they say, "Go, you got it, Bean." Got what? What the hell can you get? What can you play between these two things? But it's interesting. That's what music is—interesting. That's what music's all about anyway. Finding those things; the adventure.

The next day brought another recording session with Oliver Nelson; this included Freddie Hubbard, Roy Haynes, and Bill Evans (with whom Dolphy had played while with Gunther Schuller) on piano. Evans' moody solos contribute much to the impact of the album, "*The Blues and the Abstract Truth*," one of the finest under Nelson's leadership. Although Dolphy performs more conservatively here than in the remarkable December 1960 recordings, his work is more adventurous than on the recordings of the preceding summer, perhaps partly in contrast to the again bop-oriented format of the group, but intrinsically so as well.

As if to confirm this impression, barely a week later Nelson used Dolphy on his "*Straight Ahead*" album, this time with the same rhythm section used on Nelson's previous recording date for Prestige that had included Dolphy, the preceding spring. This turned out to be a powerful set, and Dolphy divided evenly his solo opportunities between bass clarinet and alto sax. On the longest piece, *Ralph's New Blues*, he turned in a terrific bass clarinet solo; but while generally his work is relatively conservative once again, in several places he is a bit more abstract than on any of his recordings from the previous summer. Basically, this change originates from attacking solos with an even greater intensity, phrasing more freely, and utilizing sound-effects more liberally. Also, the use of intervals in his work, always full of unexpected directions, seems to take on even wilder leaps in the more impassioned solos.

There is little opportunity to study this development in the next few recording sessions, in March and April, for the few solos he gets on Booker Little's heavily arranged "*Out Front*" album for Candid are short and not as liberated as several of the pieces with Nelson. It was clearly Little's date, as the trumpeter composed and arranged all the tunes, and is extremely prominent. The album was recorded in two sessions; the group was taken from the 22 February Abbey Lincoln date, with Don Friedman replacing Waldron on piano, and Ron Carter replacing Art Davis on bass for the second session.

Dolphy's two solos on the earlier session are fairly restrained. His solo on *Moods in Free Time* consists of excruciatingly bent notes and sound effects for the most part, and his brief solo opportunity in 5/4 on *Hazy Hues* is phrased very freely. However, he was given much more room by Little than by Ted Curson on Curson's date in April. Here, Dolphy's only exposure is limited to flute obligatos.

Opportunities for work outside the recording studios seem to have been even scarcer. It appears that Dolphy played opposite Mingus briefly at the Copa City, in early March. Later in the spring he joined George Russell's group for a short time. Russell is another jazz musician with a thorough theoretical background in music, and many of his own concepts, especially his theory of Lydian tonality (which John Lewis called "the first profound theoretical contributions to come from jazz"), have been utilized by other contemporary jazzmen. His experiments in atonality and composition led him to be involved with Third Stream music and the avant-garde of the day, yet he had been on the scene since the latter 1940s when he provided *Cubano Be / Cubano Bop* for Dizzy Gillespie's big band. The sextet concept he began working with in 1960 caused some excitement, and produced several fine recordings, with varying personnels, that revealed his use of many advanced concepts. The LP that emerged from Dolphy's association with him, recorded 8 May 1961, has more generous solo space for Dolphy than on his two previous sideman dates. *'Round Midnight* is a vehicle for Dolphy's alto, and *Honesty* and *Ezz-thetic* each offer him enough room to stretch out a bit. The work of the adventurous and imaginative trumpeter Don Ellis is also featured to advantage. The strength and imaginativeness in evidence on this date, both in the writing and in the solo work, make this one of the finest recordings that Dolphy participated in, although the general framework of Russell's arrangements are still rather bop-oriented and relatively disciplined. Though Dolphy's work is consequently more restrained than the material he recorded with his own group in December, for example, the greater sense of abandon mentioned earlier and the utilization of somewhat freer techniques on several pieces is quite evident, affirming the impression that his style continued to develop.

The recorded documentation of Dolphy's relationship with John Coltrane also began that month, with Coltrane's first record date for Impulse, that resulted in the LP "*Africa / Brass.*" As Dolphy explained in the liner notes, Coltrane told him exactly what he wanted, and Dolphy wrote the arrangements, basing some of the chords for brass on the patterns McCoy Tyner used in comping on piano. Otherwise, Dolphy's role was confined to playing in the orchestra.

However, between the two sessions for that album, Dolphy participated in Coltrane's last date for Atlantic, which also included trumpeter Freddie Hubbard. The four tunes released from that session include two ballads, one of which, *Aisha*, featured a very Parkerish alto solo. On the up-tempo pieces, Dolphy sounds thoughtful on alto for *Dahomey Dance* and rather free in his phrasing on flute for *Ole*. Unfortunately, his and Hubbard's solos sound as if they were inserted into *Ole*, rather than integral with it; the same is true of the *Original Untitled Ballad*, though Dolphy's flute is the high point of the piece. The use of an ensemble head makes *Dahomey Dance* the most cohesive of the performances, but the lovely *Aisha*, though also strung together, sounds less fragmented than the others.

It is interesting to note that Dolphy was listed under the pseudonym "George Lane" on the LP "*Ole*," which was released late that year from this session; presumably he had exceeded the terms of his contract with Prestige in making so many records for other labels. It was a fairly inauspicious beginning for a union that was to prove so vital.

Dolphy was back in the Prestige studios, as a sideman once again, for two sessions one week apart in late June, along with Ron Carter, Mal Waldron, and drummer Charlie Persip. The first session was for an LP under Carter's leadership, on which Carter played both cello and bass; George Duvivier was added on bass for titles on which Carter played cello. Dolphy appeared on four titles, using flute on two. This was a happy, swinging set, and while the flute work is relaxed and straightforward, the bass clarinet solo on *Rally* and his alto work on *Softly, as in a Morning Sunrise* alternate the charging bop-phrased style that predominated in his work with the freer phrasing and out-of-tempo passages of his more adventurous solos; indeed, the structure of Carter's *Rally* seems to encourage this.

The second set featured Carter on cello throughout, with Joe Benjamin on bass and Booker Ervin added on tenor. This was Mal Waldron's date, featuring his compositions exclusively, and is especially noteworthy to students of Dolphy in presenting his only recorded jazz solo on clarinet, on *Warm Canto*; unfortunately, it is marred by reed trouble, though the performance is otherwise lovely. He sounds uncomfortable in five on *Warp and Woof*, and on most of the rest of the set is fairly conservative; but he produces some fiery and adventurous alto work on *Status Seeking*. A second tune that was also recorded later at the Five Spot, *Fire Waltz*, does not feature Dolphy in this version.

Curiously, both of these June 1961 sessions were later reissued with Dolphy's name prominent, as if under his leadership. The reissue of Carter's "*Where?*" LP even bore Dolphy's photograph on the cover!

The first steady club work Dolphy had after leaving Mingus several months earlier was the two-week gig at the Five Spot in July 1961. Rumors that Eric was forming a group with Booker Little had been circulating since May, but evidently the cooperative organization that developed held together only during this one job. It is a fortunate and rare circumstance that Prestige recorded the entire performance of the night of July 16, and released all tracks eventually (though not for quite a few years afterward). This was about the time that Mingus had been actively proposing that musicians be recorded in clubs, and the best tracks released to make albums, rather than the usual procedure of holding studio recording sessions to produce material for LPs. It is interesting to note that Prestige did this for Dolphy not once, but twice within a few months, and that this is what Impulse did for Coltrane a few months later while Dolphy was with that group.

The ten tunes recorded on 16 July 1961, present the rare opportunity to study a night's work in the club. According to the matrix numbers assigned to the pieces by Prestige, the first piece played following the warm-up and tune-up procedure, which curiously was itself assigned a matrix number and must have been quite an ordeal since the Five Spot's piano was obviously out of tune, was *Status Seeking*. Following Dolphy's alto solo, which seems perhaps rather less potent than on the earlier version of the tune, and a good piano spot, the piece generally seems to fall apart; but it is fascinating to listen to the confusion and the manner in which it is resolved by the musicians.

The first recorded performance of Dolphy's impressive unaccompanied bass clarinet solo vehicle, *God Bless the Child*, followed. Dolphy does not sound fully involved; there is a sense of dispassion in this most relaxed of the four known versions. However the form of the solo is fully evolved by the time of this performance.

One may well wonder what an interlude of this sort was doing so early in the evening; or how the group managed such a tight, dynamic, fully-warmed-up performance of *Aggression* immediately afterwards; or how it is that *Aggression* was followed by a ballad. That the piano was out of tune is particularly noticeable on *Like Someone in Love*, and the piece is not as unified as a performance of many of the other tunes of the date.

The rest of the evening's work is quite consistent. On *Fire Waltz*, *Bee Vamp*, and *The Prophet*, the group had hit its stride; it is easy to understand why these selections were released first. All three tracks are good, tight performances with excellent solos by all concerned, rivalled only by the sheer energy of *Aggression* and the easy balance of *Booker's Waltz*. Dolphy's *Potsa Lotsa* is also an excellent piece, though more relaxed than the others and thrown off balance by a very long drum solo. The vamp that opens and closes the piece is infectious, and something of the good spirits the group was in may be heard in the way Dolphy plays a phrase of *Peanut Vender* over the vamp in the closing ensemble. *Booker's Waltz* also has this relaxed, swinging feel, and is flawed only by a fluffed return to the theme at the end. At the close of the piece Dolphy can be heard saying something about playing flute; perhaps the missing matrix number indeed implies a lost track, unless it was the alternate take of "Bee Vamp."

In any case, despite any unevenness in strength of solos or tightness of the performances, a very well-balanced and brilliant group is in evidence, and it is unfortunate and surprising in view of the critical attention and recognition it received, that the group could not sustain itself for longer than its two-week appearance at the Five Spot. At least, the unity and wide dimensions revealed by the preservation of one night's work remain to testify to the quintet's worth and vitality.

Following this important interlude, Dolphy returned to his free-lance existence, sustained by a few recording dates a month and the constant routine of practice, sitting in, and waiting for an occasional gig. It is easy to understand and sympathise with his spontaneous comment when notified of his winning the *Down Beat* International Jazz Critics' Poll as New Star on alto saxophone: "Does that mean I'm going to get work?" Actually he also placed second on flute, and on bass clarinet in the ominously titled "Miscellaneous Instrument" category, and the nature of the voting and the many comments from critics reveal how much attention he had raised in the jazz world.

During August he was reported to be playing at the Jazz Gallery with Booker Little, and he participated in several recording sessions with Max Roach in a group that included Little, Waldron, and several other musicians who had also appeared on Abbey Lincoln's Candid LP. And like hers, these recordings featured Latin rhythm and a tenor man (Clifford Jordan). A similarity is also evident in the arrangements and in the thematic material of the vocals. This time Dolphy is featured in half the tunes on the resulting LP, "*Percussion Bitter*

Sweet"; he has some good moments, particularly on *Mendacity*, though the setting of the piece as a whole distracts from the impact of his work.

Shortly after these sessions, he went to Europe for the second time, this time alone, to fulfill arrangements that had been in the works for several months, for some appearances in Scandinavia. He was also in Berlin, where on August 30 he participated in some broadcasts (from which tapes are said to exist) with members of Humphrey Lyttleton's band; and with a group, under his own name, that included trumpeter Benny Bailey. From this session with Bailey tapes of two numbers are in circulation: Dolphy's *G.W.* is treated similarly to the recorded version and includes a fiery alto solo; while the unaccompanied bass clarinet solo *God Bless the Child* is a rather brief treatment compared to the commercially recorded versions.[13]

In Copenhagen, during the week following, Dolphy performed a pair of concert-recording sessions with three top Danish musicians: Bent Axen, who already had to his credit several albums of his own; Erik Moseholm, who had led his own group at the Antibes Jazz Festival in Juan-Les-Pins the preceding year; and Jørn Elniff, a 23-year-old conservatory-trained drummer who was making his reputation in Danish jazz circles working with a big band.

There was a particular empathy in the group that makes especially vital and engaging their work on the *"In Europe"* series of LPs that came out of these sessions. The musicians all seemed to enjoy the proceedings, listened carefully to one another, and for the most part responded well. Elniff seemed especially stimulated by the sessions, and sounds occasionally as if he would run away with the rhythm, fairly bursting with energy and urgency. Axen and Moseholm both contribute sensitive solos and work hard at accompanying Dolphy, who was in very good form on the 8th. Dolphy also did his share of listening and responding to the others; the conceptions of the Danish musicians are not as advanced as Dolphy's, or as those of the musicians with whom Dolphy had been working, but they do not noticeably inhibit him. Dolphy is therefore shown to extremely good advantage, for this and for several other basic reasons, on these dates. Most obviously, these are quartet sessions; Dolphy is the only horn and a dominant voice, both intrinsically and in terms of his musical personality. Further, he was the focus of attention on the date; this was neither a "cooperative" group nor one in which arrangements were emphasized. And, possibly most importantly, there was a large output from the pair of performances. In all (with the exception of the two takes of *Miss Ann*), fourteen tunes, including the unaccompanied *God Bless the Child*, the duet *Hi-Fly* with Chuck Israels (who was in town on tour with the Jerome Robbins ballet company), and the alternate takes, were released by Prestige.

The order in which the tunes were recorded is not known with absolute certainty. On the 6th, the two takes of *Don't Blame Me* are ordered on the basis of Dolphy saying "Let's try it again" before the second take. Although the uncertain ending of the first take is cleared up on the second, the first is a more convincing rendering of the tune, though both are fine examples of Dolphy's ballad flute work. *When Lights are Low* is a marvellously effective piece for bass clarinet, and a performance with wonderful unity. Unfortunately, neither version of *Miss Ann* was released; the tune so labelled on the record is *Les*, recorded on the 8th. The mistake is not unnatural; the two pieces have similar structure and tempo, and both have angular, jagged melodies.

The version of *God Bless the Child* recorded on the 8th is the best of the three known versions, and a masterpiece. Dolphy was not only fully involved and at leisure to time it himself, but was particularly inspired, as attention to his emotional lyricism and use of dynamics demonstrates. As a result, the performance is sustained extremely well, so that its continuity, logic, and emotional content are both absorbing in process and rewarding in result, in spite of a momentary technical problem in the upper register at one point. The flute-bass duet *Hi-Fly* is an extended, mesmeric, and wholly delightful improvisation by Dolphy and Chuck Israels. It also shows a remarkable continuity. The rest of the session was with the same quartet as on the 6th, and ranged in quality from the merely interesting and vital (*Glad to Be Unhappy*, *Les*, the first two complete takes of *In the Blues*), to very fast, stimulating, dynamic tours de force (*Oleo* and *The Way You Look Tonight*) which, in spite of flaws, are immensely exciting and satisfying performances. In his ballad treatment of *Laura*, Dolphy produces one of his most intellectually rewarding alto solos, in spite of having some trouble producing freak-register notes from time to time. Every performance is worthy of close attention and full of fine moments, and several, notably *Woody'n You* and the final take of *In the Blues*, are excellent, consistent performances of particular unity.

Following this superb documentation of his work, Dolphy made a pair of television appearances in Sweden which are preserved on tape, but the exact dates of these performances are unknown. After returning from Europe, he went back to the West Coast and began working on a regular basis with John Coltrane, who was in Southern California for much of September and early October.[14]

During the last two weeks of September the group held forth from the Jazz Gallery in San Francisco, where Coltrane's regular working group of McCoy Tyner on piano, Reggie Workman on bass, and Elvin Jones on drums was augmented by Dolphy and guitarist Wes Montgomery. This is the group Coltrane presented at the Monterey Jazz Festival on 22 September, and their performance there, reviewed in detail by Don McMichael in *Down Beat* (9 November), was of interest as the first indication of the program and performances Coltrane was to present in Europe during November and December. On stage an hour, they played three tunes: *My Favorite Things*, with Dolphy on flute; *Naima*, which featured Dolphy's bass clarinet; and, with Dolphy on alto, *So What* (probably really *Impressions*, a Coltrane original based on *So What* and, in fact, misannounced as that piece on one of the European tapes). According to DeMichael, Montgomery was outstanding, with Coltrane and Dolphy exhibiting "intonation trouble" along with "animal sounds," quarter-tones, and bird calls. However, he concluded, "If Coltrane is able to keep this group together, it could turn into one of the most interesting in jazz."

While it did not stay together—Montgomery did not join the group on a regular basis—it certainly quickly became one of the most controversial groups in jazz. At the beginning of October, the group went into Hollywood's Renaissance Club for a week and provoked an attack from jazz critic John Tynan, in his "Take Five" column in *Down Beat*, which begins:

Go ahead. Call me a reactionary. I happen to object to the musical nonsense currently being peddled in the name of jazz by John Coltrane and his acolyte, Eric Dolphy.

The attack provoked a series of letters pro and con in *Down Beat* throughout the winter of 1961–62, and the controversy and attention made the entire jazz world aware of these men and of something of what they were trying to do in their music.

Meanwhile the group had moved on to the Sutherland in Chicago for two weeks, and eventually to the Village Vanguard in New York, where on four successive nights everything the group played was taped by Bob Thiele for Impulse Records. Out of these four nights' work, five tracks were eventually released, only two of which included Dolphy as a soloist, on two albums of Coltrane's music. Oddly, the released version of *Impressions* did not include Dolphy except on the final sustained note of the performance, in contrast to the effective counter-melody he played on all other circulating performances of the piece. The long, remarkably sustained Coltrane solo on the blues titled *Chasin' the Trane* begins abruptly, as if it were Coltrane's second solo on the tune or as if he played last and everything previous had been edited out of the release; this impression is strengthened by Dolphy's again being audible at the end of the piece, playing a little blurble on bass clarinet as the applause begins. He is not in evidence at all on *Softly, as in a Morning Sunrise.*

But the two pieces that do feature Dolphy, on bass clarinet, are certainly the most vital of the few pieces commercially available on which Dolphy and Coltrane played together. Of the two, *Spiritual* is the undisputable masterpiece; a classic performance by any standard, it is one of those unique pieces of art that is so well balanced, that communicates so effectively, that each note seems immutable and essential. *India* also demonstrates some of the rapport and vitality of their musical relationship, if less profoundly.

Astonishingly, this is the full extent of available commercial releases of this remarkable group's music. Impulse undoubtedly has the other material featuring their work together from those four nights, and perhaps even from other sessions. It is comforting to imagine this music being released eventually, and in fact, as of this writing, Impulse has been regularly releasing Coltrane's previously unissued music.[15]

It is incalculably important therefore to hear the tapes made from the quintet's tour in Europe to gain an adequate appreciation of its work. Evidently nothing was recorded in England, though legends of single pieces lasting over half an hour and of unusual improvisations grew out of their visit. The tapes from Scandinavia, France, and Germany from this tour document their work quite well, and Historic Performances HPLP-1 is representative of this material. *My Favorite Things* and *Impressions* were recorded in Stockholm on 23 November 1961; it is not presently known where or when *Naima* was recorded. Unfortunately, Naima is edited, fading out after a chorus of Dolphy's bass clarinet; *Impressions* is a particularly good performance, and *My Favorite Things* is at least as fine a performance as most of the versions they played in Europe that circulate among collectors. The second version of *Impressions* on HPLP-1 is from a different concert and does not include Dolphy.

Historic Performances HPLP-5, released in the summer of 1972, contains four additional performances from the group's appearance in Stockholm on 23 November 1961; alternate versions of *My Favorite Things* and *Impressions,* a complete version of *Naima,* and the other consistently featured composition at the group's appearances, *Blue Train.* HPLP-5 therefore offers a spectrum of the repertoire Coltrane featured throughout this tour, and when taken along with HPLP-1, provides for study all material recorded that day. The performance of *Impressions* on HPLP-5 is one of the most dazzling recordings documenting the careers of either figure, with Coltrane's first solo evidencing a perfectly controlled use of intervals much more in the fashion to be expected from Dolphy, and Dolphy producing some of his most fiery and exciting leaps and twists while preserving the approach to jagged intervals and phrasing which Coltrane initiated. The version of *Naima* is quite different from that on HPLP-1, although it is the same arrangement; Dolphy's solo is sensitive and lush. *Blue Train* is a good solid performance and offers solo space for Tyner following Dolphy's potent alto solo, and an additional version of *My Favorite Things* cannot be anything but welcome.

Tapes from as many as eleven separate broadcasts or appearances are said to exist from this tour, including two made apparently the same day, in Copenhagen and in Baden-Baden, and possibly two in one day in Stockholm. The program can be seen to have been consistent, and the performances are consistently of vital content. Nevertheless, contrast in performances of even the same tune from concert to concert is evident. For example, on the 26 November Baden-Baden television broadcast, *My Favorite Things* was abbreviated so that only Coltrane's solo included improvisation in both the minor and major modes; yet it is a tighter and more intense performance than the radio broadcast from Frankfurt on the 27th, which, like most versions, contained solos in both minor and major modes from Tyner, Dolphy, and Coltrane. Again at Baden-Baden, Tyner is given a solo on *Impressions,* in place of Coltrane's usual second solo and following Dolphy, before the piece is taken out. The performance on this piece in Berlin on 2 December, however, achieves a peak of intensity heard on no other versions.[16]

In general, Dolphy's solos reveal a greater intensity and concentration than evident previously; his earlier work sounds more uninhibited and gracefully fleet in some ways while his solos with Coltrane exhibit a new freedom and greater seriousness in overall conception. This direction involved an even denser texture of phrasing and wilder use of unexpected intervals, a clear development of the pattern that had been emerging in his work over the preceding year. In such a powerful group, following Coltrane's solos, he more than held his own. He developed a new vitality which added dimension to the net effect of the group, responding brilliantly to the psychic force and spiritual requirements set forth by Coltrane's opening solos on piece after piece, providing in many cases the ideal contrast or the logical extension into another plane for what Coltrane had played. His contributions within the structure of the compositions range from the flute solo, simply inserted into *My Favorite Things*, to providing harmony and unique tonal coloring on bass clarinet for the lovely melodic statement on *Naima*, as well as being the featured soloist. On *Blue Train* and *Impressions* he is present for the theme statements and follows Coltrane's tenor solos on alto.[17]

The group returned to the United States in December, played Carnegie Hall on New Year's Eve in New York City, and went into the Jazz Gallery there in January. They made at least one television appearance in the United States during this period, but whether the broadcast has been preserved in any form is not known.

Fortunately a broadcast from Birdland on 10 February 1962 was preserved and gives further evidence of the remarkable music the group was creating in this period. *My Favorite Things* is given the same treatment as other surviving versions; but the quintet performances of *Mr. P. C.* and *Miles' Mode* (later also known by the title *Red Planet*) are the only known recordings of these pieces made while Dolphy was with the group. He is present for the melody statements for both pieces and follows Coltrane's tenor solos on alto to great effect, especially on the dynamic *Mr. P. C.*, one of the most powerful of their known recordings together.

In the midst of the quintet's activity in this period, Dolphy and Elvin Jones participated in a Pony Poindexter recording session on 16 February 1962. One title remains unissued; one did not feature Dolphy at all; but *Lanyop*, a slow blues, has a double-time alto solo. His performance is rather conservative, in that he plays an essentially boppish solo that includes none of the effects or freer phrasing that had distinguished his more adventurous solos since his period with Chico Hamilton. He does nothing to disturb the easy blues mood of

John Coltrane at the Jazz Gallery session, December 1961 or January 1962.
(Photo by Joe Alper, courtesy Jackie Gibson Alper.)

the piece, and it is interesting to note his turning out this kind of performance at the height of the controversy concerning his music.

About this time, Coltrane and Dolphy were interviewed with respect to the criticism and discussion their music had inspired. Their statements in the resulting article serve as eloquent testimony to the philosophy behind the music they were developing, and to their awareness of the artistic basis from which they worked. Coltrane proved the more articulate of the two in that interview, and the key statement in his comments is revealing:

Over all, I think the main thing a musician would like to do is give a picture to the listener of the many wonderful things that he knows of and senses in the universe . . . . That's what I would like to do. I think that's one of the greatest things you can do in life and we all try to do it in some way. The musician's is through his music.

Dolphy summarized by breaking in with, "Music is a reflection of everything. And it's universal."

Their responses to the specific charges levelled against the group by critics were based on artistic license—the freedom to explore the impulses of inspiration stemming from the excitement of new discoveries in the emotional and musical possibilities opening before them as they played. The very specific point was made that much negative judgment heaped upon them was based on clear misunderstanding of their art and their directions within it, and that the musician was rarely called upon to interpret his work to his critics. The resulting negative reviews could hurt the musician both because he loves his work and because he depends on it for a living, and when this review is based on superficial analysis and lack of understanding rather than comprehension or at least insight, everyone suffers.

Dolphy left Coltrane's group as a regular member in March 1962, in order to form his own group. During the period in which he worked regularly with Coltrane, the only commercially issued recordings he appeared in were the few with Coltrane and the Poindexter date.

The best available estimate of the recording date for the peculiar set made under Benny Golson's direction for Audio Fidelity is April 1962. Evidently, two jazz groups were hired to perform routine and fairly sterile bop performances, over which a string section was dubbed playing pop tunes with which the jazz pieces share harmonic structure. Later issues of the jazz performances from this experiment fortunately omitted the string section. While Dolphy is the primary soloist on all five of the pieces in which he participates, they are certainly the least inspired and among the most conservative solos he ever recorded. The only aesthetic point of interest is the ballad *If I Should Lose You,* on which Dolphy at least sounds convincing. Many of the pieces are associated with Charlie Parker; in fact, the jazz arrangements and group sound hark back to the mid-1940s in every way. It is surprising to hear the individuals involved produce this kind of music at this time; the record is of interest for this feature alone.

Later in spring 1962, Dolphy returned to the West Coast, where, on May 19, he participated in a concert of Experimental Music and Jazz at the 1962 Ojai Festival as a featured performer in three of the five pieces on the program. The concert opened with Dolphy performing Edgar Varese's difficult solo vehicle for flute, *Density 21.5,* written in 1936 for George Barrere's platinum flute. The remainder of the first half of the program consisted of compositions by John Cage and Luciano Berio, including such performers as Berio himself, Cathy Berberian, Lukas Foss, Jean Cunningham, and Morton Subotnik. Following intermission, Dolphy appeared with bassist Jimmy Bond and drummer Milt Turner for a segment entitled "Jazz Profiles." Finally, Gunther Schuller conducted a group consisting of Dolphy, Bond, Turner, Paul Horn, John Pisano, Larry Bunker on vibraphone and piano, violinists David Frisna and Nathan Ross, cellist Howard Colf, violist Milton Thomas, and bassist Peter Mercurio in a performance of *Variants on a Theme of Thelonious Monk (Criss Cross);* this is the piece which features Dolphy to greatest advantage on the LP *"Jazz Abstractions."*

The next day, he was reunited briefly with Coltrane and Wes Montgomery at a session at the Jazz Workshop in San Francisco, on the final Sunday of Coltrane's appearance there; the group was further augmented by the violin of Mike White.

This was Eric Dolphy's last visit to the West Coast. On about 28 May he departed for Washington, D. C., to participate in the First International Jazz Festival, held 31 May through 3 June 1962. On this occasion he participated in a curious experiment involving abstract painter Paris Theodore, the 10-piece Lee Becker troupe of dancers, and his own quintet, which included Don Ellis, Eddie Costa on vibraphone, Ron Carter, and Charlie Persip, in a performance called the Jazz Ballet Theatre. This involved simultaneous improvisations by the dancers and the musicians, while Theodore executed an abstract painting on a large backdrop. Reviewer Pete Welding remarked in *Down Beat*, "Here was a vastly stimulating, fresh presentation of three art forms in conjunction," and spoke of the interplay among them in carrying off the performance. It is of vital importance to note that the instrumentation in Dolphy's group on this occasion consisted of Dolphy's reeds with trumpet, vibes, bass, and drums.

On Saturday morning a special program, a Children's Introduction to Jazz, was the setting for the premier of a specially written work by Gunther Schuller and Nat Hentoff, in which Hentoff narrates a *Journey Into Jazz*, here featuring as soloists Don Ellis and J. R. Monterose, and presumably including Dolphy on alto. The next day, 3 June, Ellis and Monterose participated with Dolphy, Carter, Persip, guitarist Barry Galbraith, trombonists Slide Hampton and Dick Lieb, and trumpeter Lou Glucken, in a Jazz Vespers service composed and conducted by Ed Summerlin, at the Church of the Epiphany in Washington, in which the jazz group performed with the church organ and choir. Welding noted, "Against this dense texture were set darting solos and exciting improvised duets." This presentation was videotaped by CBS Television and telecast on the program "Look Up and Live" on 22 June 1962.

Another performance in which Dolphy participated shortly thereafter that is of interest was the teaming of Sonny Rollins and John Lewis in a concert at the YMHA in New York. According to critic Martin Williams, who reviewed the event for *Down Beat*, Lewis' work, especially the premier performance of *The Milano Story*, was "naive in its scoring," though Rollins' performances were praised. Joe Alper's photographs from this concert show Rollins performing with a string quartet, guitarist Jim Hall, bassist Richard Davis, Ben Riley on drums, and Dolphy on flute, conducted by Lewis.

In September, Dolphy debuted his own group at the Village Gate, with Jaki Byard on piano, Richard Davis on bass, and J. C. Moses on drums; and was reportedly "besieged by record companies with offers of contracts." This, however, did not result in any known recording sessions; in fact, the first commercially issued record date after the Golson date in April in which Dolphy is known to have participated was a John Lewis Orchestra session on 5 October 1962, but neither of the two tracks released from that session features Dolphy's solo work. The lush and imaginative arrangements by Gary McFarland do occasionally contain passages in which Dolphy can be heard playing alto flute in the ensemble; these are the only known recordings of his

Eric Dolphy in orchestra at International Jazz Festival.
(Photo by Joe Alper, courtesy Jackie Gibson Alper.)

work on this instrument, and evidence that his desire to own an alto flute, expressed some two years earlier, had been fulfilled.[18]

On 12 October 1962, Charles Mingus' infamous Town Hall Concert or recording session for United Artists, originally scheduled for 15 November but unaccountably moved up, took place amid great confusion. According to commentary, reviews, and later developments, it was an "open recording session," and there is still some confusion over who was in the band. Mingus' comment in a later letter to *Down Beat*, that he ". . . knew it was impossible to make a concert out of a recording session—that one tune would have to be played again and again," indicates why he addressed the audience that night to the effect that they had been misled and should ask for their money back. Although the band had been rehearsed at Caroll Studios, these studio rehearsals had not been taped as planned to assist in rehearsing, and Mingus complained of inadequate preparation. The first piece, *Osmosis*, was stopped after a few bars, begun again, and stopped again. According to reviewer Bill Coss in *Down Beat*, considerable time and conversation among the musicians took place before the first complete piece, *Epitaph*, which featured ". . . a fascinating musical dialogue between Mingus and reed man Eric Dolphy," was played. Unfortunately, the rest of Dolphy's solo is off-mike and nearly inaudible, while the background is recorded with fine fidelity and drowns out all but short snatches of his work.

There is nothing in Coss' review to indicate that Dolphy did any other soloing that evening, and this is his only solo contribution to the record, with the questionable exception of the finale. *Finale* actually consisted of a jam on *In a Mellotone* by the larger proportion of the band, after the concert was announced as being over. Dolphy sounds as if he were trying to come in for a solo near the beginning, but is so swamped in sound that he seems to give up; the first real solo is by Jerome Richardson on baritone saxophone, followed by Pepper Adams, Clark Terry, and a trombonist. During this performance the stage hands drew the curtains on the band, an act that was interfered with by members of the audience; the audience can be heard on the record reacting to this inauspicious closing.

The incomplete takes and the second takes taped at the concert itself, and the mislabelling, strange editing, and occasionally badly unbalanced recording evident in the original issue of those performances released from this concert, lend the most direct sense of disorder. Out of all this, the achievements, failures, and occasional complete successes of the music emerge with enhanced and exaggerated effect.

Footage from a film made on this occasion is included in the movie "Mingus," by Thomas Reichman, which is marketed by Grove Press. Dolphy can be seen performing, but although music from this concert is heard in the sound track, he is not featured.

Several radio broadcasts of Mingus aggregations from Birdland during this period have been preserved on private tapings, but Dolphy was not with the groups on those occasions.

Personnel in Dolphy's own working group altered during the winter of 1962–63 to include Herbie Hancock on piano and Mingus alumnus Edward Armour on flugelhorn and trumpet; and it is this group which performed with poetess Ree Dragonette, and separately in concert, at Town Hall in a performance reviewed by Bill Coss for *Down Beat* (17 January 1963). Coss said of Dolphy's compositions on this occasion, " . . . here, given the chance of matching compositions to poetry, he wrote in a way that for all times must prove his real ability." Coss evaluated the program as ". . . the first big-league combination of the two art forms that has had moments of true brilliance."

Miss Dragonette said of working with Dolphy that his approach

. . . is original, perhaps radical, but it is so structured, and it goes back into so much jazz that went before. I feel that we are much alike, and his response to my work has been greater and better than I would normally find from some other poet. In any case there are few metaphysical poets around. Eric is working in a new field, and so am I. We're breaking ground. Here we will do it together.

Said Dolphy,

It was the first time I had ever done that kind of thing. What was most important to me was what she meant by each of the words. It was tough, but it was a wonderful experience.

Since no recordings have been circulated of Dolphy's work in this period, Coss' comments on the group's work in straightforward jazz performances are of great interest:

There was a whole concept involved, mostly revolving around the different ways that Dolphy's reeds could match with Davis' arco bass. Hancock really was supposed to be the anchor man in the middle of musical storms. Armour has a sound and mood that is a good and original reminder of the late Booker Little. All of this . . . was most evident when Dolphy played bass clarinet . . . .

At about this time, Dolphy became one of the original members of the Orchestra U.S.A., which went into rehearsal in November 1962. Conceived by John Lewis during his European tour in 1961, the concept attracted the attention of Gunther Schuller and Gary McFarland, who also did some writing for the unit. It was not meant merely to act as a vehicle for their Third Stream experiments, but also to perform contemporary compositions and to reach into the past for other non-jazz literature reflecting the full range of music available to such an organization.

Some idea of the kind of programming Schuller encouraged was evident in a concert given at about this time at the University of Chicago. An orchestra including Dolphy, Carl Leukaufe on vibraphone, Ronald Steele on guitar, Richard Davis, Sticks Evans, pianist Bob James, and members of the Chicago Symphony Orchestra, directed by Schuller, presented Mozart's *Music for Three Orchestras*, Gabrielli's *Canzona in Echo*, and Ives' suite of three short pieces ("In the Cage," "In the Inn," and "In the Night") titled *"Second Set for Theatre Orchestra."* Following intermission, they performed Stravinsky's *Ragtime for Eleven Instruments*, and four pieces by Schuller: "Little Blue Devil" from the larger work *Seven Studies on Themes of Paul Klee*; *Variants on a Theme of Thelonious Monk (Criss Cross)*; *Night Music*, written as a solo vehicle for Dolphy's bass clarinet; and *Abstraction*, with Dolphy's alto saxophone featured in place of Ornette Coleman's.

Dolphy seems to have stayed on in Chicago; in spite of being a charter member of Orchestra U.S.A., he was not present for its first concert. Instead, in December he rejoined Coltrane for an extended stay at McKie's, in Chicago. There, they were reported playing for standing-room-only audiences, and on one occasion played an 80-minute version of *So What* (again probably *Impressions*) that became an instant legend. Later, he appeared with Coltrane at the Jazz Corner in Cincinnati, evidently missing the first recording date of the Orchestra U.S.A. during this period.

Fortunately he was present for the remaining two of the three recording sessions that contributed to the Orchestra's *"Debut"* LP for Colpix. He is featured on one number from each session to good effect, bringing a spark of energy often otherwise absent from the recording. He has a nice spot in *Milesign*, which is virtually a big band setting arranged by McFarland, but on *Donnie's Theme* the setting does not seem totally conducive to supporting his overt expressionism, and almost seems to drag. Perhaps this is partially due to the Orchestra still being a new organization. In any case, these are the only commercially issued recordings of Dolphy's work with this organization; in addition, they are his only solos on record for nearly a year prior to these dates, excepting his brief exposure at Mingus' Town Hall Concert.

During this period Dolphy was also finding occasional work with his own groups. Reported personnel variations at major appearances varied from omitting Armour and substituting Eddie Kahn for Davis (for a gig at Connoley's in Boston), to reinserting Davis and Armour and omitting Hancock (at a "Recent Developments in Jazz" concert at Carnegie Hall).

The "Recent Developments in Jazz" concert was part of a series given by Gunther Schuller, and included, besides some selections from Dolphy's group, several Third Stream pieces by Andre Hodier, Lalo Schifrin, George Russell, and Schuller's transcription of Ellington's *Reminiscin' in Tempo*. Another concert in the series, billed as featuring works "related to or influenced by jazz," featured pieces by Schuller, Milton Babbitt, and Larry Austin (who also played trumpet that night), and two pieces performed in Chicago the preceding year, Stravinsky's *Ragtime for Eleven Instruments* and Ives' *Second Set for Theatre Orchestra*. Reviewer Don Heckman stated in *Down Beat*:

Alas, the only important thing that took place at this concert was the superb playing of Eric Dolphy. It was his contributions alone, on alto saxophone, bass clarinet, and flute, that brought Schuller's pieces (*Densities I, Night Music,* and *Abstraction*) to momentary life.[19]

Although Dolphy's freelance life once again found him participating in record dates as a sideman at the rate of one or two sessions a month for the first half of 1963, on most of the dates (with Freddie Hubbard for Hubbard's "*The Body and the Soul*" LP in March, and in April with Teddy Charles for United Artists in a group consisting largely of other veterans of Mingus' Town Hall Concert) he was lost in ensembles and did not solo. Only at the septet date that rounded out Hubbard's LP for Impulse, on 2 May 1963, was he given solo space, a brief couple of choruses on the medium blues *Clarence's Place*. The piece is in the usual style of the Jazz Messengers, to which many of the rest of the group belonged at the time, and Dolphy's blistering, densely textured statement is even more powerful in such a setting, though everything that follows must necessarily be anticlimactic. This violent solo is the best indication of his growth and capabilities in the long period between satisfactory exposures on record, as opposed to isolated alto saxophone solos as a sideman.

The exact recording dates of the sessions produced by Alan Douglas, evidently held on five consecutive nights in May or June 1963, are not known; but these were the first recording dates to result in material commercially issued under Dolphy's own name since the pair of recorded concerts in Copenhagen nearly two years earlier. The two LP's to come out of these sessions ("*Conversations*," first issued on the poorly distributed FM label, posthumously reissued on Vee Jay as "*The Eric Dolphy Memorial Album*," and partly re-reissued on Everest's Archives of Jazz and Folk label; and the superb "*Iron Man*") were not widely available until after Dolphy's death.

By this time, Dolphy's regular working group had altered personnel. Herbie Hancock had joined Miles Davis, and had been replaced by Bobby Hutcherson on vibraphone. Woody Shaw had replaced Edward Armour as well. This is the group with which Dolphy was appearing at the Take Three in late June, and this represents the group which appears on three of the tracks so far issued. Of course, this is also the instrumentation of the group Dolphy had played with in Washington, D. C., almost exactly a year earlier, which had included Eddie Costa and Don Ellis.

Prince Lasha and Sonny Simmons, two other musicians identified with the avant-garde, both coincidentally also from Southern California and only slightly younger than Dolphy, and Clifford Jordan in a rare recorded appearance on soprano saxophone, augmented Dolphy's basic group for *Burning Spear*, which also included both bassists. This larger group is present solely for ensemble purposes on this track, giving a tantalizing example of the kind of arranging Dolphy must have been capable of turning out. *Music Matador*, however, features all four reedmen in solos over rhythm; the piece is a joint composition by Simmons and Lasha in a kind of funky calypso vein with a lighthearted obligato from Dolphy's bass clarinet over the theme.

The three quintet tracks offer the best examples of Dolphy's working format, and all come off very well, with *Iron Man* an especially strong, vital performance. Following the jagged, vaguely Ornette Colemanish melody, Dolphy has a long alto solo full of wild plunges and effects, at his most exploratory of the performances released. The whole piece holds together very well, with effective solo contributions from Shaw and Hutcherson as well. By comparison, *Mandrake* seems rather routine, though nevertheless vital. *Jitterbug Waltz* is given a refreshing treatment with a fine skittering flute solo from Dolphy, whose occasional obligato contributions also add vitality and an unique flavor.

Of the duets with Davis, *Alone Together* is the masterpiece. Its structure has a unity and logic of classic proportions, and the interplay between the two men is breathtakingly intricate. The sensitive *Come Sunday* is only slightly less impressive, with its lovely voicings of arco bass and bass clarinet, offering a study in tonal textures and beauty, as opposed to the tour de force of *Alone Together*. Jaki Byard's *Ode to C. P.* is the weakest of the three, because of the treatment afforded it: a balladish statement at about the same tempo as the version Dolphy recorded in 1960, and involving much less interplay of ideas or tonal effects than the other duet pieces.

Finally, the unaccompanied alto saxophone rendition of *Love Me* involved an ornate treatment of the melody, effective use of intervals and glissando, and concluded with a chord—an impressive revelation of technical skills an order of magnitude beyond his unaccompanied alto saxophone solo on *Tenderly* recorded in 1960 for Prestige.

Dolphy gives clear evidence of the growth and development that had occurred in the interval since his last strong exposure on record, and, of course, the documentation of his working group at that time is invaluable. The significance of the loss to Eric's legacy resulting from its not having been more widely recorded is readily apparent from the enormous vitality and potential the group demonstrates on its three selections; and of course documentation of Dolphy's development and of his other working groups in the interval is greatly missed.

Yet, this group does not seem to have been overwhelmingly successful, for as recently as July following the Take Three engagement and these recordings, Dolphy was again in Washington, D.C., fronting the JFK Quartet at the Bohemian Caverns. That summer, he had private students studying with him as well; but at least one of them studied free in spite of Eric's own needs economically, since the student was as much in need himself.

Richard Davis has written of Dolphy's generosity even in time of his own need:

Once I saw Eric with an armful of groceries and I asked him where he was going. He replied that he was on his way to deliver the groceries to some musicians who had just gotten into town and didn't have anything to eat. I knew he didn't have any money (no work) but he did have a twenty dollar gig the night before.

By September Dolphy had rejoined Mingus, whose new 10-piece orchestra made its debut at the Village Gate early that month. The orchestra consisted of Richard Williams and Eddie Preston on trumpets; Garnett Brown on trombone; Don Butterfield on tuba; Dolphy, Booker Ervin, and Pepper Adams on reeds; Joe Albany on piano; Mingus; and Danny Richmond. According to an article by Bob Thiele in *Jazz* (October 1964), Mingus had unveiled a similar orchestra that had also included Dolphy at the Village Vangard early in 1963; this had led to Mingus' recording sessions for Impulse. Thiele stated that the recording session which included Dolphy in September came off well, and implied that the excessive editing and splicing of bits and pieces, which he typically had associated with Mingus' work for Impulse, was not necessary on that occasion. Dolphy's one solo contribution to the record, on the frantic blues *Hora Decubitus*, is an extremely violent and densely textured event reminiscent of his solo on *Clarence's Place*, also a blues, from Freddie Hubbard's recording date the preceding May; in the context of Mingus' composition, however, Dolphy's approach and impact were entirely appropriate and rewarding.

By all accounts September 1963 was an active month for Dolphy. Beside the record date with Mingus, he recorded with the Gil Evans orchestra in two sessions, which, however, resulted in no solo opportunities at all. He was with Mingus' group at the Five Spot at the beginning of the third week of September to substitute for Monk, who was off playing a festival. This group also included Richard Williams and Booker Ervin, with Roland Hanna on piano and Walter Perkins on drums. In addition, he was a member of Elvin Jones' septet performing in the Gretch Drum Show at Birdland on 30 September, along with the rest of Coltrane's rhythm section plus trumpeter Lee Morgan, trombonist Frank Rehak, and baritone saxophonist Charles Davis. On one number, the group was joined by the Japanese tenor-saxophone star Hidehiko "Sleepy" Matsumoto.

Yet another noteworthy appearance was his playing at the opening of painter Nora Jaffe's one-woman show at the Village Art Center on 11 November. On 29 November, Ochestra U.S.A., having reformed for its second season, played a concert at Hunter College featuring Gerry Mulligan as guest soloist. The usual typically anti-Third

Stream reviews nevertheless made special mention of Dolphy's work. Gene Lees wrote in *Down Beat*,

Eric Dolphy's presence in the woodwind section, however, was a distinct asset. He added a quality of moaning bite to the section work and played some distinctly lovely flute solo passages.

During December, Dolphy was featured one Sunday at the Five Spot, and New Year's Eve found him at Lincoln Center with John Coltrane, leading off a program that included Cecil Taylor's group and Art Blakey's Jazz Messengers. According to Leroi Jones' review of the concert, the group performed *My Favorite Things*, *Impressions*, and the ballad *Alabama*. Of *Impressions* Jones states, "Dolphy also played a very wild alto solo—in fact, I think it was probably the most completely satisfying effort of his I've ever heard." Significantly, there is an unconfirmed rumor that the tapes made at this concert may still exist.

Following the Lincoln Center concert, Dolphy participated in a Music Marathon held at 20 Spruce Street, appearing with the Nadi Qamar ensemble—it included two dancers—which was said to have performed at dawn.

The recording date with the Sextet of the Orchestra U.S.A. ten days later featured Dolphy's first two commercially issued solos to be recorded, excepting only the *Hora Decubitus* with Mingus, since the sessions under his own name the preceding spring. The Kurt Weill themes dominate the pieces, but Dolphy's highly abstract solos are the main points of interest. His alto solo on *As You Make Your Bed* is particularly effective, but his bass clarinet solo on *Alabama Song* is given a distracting backdrop by the other horns as they play the theme behind him.

Just a month later, one of Dolphy's alto solos was captured on film for marketing. On Saturday, 8 February 1964, at noon, the Leonard Bernstein Young People's Concert misleadingly titled "Jazz in the Concert Hall" involved the videotaping of *Journey into Jazz*, which Gunther Schuller had written for the First International Jazz Festival in Washington, D. C. nearly two years earlier. Shown on television the following March 11th, the program was later made available by McGraw-Hill's text-film division for educational and private consumption. Unfortunately, the names of both Dolphy and Schuller were misspelled (as "Dolfy" and "Schuler") in the accompanying film guide, and the erroneous impression that Aaron Copland's *Concerto*

Mingus passing out charts at Impulse recording date, 20 September 1963.

Dolphy and Jerome Richardson at same record date.
(Photos by Joe Alper, courtesy Jackie Gibson Alper.)

for Piano and Orchestra and Larry Austin's *Improvisation for Orchestra and Jazz Soloists* had a great deal to do with jazz is also perpetuated by the film. Dolphy's participation was confined to a brief alto saxophone solo on *Journey into Jazz* and a few short ensemble passages in the same piece. Bernstein's rendering of Nat Hentoff's narration manages to interrupt what brief exposure Dolphy has. Nevertheless, there is some good footage of him sitting in the section attentively, playing with the ensemble, soloing, and standing to bow; this is the only example of his work on film to be made generally available.

February also found Dolphy in Ann Arbor, Michigan, for the last night of the week-long Once Festival, performing with a bass ensemble and the Bob James Trio, which achieved legendary stature and a standing ovation when the pianist "hurled a brick through a five-foot-square piece of glass," according to *Down Beat*. Whatever aesthetic effect was achieved by this feat, however, seems not to have been recorded (though the sound of glass breaking may be heard on a Roland Kirk record made about a year later).

Fortunately, late that month the full aesthetic and creative impact of Dolphy's quintet was magnificently captured by Blue Note for the *"Out to Lunch"* LP. Freddie Hubbard replaced Woody Shaw, and Tony Williams (then with Miles Davis) replaced J. C. Moses. Dolphy again maintained his familiar position that "everyone's a leader in this session"; however, all compositions are Dolphy's, and the overall conception on the date seems to represent a clear advance of the ideas in evidence the preceding spring. Dolphy's solos seem even more abstract and the themes more angular, dissonant, and rhythmically displaced, but the other musicians match and support these conceptions with a truly fantastic sense of freedom and interplay, especially for the time of the recording, to provide a great sense of fulfillment of conception throughout. These features are especially in evidence on the title tune, where the basic rhythmic pulse is implied rather than stated throughout the piece, lending the greatest sense of freedom of the date.

Dolphy's comments in the liner notes regarding the compositions and the feeling generated on the date support the impression that he was moving in a definite direction, incorporating free time, some free-form concepts, and complex rhythmic patterns and thematic statements into a unit. Add the greater abstraction and stimulation consistently present in his own soloing, given added effectiveness in such a setting that they sound completely natural, and the aesthetic impact can be readily appreciated.

Many sections consist of pure interplay, or dialogue in several parts; while many solos are well defined, other sections seem to flow into and out of solos or scored passages. *Something Sweet, Something Tender* is an example of the new style applied to the concept of a lyrical, ballad-like piece, and has a remarkable effect when Dolphy solos: his bass clarinet work has a double-time feel in relation to the lyricism of what had preceded it, though the background has a free suspended quality; there is also a lovely scored passage for arco bass and bass clarinet near the ending. *Gazzeloni* has the most bop-like theme, but includes Dolphy's most advanced flute work available. *Straight Up and Down* and *Hat and Beard* demonstrate many of the free tendencies most evident on *Out to Lunch*, but are rather more rhythmic; Dolphy's alto work on the former is vocalized and contains some marvelous smears, and his bass clarinet on the latter is particularly wild. The contributions of the other musicians are potent and striking; the success of the date is to a large degree due to their capacities not only as soloists relating to themes and the other soloists, but in the collective interaction and interplay implicit in Dolphy's conception of the music.

About a month later, Dolphy made his other appearance for the Blue Note label, on Andrew Hill's *"Point of Departure"* date. The music on this occasion was not so uninhibitedly avant-garde; Dolphy's alto solo on *New Monastery* even echoes his style as it was on 1960-vintage recordings. Nevertheless, Hill exhibits rather advanced conceptions in his compositions, style of accompaniment, and soloing. As the rest of the rhythm section was made up of Richard Davis and Tony Williams, the date managed to bear some superficial resemblance to the less formal nature of *Out to Lunch*. Kenny Dorham provided much the same effect as Hubbard at times; Joe Henderson's Coltrane-like tenor, also an effective factor on the set, contributes strong solos. Dolphy manages to emerge as one of the most vital factors in the album's artistic success: he is featured for two solos on *Spectrum*, using alto saxophone and bass clarinet, with a flute interlude in ensemble; his bass clarinet is marvelously effective in solo and obligato passages for *Dedication*, a lovely slow piece with an expressive, moving theme; and his alto work is a burning, slashing fury on *Refuge*.

Coincidentally, this instrumentation was the same as that of the group Mingus organized in March, with Johnny Coles on trumpet, Clifford Jordan on tenor, Dolphy, Jaki Byard, and Danny Richmond. Dolphy had rejoined Mingus in early March, while the group had been undergoing rapid personnel changes during its tenure at the Five Spot. During this period he is also known to have performed with Coltrane's group at the Half Note; and he once again recorded as a sideman in Gil Evans' orchestra, shortly before leaving for Europe with Mingus on a tour organized by George Wein. He was not featured with Evans' orchestra, so his last exposure on record prior to leaving the United States was at the concert with Mingus on 4 April at Town Hall.

The commercially issued material from this concert featured two compositions common to the tour repertoire, the blues ominously titled *So Long Eric* and the extended composition *Meditations* (retitled *Prayin' with Eric* on the record). These performances are among the most vital to have been preserved, as comparisons with later concert performances from their tour reveal. *Meditations* seems to have been rearranged, and comparisons with later versions are therefore very revealing. This version of *So Long Eric* is especially strong, with Clifford Jordan in good form.

Meditations was certainly a major composition by Mingus, and comments in jazz magazines on later performances with other musicians in the United States greeted it with accolades that described it as "hypnotic" and as "running the gamut of human emotion." In later recordings, Mingus orchestrated the piece much more heavily, but kept the same form. Mingus describes it as being inspired by an article Dolphy showed him, and can be heard relating the story at various performances in introducing the piece. In Oslo on 12 April, he said, approximately:

Meditations grew out of a newspaper article that Eric Dolphy read that had some descriptions in the South; black, white, and red, different colored people, was being separated into dungeons built especially . . . prisons for darker skinned people with barbed wire and electric fences . . . electric fences. They don't have the ovens and gas faucets yet but—uh—so we, I wrote the pieces, along with these other fellows, titled *Meditations*—meditations and prayer that we get some wire cutters before guns, get out of them . . . .

Whatever Mingus' intentions in proclaiming the social context of any of his works, the music usually stands alone, its aesthetic impact unenhanced by such messages or social relevance. *Freedom* and *Fables* of *Faubus* are two that carry social criticism as part of their content, and Dolphy participated in them more than once on records. The vocals are effective documents in context, but the music transcends these messages. *Meditations* bears no such direct exhortation beyond the introductory remarks; it is unadulterated music of the highest emotional content, and in its intrinsic nonspecificity, attains universal significance beyond the scope of any intentions expressed in the introductions. As performed by this group in Europe or at Town Hall, *Meditations* transcends its inspiration, and its context, and is clearly more than the sum of its parts. Dolphy's work is particularly vital, not only for the superb flute passages and duets with Mingus' arco bass, but for the tonal colors of the bass clarinet in ensemble passages and, of course, for his solo work on that instrument as well.

Performances of *Meditations* recorded during the tour reveal a consistently rendered composition, although, as revealed on surviving tapes, in the performances of most tunes wide variations were apparent. These range from the variety in length of treatment afforded an individual composition, to complete omission of solo contributions by one individual or another from one performance to another. For example, the television broadcast from Liege on 19 April offers short versions of *So Long Eric* and *Peggy's Blue Skylight*, so that as much time as possible can be given over to *Meditations;* solos are offered from Dolphy on *Orange Was the Color of Her Dress, Then Blue Silk* at most performances, but not in Oslo on the 12th, and while he solos on *Fables of Faubus* there, he does not do so in Stockholm the next day.

But unquestionably the most significant variation was the omission of Coles for the last half of the tour. Evidently, he had resumed playing too soon after an operation for ulcers, and suffered a gastric perforation on stage in Paris on April 17. This led to his hospitalization at the American Clinic at Nuilly for about three weeks, and necessitated another operation. Jordan was reportedly also absent from the Wuppertal concert, but tapes apparently existing of that performance were not available for review at this writing.[20]

Therefore the second half of the tour was made with a quintet recalling the instrumentation of other great Mingus recording quintets featuring alto and tenor saxophones in the front lines—those with Jackie McLean and J. R. Monterose, or later with John Handy and Booker Ervin. However, the great versatility of tonal coloration offered by Dolphy's doubling was not present in these earlier groups.

The aesthetic impact and distinctiveness of this particular group is, astonishingly, hardly affected by Coles' absence, aside from the reduction of available depth of tonal coloring, despite the generally high quality of his Miles Davis-type solos. In fact, his and Byard's tendencies to play derisive cliche-quotes (inserting distracting segments of *Yankee Doodle* or *Ghost Riders in the Sky*, among others, into their solos) are happily fewer in the reviewed performance of the group's music from concerts following Coles' illness. No doubt this consistency of effect even in the face of such a major alteration in personnel is due to the distinctive qualities lent by Dolphy's range of tonal coloring being so integral to the group, to Jordan's straightforward and thoughtful solos offering a perfect contrast to Dolphy's complexity, to Byard's ability to reflect various phases of jazz history in his solos almost simultaneously, and of course to the strength of Mingus' conceptions as a unifying force. However, the balance and texture of the unique musical personalities making up this particular group is of classic proportion, and has a refined flavor of appropriateness with or without Coles.

All these aspects are well represented in the commercially issued recordings finally made available some seven years after the fact, from Town Hall with Coles, and from Paris immediately following his illness. The one solo by Coles included in the three-record set from the Paris concerts was made on the evening before the rest of the recordings were made, and represents the one complete piece in which he participated that night; he collapsed before the next tune. This long version of *So Long Eric* (unaccountably mistitled on the record *Goodbye Pork Pie Hat*) is unfortunately edited; what alleges to be the conclusion of the piece is actually part of the next evening's performance of *So Long Eric*, which begins on the record just as Dolphy's solo is ending.

While these performances from Paris are not necessarily the finest performances the group turned out during the tour, and several of the compositions are issued in two parts, several performances are typically vital representations of what the group was offering; the broad survey of their repertoire is particularly attractive, and when the three-disc set is taken together with the Town Hall release, the group may be said to be well represented on commercially issued records. Nevertheless, the frequently superior performances and fascinating variety in treatment preserved on private tapes from the tour add enormous insights into the work of the group.

But if the tour was an artistic success, it seems to have been a social disaster, as contemporary accounts testify. The European press reported consistently that concerts were started late: in Wuppertal and Frankfurt, 45 minutes; in Hamburg and Zurich, an hour. According to *Down Beat*, "In Biel, Switzerland, the musicians were observed leaving to eat when the hall was filled and the concert due to start." The German newspaper *Die Welt* is quoted with the statement, "His musicians drink schnappes and smoke on the stages . . ." Mingus' harrangues from the stage concerning "criminal booking agents" also drew comment. Surviving tapes of performances contain social commentary from Mingus delivered in the course of introducing tunes, and in Bremen and Hamburg he is said to have told his audiences to go home because they wouldn't understand the music.

At the Biel concert he is reported to have destroyed a tape recorder with his feet, and had the film confiscated from a camera filming the program, on the grounds that they were unauthorized. In Hamburg, backstage, he put his fist through a door and brandished a knife, resulting in the police being called. In rebuttal, Mingus wrote to *Down Beat*, stating that the recording equipment was being used for possible television sale without payment to the musicians. He also accused George Wein of complicity in this; Wein had no comment. It appears that Mingus' fabled volatility was running at peak efficiency, but the recordings clearly indicate that the same can be said of his creative powers, and one is left to reflect on the supposed relationship between creativity and eccentricity.

Following the tour, Dolphy left Mingus to settle in Paris, where he stayed with an old Army friend for a while and was playing frequently at the Chat Qui Pêche with Donald Byrd and Nathan Davis. Davis was making his debut in that club, and Byrd and Dolphy joined him. Davis has said of this period in his own development that—

Eric helped me get over the complex that it's wrong to play a lot of wind instruments. He also showed me how to split tones. He and I each played two notes at the same time, Donald Byrd played one: so with three men we got five-tone chords.

On 2 June he was in Hilversum, in the Netherlands, for a recording date with the Misja Mengelberg trio, for which applause was supplied by an invited audience of studio hands and recording executives. The LP released from this session, erroneously titled *"Last Date"* (leading to the false impression that it was the last known recording involving Eric Dolphy), contains one of his finest recorded performances on flute, the mesmerically beautiful *You Don't Know What Love Is.* The two tracks on which he plays bass clarinet, Thelonious Monk's *Epistrophy* and Mengelberg's *Hypochristmutreefuzz*, are both superior performances; it is of interest to note that the existence of an alternate take of *Epistrophy* has been confirmed. The three shorter tracks are also excellent, and his alto solo on *The Madrig Speaks, the Panther Walks* is particularly fascinating, with shifting rhythms beneath his leaping intervals and flurries. This composition had undergone slight alteration, in adding shifting rhythm from four to three in the theme statement, since it was recorded the year before as *Mandrake* (on the "*Iron Man*" LP). The bop orientation of the music is a slight letdown after the brilliant "*Out to Lunch*" of only three months before, but it is nevertheless a vital set of performances, and is indeed the last recorded example of Dolphy's work to have become available. The Scandinavian musicians perform admirably, and Mengelberg's solos are particularly fine. Dolphy also seems to have appreciated their work, as he later wrote Mengelberg concerning plans for the group to work together again.

During the period he was in Paris, Dolphy also participated in several radio broadcast tapings with the French pianist Jacques Dieval; Dieval's recollection is that the sessions took place in late June, perhaps as little as a week prior to Dolphy's death. Certainly the actual last known recording session took place in a Paris radio station, but without accurate dates it is an open question whether it was the session or two with Dieval, or the one with Donald Byrd, concerning which no further details have come to light, except that it was apparently never broadcast.[21]

Some of Dolphy's other plans at the time of his death are also known with reasonable definition. He was quoted as telling German critic Joachim Berendt a few weeks before he died, "I'd like to stay in Europe. There is no race trouble. I'll live in Paris." Writer A. B. Spellman quoted him as saying, before he left with Mingus:

I'm on my way to Europe to live for a while. Why? Because I can get more work there playing my own music, and because if you try to do anything different in this country, people put you down for it.

However, he does not seem to have been considering becoming an expatriate, as many have speculated. In an eerie dialogue with Mingus, captured between numbers on the Stockholm rehearsal tape, Mingus tells Dolphy that he is going to miss him, then asks,

"How many years you going to stay?"
Dolphy can be heard replying,
"I don't know. Not long."
Mingus repeats his question,
"What's not long, Eric? A year? A month?"
To which Dolphy answers,
"Not more than a year."

And during that summer in Paris, say Eric's parents, he was to have married Miss Joyce Mordecai, from New York.

By all accounts, Eric Dolphy was a warm, generous, kind, gentle, highly intelligent and enormously talented man who devoted his gifts to a lifetime of music. Ultimately one can only agree with the statement made by John Coltrane upon learning of Dolphy's death:

Whatever I'd say would be an understatement. I can only say my life was made much better by knowing him. He was one of the greatest people I've ever known, as a man, a friend, and a musician.

Eric Dolphy at First International Jazz Festival, Washington, D.C., 31 May–3 June 1962.
(Photo by Joe Alper, courtesy Jackie Gibson Alper.)

Notes and Updates

[1]This list should read: "Les," "G.W.," "Serene," and "Miss Ann," plus "245" (if incomplete theme statement takes are included), all appeared in several versions over the years. "Out There" (15 August 1960) appeared, with different instrumentation, retitled "Far Cry" (21 December 1960). "Miss Ann" also reappeared with different instrumentation. "Mandrake" (1963) reappeared, with shifting rhythmic foundation, as "The Madrig Speaks, the Panther Walks" (1964). In general, thematic interpretation was quite consistent.

[2]The roughly 20 lp's under Dolphy's nominal leadership include formal recording sessions, informal sessions and broadcasts issued many years after his death, and in some cases material not originally considered under his leadership. Formal studio record dates are represented on 7 full albums and a scattering of out-takes mixed with other sessions and issued posthumously.

[3]ENJA Records has also issued 3 lp's of material from Dolphy's 1961 European tours, reissued on Inner City in the 1980's and also available on CD in the 1990's. One of these sessions occurred during Dolphy's tour with John Coltrane. This tour also provided a bootleg issue from a jam session away from the itinerary, but including musicians from Coltrane's and Dizzy Gillespie's groups, who were touring together.
A broadcast from the Gaslight Inn in New York City in October 1962 provided material for a collectors' label album documenting Dolphy's working group at that time. Also, ENJA again was responsible for issuing an album, titled "Vintage Dolphy," with some so-called Third Stream pieces and some items by Dolphy's own group, from concerts in 1963, plus another long jam session track. Also, Blue Note issued

some private tapes and other unissued material, discovered by James Newton, called "Other Aspects." This was generally quite unlike most of Dolphy's other recordings discussed in the text.

[4]The date for Dolphy's actual last recording session was given as June 11, 1964. This was reported to have been for a radio broadcast and was recorded in a Paris studio. Ultimately, these recordings appeared on collectors' label lp's and CD's beginning in the late 1980's. As with the ENJA recordings from his 1961 European tour, personnel consisted of musicians from both Europe and the United States.

[5]As more material from Dolphy's legacy became available, it became apparent that most of Dolphy's issued material under his own name was featuring more or less conventional bop group lineups: trumpet, woodwind, piano, bass and drums, or quartets without the trumpet. These groups often included European sidemen. There were also performances where he was backed by only a bassist, or only bass and drums, with or without a trumpet sharing the front line, and, of course, many solo performances.

[6]Impulse's eventual issuing of most of the Village Vanguard recordings, and the eventual proliferation on collectors' label issues of the 23 November 1961 Stockholm concert and 10 February 1962 Birdland broadcast, has ultimately provided a rich harvest from that phase of their work together. In addition, the TV broadcast from Baden-Baden on 26 November 1961 appeared on the Video Artists International Jazz Video Collection release, "John Coltrane: The Coltrane Legacy" (VAI69035). This provided the opportunity of seeing the Quintet in action.

[7]Fortunately, ENJA issued 3 pieces recorded at one of these recitals, the Carnegie Hall concert of 14 March 1963. Dolphy can at last be heard performing pieces written for him by Schuller, "Densities" and "Night Music," as well as "Abstractions," which had been a feature for Ornette Coleman on the "Jazz Abstractions" lp.

[8]Unfortunately, as noted, testimony from those present indicated Dolphy did not solo with Porter's band, and that solos were taken by Leroy "Sweetpea" Robinson. However, after Savoy reissued the sessions from early 1949 in an album titled "Black California," it became very clear that it had, in fact, been Dolphy soloing. When both alto saxophonists

took solos on the double-length performance titled "Sippin' With Cisco," the other alto soloist sounded totally unlike anything Dolphy would have played. This validated the opinions derived from aural evidence as given in the original discussion.

[9]Fortunately, 3 additional numbers were issued along with the 3 titles originally discussed (see discography). Dolphy performed on bass clarinet on one of these pieces, "What Love?"

[10]According to the liner notes to the Blue Note album titled "Other Aspects" (BT85131), Dolphy recorded the piece called "Improvisations & Tukras" on 8 July 1960, between the Newport appearance and the trip to Europe. While this private recording documented Dolphy's interest in the music of India, it was not actually a musical performance at all, but a practice tape on which Miss Lalli chanted the rhythm (tala) and Dolphy provided a repetitive motif on flute throughout. This is a common technique traditionally used for accompanying Kathak dancers in India, but should not be confused with a purely musical exposition.

[11]Mosaic Records issued the complete Mingus Candid sessions in a 4-lp boxed set in the mid-1980's, providing correct data on the recordings and several previously unissued items. The first of two versions of "Reincarnation of a Love Bird" included excellent exposure for Dolphy's flute, in an improvised introduction and soloing at length between solos by Ted Curson and Charles McPhereson. His bass clarinet also provided interesting counter-lines in theme statements (although the performance had a fadeout ending). Dolphy did not solo on the second version, also previously unissued, made at the session on November 11th. The long version of 'Body and Soul' from the session with Eldridge, which appeared for the first time in the Mosaic boxed set, is particularly vital, with a viscerally powerful Dolphy contribution. An alternate take of this title emerged even later.

Also dated as November 1960, Dolphy's collaboration with Ron Carter may be the session referred to earlier in the context of their tenure with Chico Hamilton's group. When private tapes of these 4 pieces began to circulate widely, it was suggested these were the recordings that Carter referred to as "so far out they never released [it]." However, the date attributed to these titles on the Blue Note release place them a year later, well after they had left Hamilton.

The two takes of Dolphy's unaccompanied flute composition, titled "Inner Flight," are quite different, although similar in mood. These are his earliest unaccompanied recordings to have surfaced. Similarly, the alto sax / bass duet would be the first in the series of duets with bassists which punctuate the discography periodically. While these 3 performances are excellent additions to the legacy, the track titled "Triple Mix" represents an experiment in multi-tracking which sounds unfortunately clumsy and a bit muddy. Bass clarinet and flute are overdubbed along with multiple bass parts, and Dolphy solos on flute. The effect is of a Third Stream composition exhibiting a whacky sense of humor and some effective solo work, and is of particular interest in Dolphy's flute duet with himself.

[12]"The First Take" is literally the group's first run through the musical idea that became "Free Jazz," and particularly interesting as a consequence. At less than half the length of the initially released version, it sustains the mood well, and Dolphy's bass clarinet work is even more outstanding, almost stealing the show.

[13]The same group recorded two longer performances later that evening, "I'll Remember April" and "Hot House," affording Dolphy room to stretch out comfortably in his alto sax solos. Dolphy also performed two extended trio numbers with just bass and drums accompanying, playing bass clarinet for "When Lights are Low," and flute for "Hi Fly." Both pieces were recorded later in Copenhagen, with piano added for the former, and with drums ommitted for "Hi Fly." The latter became an impressive, mesmerising duet with bassist Chuck Israels. It is interesting to hear Dolphy performing these same pieces with varying instrumentation, so close together in time (see discography).

[14]The audio portions of these broadcasts have surfaced since the 1970's. The Copenhagen broadcast, replacing the drummer Jorn Elniff with William Schiopffe, but including Axen and Moseholm, has circulated among collectors as a private tape. It revealed the group and Dolphy in consistently good form. The Stockholm set contains two generously timed performances, plus a briefer version of "Les," and has been issued on lp by ENJA (see discography). Of course, it would be of great interest if the video portion of these broadcasts survived and could be made available eventually.

[15]About two decades after this remarkable music from this vital partnership was recorded, a pair of 2-lp sets appeared containing most of the unissued material from the other nights, along with unissued material from the "Africa" sessions. Even later, a CD issue also appeared which included two additional titles not formerly available from the Vanguard. Speculation on the impact such material might have made, had it been released when current, is futile. The music is of such power and quality, one can only lament the decades of cultural deprivation needlessly suffered, while simultaneously being grateful it has eventually surfaced after all. The augmented ensembles were for texture only, but provided settings which sounded eerily appropriate and deep, reminding many listeners that Coltrane had been communicating with Sun Ra over his developing years, prior to these recordings. On the other extreme, several pieces featured Coltrane and Dolphy backed by bass and drums only, with fiery solo work from both saxophonists, Dolphy performing on alto.

Following these important sessions, the quintet toured Europe along with the Dizzy Gillespie Quintet as a concert package, and were fortunately recorded at many of their appearances.

[16]The release of the video recording of the John Coltrane Quintet in Baden-Baden on "The Coltrane Legacy" issue provided the rare treat of seeing this group perform two pieces from their standard repertoire for this tour. Although awkwardly photographed with an irrelevant metal structural framework surrounding the group (perhaps symbolically pointing out the encroachment of technology upon the spirit), the footage is presented uncut and the performances are excellent. Private tapes from many other concerts from this tour are in wide circulation as well, providing a basis for comparison in studying their work that season.

[17]Dolphy also was recorded twice away from the Coltrane unit during the course of this tour. A T.V. Special from Stockholm, dated 19 November 1961, was issued by ENJA featuring quintet performances of "G.W." and "Miss Ann," including Idries Sulieman on trumpet; a quartet version of "Left Alone"; and a fourth (and so far the last available) version of Dolphy's unaccompanied bass clarinet feature "God Bless the Child." Again, the possibility of the video portion surviving and eventually becoming available remains an open question.

An unusual jam session has also been preserved and issued on CD's and collectors' label lp's, usually identified as from Munich on December 1st, 1961. While aural evidence indicates the pianist is McCoy Tyner, at least most of the time, the rhythm section has also been identified as being the members of Gillespie's band also on the tour, which included Lalo Schifrin (piano), Bob Cunningham (bass), and Mel Lewis (drums). Dolphy played only bass clarinet, and the long, rambling performances did not set him off as well as most of the other performances under discussion. "Oleo," for example, is apparently a long trio performance until eventually Dolphy joins in, tossing off the theme almost as an afterthought after some good solo work. On "Softly..." he opens the piece and takes a typically visceral solo, and then leaves the trio to take solos and finish the performance without him. The casual atmosphere is evident throughout, although Dolphy plays well. This session documents the jam sesson environment of presumably hundreds of evenings of his career, a raggedly informal but vivid item.

[18]Dolphy's working group at this time was broadcast from the Gaslight Inn in New York City on October 7th, 1962. Eddie Armour, the young former Berklee student working with Mingus that fall, was also a regular with Dolphy's working groups that 1962-63 season. Herbie Hancock, then 22 years old but already having recorded with Donald Byrd and as a leader for Blue Note the preceeding spring, was the pianist. Dolphy's old friend Richard Davis on bass, and Edgar Bateman on drums, completed the quintet, but they were joined on 2 numbers by vocalist Joe Carroll. Dolphy was interviewed briefly during the course of the broadcast. He mentioned playing in Pittsburgh and being uncertain where the group would go next, but the interview had little substance.

The quintet performed typically fiery versions of "G.W." and "Miss Ann," plus an incomplete version of "245" as the broadcast closed. The usual quartet treatment of "Left Alone" was also featured, indicating Dolphy's performing repertoire since the broadcasts the preceeding year in Europe had retained consistency. Joe Carroll's exuberant vocals occupy much of "I Got Rhythm," which nevertheless contains an interesting bass clarinet solo from Dolphy, and all of "Lady Be Good," a basically annoying performance except for Joe Carroll fans. This broadcast remains the only documentation of Dolphy's working unit between 1961 and spring 1963, with the possible exception of the unusual "Jim Crow" performance issued from a private tape with unidentified personnel on Blue Note's "Other Aspects" album. "Jim Crow" featured a classically-trained singer, and lyrics sounding like a scored poem. Dolphy soloed on all 3 instruments as the shifting moods evolved. Circumstantial evidence leads to the obvious speculation that there may be some connection between this performance and Dolphy's collaboration with poetess Ree Dragonette that winter, as discussed in the text.

[19]The issuing of the pieces featuring Dolphy, by ENJA in the mid-1980's, provided vital documentation of Dolphy's activity with the Third Stream Movement and some of the most interesting and successful pieces in the repertoire of their concerts. In addition, Dolphy's set from the "Recent Developments in Jazz" concert at Carnegie Hall that spring also was issued on the same release, providing opportunity to hear Dolphy and Armour over a rhythm section cosisting only of bass and drums. While the instrumentation is reminiscent of the Mingus Candid Quartet, the effect of the music is distinctively evocative of Dolphy's own musical personality, having quite a different "feel" than the Mingus group or Ornette Coleman's famous pianoless quartet with Don Cherry.

[20]Actually, Jordan was present at Wuppertal. ENJA and various collectors' label lp's have issued many additional sets of records, usually documenting the entire concert recorded (see discography). ENJA's release of the Wuppertal recital seems to offer the best fidelity, while quality of the performances seem consistently at a high level. The release of the 28 April 1964 Stuttgart recital by Unique Jazz suffers from inappropriate editing. Outstanding performances on Ulysse Music of the Amsterdam recital on April 10, and the Ingo releases of the Bremen concert on April 16, are difficult to acquire, but document the sextet particularly well, and there are no significant problems with fidelity. Videos of the T.V. broadcasts are known to exist (some even circulate among groups of collectors), but have not yet achieved general distribution at this writing.

[21]Dolphy's actual last recording session is known to have taken place in the O.R.T.F. radio station studios around mid-June 1964. Issued material dated 11 June 1964 from this series of sessions may not all be from the same session or date, and there is certainly considerable additional material known to exist. Nathan Davis has been quoted as stating Dolphy was going into recording studios almost every day in this period, with Sonny Grey's big band, Jacques Dieval's All-Stars (see discography), and varying ensembles of his own, performing mostly original compositions. Issued material includes a pianoless quintet, on "Naima" adding a conga player. There are the usual quartet and quintet lineups

performing in a style closer to Dolphy's 1960-61 recordings in this format than his later material, as well. Obviously the Sonny Grey Big Band material featuring Dolphy's arrangements would be of great interest should they ever surface.

His Recordings

The listing which follows contains, as accurately and as completely as possible, given our available sources and their limitations, full data for every traceable recording in any form in which the late Eric Dolphy participated. As might be expected with a musician of Dolphy's stature, there are a number of "phantom" recordings, commonly discussed, whose existence could not be substantiated; we have chosen to let these remain as legend until more concrete evidence appears. The sessions listed here are those for whose existence, and for Eric Dolphy's participation in them, there is unimpeachable objective evidence.

The format followed in this listing is in all cases similar to the standard discographical format, and should present no problems of understanding to the user. Mistitled selections or changes of title are noted where appropriate in the listing, and wherever possible (i.e., where the appropriate recordings were available for review by the compilers) "false starts" (recordings breaking down before any solos take place) are distinguished from "incomplete takes" (selections breaking down during or after solos). Sessions of whose existence we know for certain, but for which the available data was largely incomplete at the time of final compilation of this listing, are included as session footnotes in their proper chronological place in this catalogue.

The following notations, placed after a selection title, indicate that we are able to review the recording in question, and designate the presence or absence on that title of a solo by Dolphy. (For our purposes, a "solo" is defined as a passage, or passages, of featured improvisation of length four bars or greater; this definition therefore excludes written passages or featured melody statements played by Dolphy.) The absence of any of the following solo notations indicates only that we had not, to the time of final compilation of this listing, been able to obtain a copy of the piece in question for review.

(NS) no solo by Dolphy
(as) alto saxophone solo by Dolphy
(bcl) bass clarinet solo by Dolphy
(cl) clarinet solo by Dolphy
(fl) flute solo by Dolphy

The following abbreviations for the names of musical instruments have been used throughout the text of this catalogue:

arr	arranger	gtr	guitar
as	alto saxophone	perc	percussion
bars	baritone saxophone	picc	piccolo
bass	bass viol	pno	piano
bcl	bass clarinet	ss	soprano saxophone
btpt	bass trumpet	tbn	trombone
cel	cello	tpt	trumpet
cl	clarinet	ts	tenor saxophone
comp	composer	tu	tuba
cond	conductor	vcl	vocal
dir	musical director	vib	vibraphone
fl	flute	vla	viola
frh	french horn	vln	violin

The following abbreviations, parenthesized and suffixed to the name of a recording company, indicate country of origin (other than U.S.A.) of that edition of a commercial disc or tape recording. Issues originating in the U.S.A. bear no such suffix:

C	continental Europe	G	West Germany
D	Denmark	J	Japan
E	United Kingdom	S	Sweden
F	West Germany		

For contributions to our undertaking, in addition to the usual serial publications, liner notes, etc., we acknowledge the assistance of the following people who have supplied information or needed recordings, read drafts, offered advice or inspiration, or otherwise generally made themselves indispensible in the compilation and completion of this listing:

George Avakian	Ron Carter
Eddie Beal	Buddy Collette
Richard Bock	Michael Cuscuna
Donald Byrd	Martin Davidson
Red Callender	Jacques Dieval

Mr. and Mrs. Eric Dolphy Sr.   Roy Porter
Ron Eyre   Brian Priestly
Ross Firestone   Erik Raben
Mark Gardner   Robert Rusch
Laurent Goddet   Roger B. Rowland
Michael Hames   Richard Seidel
Michael Head   Bill Smith
P. L. Koster   Nicholas Spanos
Dietrich Kraner   Bob Thiele
Jan Lohmann   Keith Thompson
Martin Milgrim   Malcolm Walker
Charles Moffett   Roy Wilbraham
Martine McCarthy   Gerald Wilson
Alan Offstein   Nils Winther-Rasmussen
Lillian Polen   Barry Witherden
Bob Porter

Unfortunately, a discographic listing is never fully completed or completely accurate. While we have taken all possible pains to ensure the accuracy and completeness of this listing, the need for amendments or additions will undoubtedly arise, and any information regarding omissions, additions, or amendments sent to either of the compliers would be most welcome.

B.T.
V.S.

Barry Tepperman
548 Palmerston Blvd.
Toronto, Ontario M6G 2P5
Canada

Vladimir Simosko
1E Hibben Apartments
Faculty Road
Princeton, New Jersey 08540
U.S.A.

Introduction to the
Updated Discography

For this second edition, I have finally been able to incorporate the additional information on Eric Dolphy's recorded legacy which has been emerging since the original edition of this book. It is worth noting that Uwe Reichardt's excellent "Like A Human Voice," a discography on Eric Dolphy published in 1987, pays detailed attention to reissues and equivalent issues as well as new material appearing up to that time. However, a number of previously "unknown" items in Dolphy's legacy have appeared since, perhaps most notably the "surfacing" of some videos of his work with Chico Hamilton and Charles Mingus. We hope more such material will continue to emerge and be issued, as his work remains some of the most vital and exciting that jazz has to offer.

In this revised discography, I have kept the original form agreed upon by Barry Tepperman and myself for the original edition, except for adding timings for most items. As I was not concerned with the timings on material on which Dolphy does not solo, I have not been diligent in tracking these down, but I have tried to incorporate this information when I could gain access to it. For performances on which Dolphy solos, I have used published timings in most cases, or timed the performances myself when published information did not exist. These timings are to be understood as approximate, taking into consideration the occasional inaccuracy of published timings and variations in playback speed among equipment. However, it was apparent that this information would be helpful since obviously there is a significant difference in what can happen in a performance of 20-30 minutes, compared to one of 2-3 minutes! I have also developed indexes listing Dolphy's solos by instrument, and of tune titles showing instruments used where known, with dates of recording for reference in the discography; and an index of musicians listed in the discography with dates of the recording sessions. I have also updated the original list of Dolphy's recordings of his own compositions. In response to suggestions, I have noted (primarily on sessions with Chico Hamilton) situations where Dolphy plays 'lead' so prominently, he can be considered to be featured, but does not perform an improvised solo. For these pieces I have noted "(NS)" after the notation for the instrument. Finally, I have not been concerned with equivalent issues in the discography, although I have included information on Compact Discs where such data has come to my attention. Most material goes out of print very quickly, and I did not wish to clutter the discography with useless and dated details. Thanks to Alan Saul and Martin Milgrim for information on recent CD issues, and to Chris Rutkowski for assistance with the computer.

Vladimir Simosko
Summer, 1992

Discography

Roy Porter's 17 Beboppers: Los Angeles, 19 January 1949

Art Farmer, Bob Ross, Eddie Preston, James Metlock(tp), Jimmy Knepper, Danny Horton, William Willington(tb), Eric Dolphy, Leroy Robinson(as), Clifford Solomon, Joe Howard(ts), Clyde Dunn(bar), Joe Harrison(p), Ben White(g), Roger Alderson(b), Roy Porter(d), Alvy Kidd(cga), Paul Sparks(v).

1100	2:36	Pete's Beat	(NS)	Savoy MG9026, SJL2215
1101		Sippin' With Cisco A	(as)	–
1102		Sippin' With Cisco B	(NS)	–
1103	2:50	This Is You (vPS)	(NS)	–
1104	2:44	Gassin' the Wig	(as)	Savoy 944, –

Note: "Sippin'..." was issued uninterrupted; total timing = 4:50.

Roy Porter's 17 Beboppers: same.   Los Angeles, 23 February 1949

512	2:55	Phantom Moon	(NS)	SJL2215
513	2:58	Howard's Idea	(NS)	–
514	2:49	Love Is Laughing At Me (vPS)	(NS)	–
515	2:34	Little Wig	(as)	Savoy 944, –

Probably from above sessions:

	Minor Mode		Savoy unissued
	(3 unknown titles)		–

Roy Porter's 17 Beboppers: Los Angeles, spring 1949

Art Farmer, Reuben McFall, Bob Ross, Kenny Bright(tp), Jimmy Knepper, Danny Horton, William Willington(tb), Eric Dolphy, Joe Maini(as), Hadley Caliman, Joe Howard(ts), Bob Gordon(bar), Russ Freeman(p), Harold Grant(g,v), Addison Farmer(b), Roy Porter(d), Alvy Kidd(perc).

	Hunter's Hunters	Knockout (issue numbers unknown)
	Blues A La Carte	–
	Sampson's Creep	–
3:02	Moods at Dusk	(as)(NS) –

Note: Information on the Knockout session from Roy Porter & Mark Gardner. "Knockout" was a small Los Angeles-based record company with no distribution outside the immediate local Los Angeles area.

Gerald Wilson and His Orchestra: Los Angeles, c. early 1950's

Note: Gerald Wilson & Mrs. Sadie Dolphy have confirmed for us that Eric Dolphy did record with a large orchestra led by Wilson at some time in the early-to-mid 1950's. No further details are available at this time.

Eddie Beal Combo: Los Angeles, c. 1956-57

Note: Eddie Beal & Mrs. Sadie Dolphy have confirmed for us that Eric Dolphy did record with Beal's group in 1956 or 1957. No further details are available at this time. These may be the titles, personnel and dates unknown, listed by Jepsen in Jazz Records 1942-1962, Volume 1, page 286, under Eddie Beal Combo.

Chico Hamilton Quintet: Los Angeles, April 1958

Eric Dolphy(as), Nathan Gershman(cello), John Pisano(g), Hal Gaylor(b), Chico Hamilton(d).

2:30	In a Sentimental Mood	(as)(NS)	Pacific Jazz 10108, CP325364
2:59	I'm Beginning to See the Light	(as)	– –
	In a Mellotone		–
	Sophisticated Lady		(unissued)

Note: Information on "In a Mellotone" from the Japanese "Swing Journal".

Chico Hamilton Quintet: Newport Jazz Festival, 4 July 1958

Eric Dolphy(as,cl,fl), Nathan Gershman(cello), John Pisano(g), Hal Gaylor(b), Chico Hamilton(d,v).

2:54	I'm In Love With a Wonderful Guy	(fl)	FDC(I)-1024
2:30	I'm Gonna Wash That Man Right Out of My Hair	(cl)(NS)	–
8:18	Pottsville, U.S.A. (vCH)	(as)	(unissued)
6:03	Blue Sands	(fl)	NYV16590(video)
0:30	Lord Randall (Intro. only)	(fl)(NS)	

Note: New Yorker Video NYV16590 contains "Jazz on a Summer's Day", a documentary on the Newport Jazz Festival directed by Bert Stern. Dolphy is not shown very clearly except for hazy, full-face views as he solos. The "Lord Randall" excerpt is from rehearsal footage, but Dolphy is only visible in silhouette. Unfortunately, the full group on stage is never depicted.

Ernie Andrews: Los Angeles, October 1958

Al Porcino, Conrad Gozzo, John Anderson(tp), Bob Pring, Dave Wells(tb), Marshall Cram(btb), Eric Dolphy, Gene Cipriano(as), Plas Johnson, Bill Green(ts), Jewell Grant(bar), Gerald Wiggins(p), Joe Comfort(b), Earl Palmer(d), Ernie Andrews(v).

Slide, Mr. Trombone (vEA)	(NS)	GNP-42
I'm Gonna Move to the Outskirts of Town (vEA)	(NS)	–
I'm Afraid the Masquerade is Over (vEA)(NS)	(NS)	–
Just You, Just Me (vEA)	(NS)	–
Travelin' Light (vEA)	(NS)	–
Until the Real Thing Comes Along (vEA)	(NS)	–
Bernie's Tune (vEA)	(NS)	–
Don't Be Afraid (vEA)	(NS)	–
Someone I Love (vEA)	(NS)	–
Julie Is Her Name (vEA)	(NS)	–

Note: Data from Uwe Reichardt's "Like a Human Voice" discography on Dolphy.

Chico Hamilton Quintet: Los Angeles, 26 October 1958

Eric Dolphy(as,fl,bcl), Nathan Gershman(cello), Dennis Budimer(g), Wyatt Ruther(b), Chico Hamilton(d,v).

8126K-14	2:25	Andante	(as)(NS)	Warner Bros. B(S)1245
8126K-25	6:32	Modes	(as)	–
8126K-35	2:58	Fair Weather	(fl)	–
8126K-42	5:38	Pottsville, U.S.A. (vCH)	(as)	–
8126K-53	5:40	Don's Delight	(fl)	–
8126K-63	4:21	Under Paris Skies	(as)	Warner Bros. W(S)1281

add unidentified string section, Fred Katz(cond). Los Angeles, 27 October 1958

8127K-13	3:50	Something to Live For	(fl)	Warner Bros. B(S)1245
8127K-29	4:36	Close Your Eyes	(as)	–
8127K-34	3:05	Strange	(as)	–
8127K-44	2:00	Ev'rything I've Got	(fl)(NS)	–
8127K-58	2:30	Speak Low	(bcl)	–

Note: Arrangements for the string section by Fred Katz. "Speak Low" was omitted from some early pressings of B(S)1245.

Chico Hamilton Quintet: Los Angeles, 29/30 December 1958

Eric Dolphy(as,bcl,cl,fl), Nathan Gershman(cello), Dennis Budimir(g), Wyatt Ruther(b), Chico Hamilton(d).

A10200	2:58	Long Ago and Far Away	(cl)(NS)	Warner Bros. W(S)1271
A10201	4:40	I Gave My Love a Cherry	(cl,fl))(NS)	–
A10202	3:04	Beyond the Blue Horizon	(fl)	–
A10203	5:04	Nature By Emerson	(as)	–
A10204	2:57	Tuesday at Two	(as)	–
A10205	4:48	Gongs East	(bcl)	–
A10206	4:03	Far East	(fl)	–
A10207	3:08	Good Grief Dennis	(cl)(NS)	–
A10208	3:19	Passion Flower	(as)	–
A10209	3:59	Where I Live	(fl)	–

same personnel: Los Angeles, 4 February 1959

B10798	5:43	More Than You Know	(as)	W(S)1344, Atl.WS4671
B10801	4:38	Newport News	(as)	– –
B10802	2:15	Miss Movement	(as)	– –

add Paul Horn(as), Buddy Collette(ts), Bill Green(bar), unk.(p); Chico (d,v).

B10803	She's Funny That Way (vCH)	(NS)	W(S)1344
B10804	The Best Things in Life Are Free (vCH)	(NS)	–
B10805	I Don't Know Why (vCH)	(NS)	–
B10806	Where or When (vCH)	(NS)	–

Note: The above 4 performances are vocal features for Chico Hamilton. Three additional tracks on the album are unaccompanied drum solos.

same as 29/30 December 1958:   Los Angeles, 19 May 1959

3:12	Truth	(as)(NS)	Jazz Vault JVll
1:41	Opening	(as)	–
2:49	Fat Mouth	(as)	–
2:38	Theme for a Starlet	(fl)(NS)	–
1:42	Little Lost Bear	(bcl)(NS)	–
2:25	Champs Elysee	(as)	–
3:12	Lost in the Night	(as)	–
3:05	Frou Frou	(as)	–
2:57	Lullaby for Dreamers	(fl)(NS)	–

Ralph Pena(b) for Ruther: Los Angeles, 20 May 1959

2:39	Cawn Pawn	(bcl)(NS)	Jazz Vault JVlll
2:41	Lady E	(fl)	–

Note: The May 1959 sessions were originally recorded for Sesac transcriptions.

Chico Hamilton Quintet: TV broadcast, c. 1958-59

Eric Dolphy(fl,cl), Nathan Gershman(cello), Dennis Budimer(g), Wyatt Ruther(b), Chico Hamilton(d).

1:25	Sleep	(fl)(NS)	TV broadcast
1:45	The Morning After	(cl)(NS)	–

Note: The group is introduced for the first number by Bob Crosby, after which Hoagy Carmichael makes some comments before introducing the second performance.

Sammy Davis Jr. with Sy Oliver Orchestra: New York, c. early 1960

William "Cat" Anderson, Thad Jones, Joe Newman, Ernie Royal, Snooky Young(tp), Henry Coker, Al Grey, Benny Powell(tb), Marshall Royal, Eric Dolphy(as), Frank Foster, Billy Mitchell(ts), Charlie Fowlkes(bar), George Rhodes(p), Ed Jones(b), Sonny Payne(d), Sammy Davis Jr.(v), Sy Oliver(cond).

There Is No Greater Love (vSD)	(NS)	Decca DL(7)8981
This Little Girl of Mine (vSD)	(NS)	–
Gee Baby Ain't I Good To'You (vSD)	(NS)	–
Mess Around (vSD)	(NS)	–

Eric Dolphy Quintet: Hackensack, New Jersey, 1 April 1960

Freddie Hubbard(tp), Eric Dolphy(as,bcl,fl), Jaki Byard(p), George Tucker(b), Roy Haynes(d).

2101-1	12:07	G.W.	(as)	Prestige MP2517
2101-2	7:55	G.W.	(as)	New Jazz NJLP8236, OJC022CD
2102-1	7:54	245	(as)	Prestige MPP2517
2102-2	6:45	245	(as	New Jazz NJLP8236, –
2103	5:40	On Green Dolphin Street	(bcl)	– –
2104	5:22	Glad To Be Unhappy -1	(fl)	– –
2105	5:11	Les	(as)	– –
2106	5:34	Miss Toni	(bcl)	– –
2107	4:07	April Fool –1	(fl)	Prestige PR7382

-1: Omit Hubbard.

Ruth Brown: New York, 19 April 1960

Burt Collins, Ernie Royal, Richard Williams, Danny Moore(tp), Charles Greenlea, Bernard McKinney, Julian Priester(tb), Charlie Mariano, Eric Dolphy(as), George Coleman, Bob Newman(ts), Jay Cameron(bar), Tommy Flanagan(p), Kenny Burrell(g), Nobby Totah(b), Pete Sims(d), Ruth Brown(v).

4376	Don't Cha Go Away Mad (vRB)	Atlantic unissued
4377	Baby Don't You Cry (vRB)	–
4378	Just the Way You Look Tonight (vRB)	–
4379	Shine On (vRB)	–

Note: Information from Michel Ruppli's "Atlantic Discography" via Uwe Reichardt.

Charles Mingus Orchestra: New York, 24 May 1960

Marcus Belgrave, Ted Curson, Hobart Dotson, Clark Terry, Richard Williams(tp), Eddie Bert, Charles Greenlea, Slide Hampton, Jimmy Knepper(tb), Don Butterfield(tu), Robert DiDomenica(fl), Harry Shulman(oboe), Eric Dolphy(as,bcl,fl), John LaPorta(as,cl), Yusef Lateef(fl,ts), Bill Barron, Joe Farrell(ts), Danny Bank(bar), Roland Hanna(p), Charles McCracken(cello), Charles Mingus(b), Danny Richmond(d), Sticks Evans, George Scott, Max Roach(perc), Gunther Schuller(conductor on 20093).

20093	8:12	Half-Mast Inhibition	(NS)	Mercury MG20627

20094	3:22	Mingus Fingus Number Two	(NS)	–
20095	4:32	Bemoanable Lady	(as)	–
20096		Yusef Isef Too		Mercury unissued

Note: All titles on MG20627 on CD on Emarcy 826496-2.

Charles Mingus Orchestra: New York, 25 May 1960

Ted Curson(tp), Jimmy Knepper(tb), Eric Dolphy(as,bcl,fl), Yusef Lateef(fl,ts), Booker Ervin, Joe Farrell(ts), Roland Hanna [-1] or Paul Bley [-2](p), Charles Mingus(b), Danny Richmond(d), Lorraine Cousins(v).

20100	3:35	Weird Nightmare (vLC)	(NS)	Mercury MG20627
20101	3:49	Prayer for Passive Resistance	(NS)	–
20102	3:45	Eclipse (vLC) -1	(NS)	–
20103	3:33	Do Nothing 'Till You Hear It From Me/		
		I Let a Song Go Out of My Heart	(NS)	–
20104	3:34	Take the A Train / Exactly Like		
		You -2	(NS)	–

Note: Emarcy 826496-2 is a CD reissue of Mercury MG20627. Band(v) on 20102. It has not been possible to determine which pianist was used on the other titles.

Oliver Nelson Sextet: Hackensack, New Jersey, 27 May 1960

Richard Williams(tp), Eric Dolphy(as,bcl), Oliver Nelson(as,ts), Richard Wyands(p), George Duvivier(b), Roy Haynes(d).

2271	6:24	Three Seconds	(as)	New Jazz NJLP8324, OJC080CD
2272	4:59	Alto-itis	(as)	– –
2273	6:39	The Meetin'	(as)	– –
2274	5:48	The Drive	(as)	– –
2275	5:00	March On, March On	(as)	– –
2276	10:57	Screamin' the Blues	(bcl)	– –

Ken McIntyre - Eric Dolphy Quintet: Hackensack, New Jersey, 28 June 1960

Ken McIntyre(as,fl), Eric Dolphy(as,bcl,fl), Walter Bishop(p), Sam Jones(b), Art Taylor(d).

2333	7:15	Geo's Tune	(as)	New Jazz NJLP8247
2334	5:07	They All Laughed	(as)	–
2335	9:07	Dianna	(bcl)	–
2336	5:49	Curtsy	(as)	–
2337	4:04	Lautir	(fl)	–
2338	10:48	Head Shakin'	(as)	–

Eric Dolphy - Gina Lalli: New York, 8 July 1960

Eric Dolphy(fl), Gina Lalli(tabla,v), Roger Mason(tamboura).

| | 10:47 | Improvisations & Tukras (vGL)(fl) | | Blue Note BT85131,CDP48041 |

Charles Mingus Jazz Workshop: Antibes Jazz Festival, 13 July 1960

Ted Curson(tp), Eric Dolphy(as,bcl), Booker Ervin(ts), Charles Mingus(b,p), Danny Richmond(d).

	11:54	Wednesday Night Prayer Meeting	(as)	Atlantic 2ASD3001, CD90352
	8:06	Prayer for Passive Resistance	(as)	– –
	13:34	What Love?	(bcl)	– –
	13:39	I'll Remember April -1	(as)	– –
	11:08	Folk Forms #1	(as)	– –
	11:00	Better Git Hit in Your Soul	(as)	– –

-1: add Bud Powell(p).

Eric Dolphy Quartet: Hackensack, New Jersey, 15 August 1960

Eric Dolphy(as,bcl,cl,fl), Ron Carter(cello), George Duvivier(b), Roy Haynes(d).

2395	6:52	Out There	(as)	New Jazz NJLP8252, OJC023CD
2396	5:00	Feathers	(as)	– –
2397	2:54	The Baron	(bcl)	– –
2398	7:00	Serene	(bcl)	– –
2399	4:40	Sketch of Melba	(fl	– –
2400	4:50	17 West	(fl)	– –
2401	2:47	Eclipse	(cl)	– –

The Latin Jazz Quintet With Eric Dolphy: Hackensack, New Jersey, 19 August 1960

Eric Dolphy(as,bcl,fl), Charlie Simons(vibes), Gene Casey(p), Bill Ellington(b), Manuel Ramos(d,timbales), Juan Amalbert(cga).

2408	5:48	Sunday Go Meetin'	(fl)	New Jazz NJLP8251
2409	4:04	First Bass Line	(bcl)	–
2410	7:18	Mambo Ricci	(as)	–
2411	5:46	Blues in 6/8	(as)	–
2412	5:00	Spring is Here	(fl)	–
2413	8:30	Caribe	(as)	–

Ruth Brown: New York, 30 August 1960

Personnel given as for the previous Ruth Brown session of 19 April 1960.

4873	Takin' Care of Business (vRB)	(NS)	Atlantic 2075, 8080
4874	Honey Boy (vRB)	(NS)	–
4875	It Tears Me All To Pieces (vRB)	(NS)	Atlantic 2104

John Lewis and His Orchestra: New York, 9 September 1960

Herb Pomeroy(tp), Gunther Schuller(frh), Eric Dolphy(as), Benny Golson(ts), Jimmy Giuffre(bar), John Lewis(p), Jim Hall(g), George Duvivier(b), Connie Kay(d).

4924	9:55	Afternoon in Paris	(as)	Atlantic 1375, CD90979-2
4925	4:14	Night Float	(NS)	Atlantic 1425
4926		If You Could See Me Now		Atlantic unissued
4927		'Round Midnight		–

Eddie "Lockjaw" Davis Big Band: Hackensack, New Jersey, 20 September 1960

Bobby Bryant, Clark Terry, Richard Williams(tp), Jimmy Cleveland, Melba Liston(tb), Eric Dolphy(as,bcl), Oliver Nelson(as), George Barrow, Jerome Richardson(fl,ts), Eddie "Lockjaw" Davis(ts), Bob Ashton(bar), Richard Wyands(p), Wendell Marshall(b), Roy Haynes(d).

2498	Walk Away	(NS)	Prestige PR7206, OJC429CD
2499	Trane Whistle	(NS)	– –
2500	Whole Nelson	(NS)	– –
2501	Stolen Moments	(NS)	– –
2502	Jaws	(NS)	– –
2503	You Are Too Beautiful	(NS)	– –

Note: Arrangements by Oliver Nelson (2498-2501) & Ernie Wilkins(2502 & 2503).

Charles Mingus Jazz Workshop: New York, 20 October 1960

Ted Curson(tp), Eric Dolphy(as,bcl,fl), Charles Mingus(b,v), Danny Richmond(d,v).

12:57	Folk Forms #1	(as)	Candid CJM8005, Mosaic MR4-111
9:10	Original Faubus Fables (vCM,DR)(as)		− −
15:17	What Love?	(bcl)	− −
8:32	All the Things You Could Be		
	By Now If Sigmund Freud's		
	Wife Was Your Mother	(as)	− −
13:25	Stormy Weather	(as)	Candid CJM8021,CCD79033, −

add Lonnie Hillyer(tp), Charles McPherson(as), Nico Bunick(p).

9:17	Reincarnation of a Love Bird	(fl)	Mosaic MR4-111,Candid CCD79033

add Booker Ervin(ts).

6:35	Vassarlean	(NS)	Candid CJM8019, Mosaic MR4-111

add Jimmy Knepper, Britt Woodman(tb).

19:07	MDM	(as,bcl)	Candid CJM8021, Mosaic MR4-111

Abbey Lincoln - Jazz Artists' Guild: New York, 1 November 1960

Benny Bailey(tp), Eric Dolphy(as), Kenny Dorham(p), Peck Morrison(b), Jo Jones(d), Abbey Lincoln(v).

7:02	'Tain't Nobody's Bizness If I Do (vAL)	(as)	Candid CJM8022
7:42	'Tain't Nobody's Bizness If I Do (vAL)	(as)	Candid CCD79033

Charles Mingus Jazz Workshop - Jazz Artists' Guild: New York, 11 November 1960

Ted Curson, Lonnie Hillyer(tp), Charles McPherson(as), Eric Dolphy(as,bcl), Booker Ervin(ts), Paul Bley(p), Charles Mingus(b), Danny Richmond(d).

6:47	Lock 'em Up	(NS)	Candid CJM8021, Mosaic MR4-111
6:56	Reincarnation of a Love Bird	(NS)	−

Newport Rebels - Jazz Artists' Guild: New York, 11 November 1960

Roy Eldridge(tp), Jimmy Knepper(tb), Eric Dolphy(as), Tommy Flanagan(p), Charles Mingus(b), Jo Jones(d).

8:38	Mysterious Blues	(as)	Candid CJM8022, Mosaic MR4-111
10:43	Body and Soul	(as)	Candid CCD79033,79042
13:46	Body and Soul	(as)	Candid CCD79026, −
11:48	R & R	(as)	Candid CJM8019,CCD79026, −

Eric Dolphy - Ron Carter: New York, c. November 1960

Eric Dolphy(as), Ron Carter(b).

6:53	Dolphy-N	(as)	Blue Note BT85131,CDP48041

Eric Dolphy(fl).

4:11	Inner Flight #1	(fl)	− −
4:08	Inner Flight #2	(fl)	− −

Eric Dolphy(2-fl,bcl), Ron Carter(3-b)(overdubbed).

9:01	Triple Mix	(fl)	Jazzway Mutt 1502

Gunther Schuller and His Orchestra: New York, 20 December 1960

Eric Dolphy(as,bcl,fl), Robert DiDomenica(fl), Eddie Costa(vibes), Bill Evans(p), Jim Hall(g), Charles Libove, Roland Vamos(vln), Harry Zaratzian(vla), Joseph Tekula(cello), George Duvivier, Scott LaFaro(b), Sticks Evans(d), Gunther Schuller(cond).

5235	10:15	Variants on a Theme of John Lewis(Django)	(fl)	Atlantic LP/SD1365

add Ornette Coleman(as).

5236	15:23	Variants on a Theme of Thelonious Monk(Criss-Cross)	(fl,bcl)	

Ornette Coleman Double Quartet: New York, 21 December 1960

Freddie Hubbard(tp), Don Cherry(pocket-tp), Ornette Coleman(as), Eric Dolphy(bcl), Charlie Haden, Scott LaFaro(b), Ed Blackwell, Billy Higgins(d).

5247-1	17:00	The First Take	(bcl)	Atlantic SD1588, CD1364
5247-2	36:23	Free Jazz	(bcl)	Atlantic LP/SD1364, –

Eric Dolphy - Booker Little Quintet: Hackensack, New Jersey, 21 December 1960

Booker Little(tp), Eric Dolphy(as,bcl,fl), Jaki Byard(p), Ron Carter(b), Roy Haynes(d).

2772	8:00	Ode to Charlie Parker	(fl)	New Jazz NJLP8270, OJC400CD
2773	8:45	Mrs. Parker of K.C.	(bcl)	– –
2774	5:40	It's Magic -1	(bcl	– –
2775	6:38	Serene	(bcl)	Prestige P24046,MPP2517,
2776	4:15	Miss Ann	(as)	New Jazz NJLP8270,
2777	3:50	Far Cry	(as)	– –
2778	6:40	Left Alone -1	(fl)	– –

-1: Omit Little.

Eric Dolphy(as).

2779	4:15	Tenderly	(as)	New Jazz NJLP8270, OJC400CD

The Latin Jazz Quintet With Eric Dolphy: New York, c. late 1960-early 1961

Eric Dolphy(as,bcl,fl), Felipe Diaz(vibes), Arthur Jenkins(p), Bobby Rodriguez(b), Tommy Lopez(cga), Louis Ramirez(timbales).

	3:12	You're the Cutest One	(bcl)	United Artists UAI4071
	4:58	Speak Low	(fl)	–
	2:38	I Got Rhythm	(bcl)	–
	3:52	Night in Tunisia	(as)	–
	2:33	Cha-Cha King	(fl)	–
	3:08	I Wish I Were In Love Again	(bcl)	–
	2:49	Lover	(fl)	–
	2:10	Mangolina	(fl)	–
	6:33	April Rain	(fl)	–

Note: Eric Dolphy is not present on the remaining title from this session.

Abbey Lincoln: New York, 22 February 1961

Booker Little(tp), Julian Priester(tb), Eric Dolphy(as,bcl,fl,picc), Coleman Hawkins, Walter Benton(ts), Mal Waldron(p), Art Davis(b), Max Roach(d), Abbey Lincoln(v).

110

	5:15	Straight Ahead (vAL)	(NS)	Candid CJM8015
	4:00	When Malindy Sings (vAL)	(NS)	– , New World NW295
	8:23	In the Red (vAL)	(NS)	–
	6:32	Blue Monk (vAL)	(NS)	–
	6:42	Left Alone (vAL)	(NS)	–
	3:45	Retribution (vAL)	(NS)	–

add Roger Sanders, Robert Whitley(cgas).

	3:42	African Lady (vAL)	(NS)	Candid CJM8015
	3:36	African Lady (vAL)	(NS)	Candid CCD79033

Oliver Nelson Septet: New York, 23 February 1961

Freddie Hubbard(tp), Eric Dolphy(as,fl), Oliver Nelson(as,ts), George Barrow(bar), Bill Evans(p), Paul Chambers(b), Roy Haynes(d).

	8:45	Stolen Moments	(fl)	Impulse AS-5, MCAD-5659(CD)
	4:43	Hoe Down	(as)	– –
	5:30	Cascades	(NS)	– –
	6:20	Yearnin'	(as)	– –
	4:35	Butch and Butch	(as)	– –

omit Hubbard & Barrow.

	6:31	Teenie's Blues	(as)	– –

Oliver Nelson Quintet: New York, 1 March 1961

Eric Dolphy(as,bcl,fl), Oliver Nelson(as,cl,ts), Richard Wyands(p), George Duvivier(b), Roy Haynes(d).

2899	7:17	Six and Four	(as)	New Jazz NJLP8255, OJC099CD
2900	5:03	Mama Lou	(as)	– –
2901	5:45	Images	(bcl)	– –
2902	9:54	Ralph's New Blues	(bcl)	– , FCD60-022, –
2903	3:28	111-44	(bcl)	– –
2904	5:35	Straight Ahead	(as)	– –

Booker Little Sextet: New York, 17 March 1961

Booker Little(tp), Julian Priester(tb), Eric Dolphy(as,fl), Don Friedman(p), Art Davis(b), Max Roach(d).

	6:41	We Speak	(as)	Candid CJM8027, JDC106, NW275
	5:23	A New Day	(NS)	– –
	8:00	Quiet, Please	(as)	– –
	8:09	Quiet, Please	(as)	Candid CCD79033

Ron Carter(b) replaces Davis: New York, 4 April 1961

	5:42	Hazy Hues	(as	Candid CCD79033
	6:32	Hazy Hues	(as)	Candid CJM8027, JDC106
	5:34	Moods in Free Time	(as)	– –, CCD79033
	4:44	Man of Words	(NS)	– –
	6:39	Strength and Sanity	(NS)	– –, NW275
		Strength and Sanity	(NS)	– –

Ted Curson Quintet: New York, c. April 1961

Ted Curson(tp), Eric Dolphy(fl), Kenny Drew(p), Jimmy Garrison(b), Roy Haynes(d).

	The Things We Did Last Summer	(NS)	Old Town 2003
	Bali H'ai	(NS)	–

George Russell Sextet: New York, 8 May 1961

Don Ellis(tp), Dave Baker(tb), Eric Dolphy(as,bcl), George Russell(p),Steve Swallow(b), Joe Hunt(d).

8:57	Ezz-Thetic	(as)	Riverside RLP9375, OJC070CD
4:34	Nardis	(bcl)	–	–
8:06	Lydiot	(as)	–	–
5:26	Thoughts	(bcl)	–	–
8:55	Honesty	(as)	–	–
6:29	'Round Midnight	(as)	–	–

John Coltrane: New York, 23 May 1961

Booker Little, Freddie Hubbard(tp), Julian Priester, Charles Greenlea(euphonium), Julius Watkins, Donald Corrado, Bob Northern, Jim Buffington, Bob Swisshelm(frh), Bill Barber(tuba), Eric Dolphy, Garvin Bushell(reeds), Pat Patrick(bar), John Coltrane(ss,ts), McCoy Tyner(p), Paul Chambers, Reggie Workman(b), Elvin Jones(d).

9:55	Greensleeves	(NS)	Impulse AS-6, MCAD42001
6:37	Song of the Underground Railroad	(NS)	Impulse 9273
10:49	Greensleeves	(NS)	–
7:38	The Damned Don't Cry	(NS)	Impulse IZ9361/2
14:06	Africa	(NS)	–

Note: Orchestrations by Eric Dolphy.

John Coltrane Sextet/Septet: New York, 25 May 1961

Freddie Hubbard(tp), Eric Dolphy(as,fl), John Coltrane(ss,ts), McCoy Tyner(p), Art Davis, Reggie Workman(b), Elvin Jones(d).

5556	18:05	Ole		(fl)	Atlantic 1373, 1373CD
5557	10:50	Dahomey Dance		(as)	–	–
5558	7:32	Aisha	–1	(as)	–	–
5559	8:54	To Her Ladyship	–2	(fl)	Atlantic 1553,	–

–1: omit Davis; –2: omit Workman.

Note: 5559 issued as 'Original Untitled Ballad' on Atl.1553. Eric Dolphy listed as'George Lane' on Atl.1373.

John Coltrane: New York, 7 June 1961

Booker Little(tp), Britt Woodman(tb), Carl Bowman(euphonium), Julius Watkins, Don Corrado, Bob Northern, Bob Swisshelm(frh), Bill Barber(tuba), Eric Dolphy(reeds), John Coltrane(ts), Pat Patrick(bar), McCoy Tyner(p), Art Davis, Reggie Workman(b), Elvin Jones(d).

16:26	Africa	(NS)	Impulse AS-6, MCAD-42001
16:01	Africa	(NS)	Impulse 9273

omit Davis.

7:20	Blues Minor	(NS)	Impulse AS-6,	–

Note: Orchestrations by Eric Dolphy.

Ron Carter: New York, 20 June 1961

Eric Dolphy(as,bcl,fl), Mal Waldron(p), Ron Carter(cello), George Duvivier(b), Charlie Persip(d).

3086	5:35	Rally	(bcl)	New Jazz NJLP8265, OJC432CD
3088	5:47	Yes Indeed	(fl)	–	–

omit Duvivier; Carter plays bass.

3090	5:06	Saucer Eyes	(fl)	–	–
3091	7:40	Softly as in a Morning Sunrise	(as)	–	–

Mal Waldron: New York, 27 June 1961

Eric Dolphy(as,cl), Booker Ervin(ts), Mal Waldron(p), Ron Carter(cello), Joe Benjamin(b), Charlie Persip(d).

3110	4:45	Thirteen		(as)	New Jazz NJLP8269, OJC082CD
3111	4:10	Duquility		(NS)	–	–
3112	8:50	Status Seeking		(as)	–, FCD60-022	–
3113	5:35	Warp and Woof		(as)	–	–
3114	5:37	Warm Canto	–1	(cl)	–	–
3115	7:55	Fire Waltz		(NS)	–	–
3116	4:23	We Diddit		(as)	–	–

–1: omit Ervin.

Eric Dolphy – Booker Little Quintet: Five Spot, New York, 16 July 1961

Booker Little(tp), Eric Dolphy(as,bcl,fl), Mal Waldron(p), Richard Davis(b), Ed Blackwell(d).

3146		(warming up & tuning)		unissued	
3147	11:30	Status Seeking		(as)	Prestige PR7382, OJC673CD
3148	5:16	God Bless the Child	–1	(bcl)	–	–
3149	16:38	Aggression		(bcl)	Prestige PR7294, OJC247CD
3150	19:25	Like Someone In Love		(fl)	–	–
3151	13:14	Fire Waltz		(as)	New Jazz NJLP8260, OJC133CD
3152	12:13	Bee Vamp		(bcl)	–	–
3153	21:00	The Prophet		(as)	–	–
3154	17:00	Number Eight (Potsa Lotsa)		(as)	Prestige PR7334, OJC353CD
3155	15:00	Booker's Waltz		(bcl)	–	–
	9:33	Bee Vamp		(bcl)	Prestige MPP 2517

–1: omit tp,p,b,d.

Max Roach: New York, 1 August 1961

Booker Little(tp), Julian Priester(tb), Eric Dolphy(as,bcl,fl), Clifford Jordan(ts), Mal Waldron(p), Art Davis(b), Max Roach(d), Carlos Valeler(cga), Carlos Eugenio(bell), Abbey Lincoln(v).

	7:55	Garvey's Ghost (vAL)		(NS)	Impulse AS-8
	8:56	Mendacity (vAL)	–1	(as)	–

omit Lincoln.   New York, 3 August 1961

	4:50	Mama	–1	(NS)	Impulse AS-8
	6:54	Tender Warriors		(bcl)	–

same.   New York, 8 August 1961

	7:13	Praise for a Martyr	–1	(NS)	Impulse AS-8

same.   New York, 9 August 1961

| | 5:15 | Man From South Africa | (as) | | Impulse AS-8 |

−1: omit Valeler, Eugenio.

Eric Dolphy Quintet: Funkturm Exhibition Hall, Berlin, 30 August 1961
Eric Dolphy(as,fl,bcl), Benny Bailey(tp), Pepsi Auer(p), Jamil Nasser(b), Buster Smith(d).

	2:56	G.W.		(as)	IC-3017, ENJA 3007/9, RH79636CD
	3:15	God Bless the Child	−1	(bcl)	− − −
	5:25	245		(as)	−

−1:omit tp,p,b,d

same.   Jazz Salon, Berlin, 30 August 1961

| | 13:00 | I'll Remember April | (as) | IC-3017, ENJA 3007/9, RH79636CD |
| | 19:04 | Hot House | (as) | −   −   − |

Eric Dolphy(bcl,fl), Jamil Nasser(b), Buster Smith(d).   same session

| | 13:20 | When Lights Are Low | (bcl) | IC-3017, ENJA 3007/9, RH79636CD |
| | 14:55 | Hi Fly | (fl) | −   −   − |

Eric Dolphy Quartet: Vastmanland-Dala Nation, Uppsala, Sweden,
4 September 1961

Eric Dolphy(as,bcl,fl), Rony Johansson(p), Kurt Lindgren(b), Rune Carlsson(d).

	4:23	What Is This Thing Called Love		(bcl)	Serene SER 03
	20:38	245		(as)	−
	6:56	Laura	−1	(as)	−
	1:44	52nd Street Theme		(as)	−
	14:08	Bags' Groove		(fl)	−
	12:43	Out of Nowhere		(as)	Serene SER 04
	14:31	I'll Remember April		(as)	−
	:45	52nd Street Theme		(as)	−
	15:58	When Lights Are Low		(bcl)	−

−1: omit p,b,d.

Note: This concert was recorded privately and first surfaced on CD in 1992. The rhythm section is the least attuned to Dolphy of any with which he is known to have recorded.

Eric Dolphy Quartet: Berlingske Has, Copenhagen, 6 September 1961
Eric Dolphy(as,fl,bcl), Bent Axen(p), Erik Moseholm(b), Jorn Elniff(d).

	11:30	Don't Blame Me	(fl)	Prestige PR-7350, OJC414CD
	13:30	Don't Blame Me	(fl)	Prestige PR-7382, OJC673CD
	12:10	When Lights Are Low	(bcl)	Prestige PR-7366, OJC416CD
		Miss Ann		unissued
		Miss Ann		−

Note: Although Prestige PR-7350 lists "Miss Ann" on liner notes and label, the composition performed is "Les" recorded at the concert on September 8th.

same.   Studenterforeningen Foredragssal, Copenhagen, Denmark,
8 September 1961

	6:05	Glad To Be Unhappy	(fl)	Prestige PR-7304, OJC413CD
	7:12	Oleo	(bcl)	− −
	9:30	The Way You Look Tonight	(as)	Prestige PR-7350, OJC414CD

13:40	Laura	(as)	–	–
5:30	Les	(as)	–	–
10:20	Woody'n You	(as)	Prestige PR-7366, OJC416CD	
	In the Blues #1	(as)	–	–
	In the Blues (false start)	(NS)	–	–
	In the Blues #2	(as)	–	–
	In the Blues 3	(as)	–	–

Note: The 3 versions of "In the Blues" with the false start in place occupy one side of Prestige PR-7366. Total timing for that side is 17:30.

Eric Dolphy(fl), Chuck Israels(b).   same concert

| 13:14 | Hi Fly | (fl) | Prestige PR-7304, OJC413CD |

omit Israels.

| 6:50 | God Bless the Child | (bcl) | – | – |

Eric Dolphy Quartet: Copenhagen, c. September 1961

Eric Dolphy(as,bcl,fl), Bent Axen(p), Erik Moseholm(b), William Schiopffe(d).

9:10	Don't Blame Me	(fl)	TV broadcast
6:10	Green Dolphin Street	(bcl)	–
2:50	Miss Ann	(as)	–
245	(incomplete)	(NS)	–

Note: A private tape of the audio portion of this broadcast circulates in low fidelity among collectors.

Eric Dolphy Quartet: TV broadcast, Stockholm, c. September 1961

Eric Dolphy(as,bcl,fl), Knud Jorgensen(p), Jimmy Woode(b), Sture Kallin(d).

12:07	Don't Blame Me	(fl)	Inner City IC-3007, ENJA 3055
12:00	Serene	(bcl)	–
3:58	Les	(as)	–	–

Note: Date given in liner notes is 25 September 1961. This may be erronious as Dolphy was reported in San Francisco with John Coltrane during the last 2 weeks of September 1961. Unfortunately the video portions of the above TV broadcasts have not become available at this writing. CD issue on RH79647.

John Coltrane: Village Vanuard, NYC, 1 November 1961

John Coltrane(ts,ss), Eric Dolphy(as,bcl), McCoy Tyner(p), Reggie Workman(b), Elvin Jones(d).

9:51	Chasin' the Trane	–1	(as)	Impulse 9325
8:50	Impressions	–2	(as)	Impulse IZ-9361/2
13:35	Spiritual		(bcl)	Impulse 9325
10:00	Miles' Mode		(as)	Impulse IZ-9361/2
7:39	Naima		(bcl)	–
18:40	Brasilia	–1	(as)	Impulse 9325
	India	–3		rejected

–1: omit (p); –2: Jimmy Garrison(b) for Workman; –3: add Achmed Abdul-Malik(oud) and Jimmy Garrison(b).

John Coltrane: Village Vanguard, NYC, 2 November 1961

John Coltrane(ts,ss), Eric Dolphy(as,bcl), McCoy Tyner(p), Jimmy Garrison, Reggie Workman(b), Elvin Jones(d), Garvin Bushell(oboe,contrabassoon).

15:34 Chasin' the Trane	−1	(as)	Impulse IZ-9361/2
13:20 India	−2	(bcl)	MCAD-5541
15:00 Spiritual	−3	(bcl)	−
10:55 Impressions	−4	(as)	Impulse IZ-9361/2

−1: omit Tyner, Bushell, Garrison; Roy Haynes(d) for Jones.
−2: add Ahmed Abdul-Malik(oud); −3: omit Garrison; −4: omit Workman, Bushell.

John Coltrane: Village Vanguard, NYC, 3 November 1961

John Coltrane(ts), Erlc Dolphy(as,bcl), McCoy Tyner(p), Reggie Workman(b), Elvin Jones(d).

13:30 Spiritual	(bcl)	Impulse A(S)-10
Naima		rejected

add Jimmy Garrison(b).

13:52 India	(bcl)	Impulse A(S)-42
Miles' Mode		rejected

John Coltrane: Village Vanguard, NYC, 5 November 1961

John Coltrane(ts,ss), Eric Dolphy(bcl), McCoy Tyner(p), Jimmy Garrison, Reggie Workman(b), Elvin Jones(d), Garvin Bushell(oboe,contrabassoon), Ahmed Abdul-Malik(oud).

15:10 India	(bcl)	Impulse 9325

omit Garrison, Malik.

20:32 Spiritual	(bcl)	−

John Coltrane Quintet: Theatre de Olympia, Paris, 18 November 1961

John Coltrane(ss,ts), Eric Dolphy(as,fl), McCoy Tyner(p), Reggie Workman(b), Elvin Jones(d).

10:55 Impressions	(as)	Magnetic Records MRCD-114
16:04 Blue Train	(as)	−
12:40 Blue Train	(as)	Magnetic Records MRCD-115
25:11 My Favorite Things	(fl)	−
4:39 Impressions (incomplete)	(as)	unissued

Note: There were 2 concerts, at 6:30 pm (MRCD-114) and 11:30 pm (MRCD-115).

Eric Dolphy Quintet: TV Special, Stockholm, 19 November 1961

Idries Sulieman(tp), Eric Dolphy(as,bcl,fl), Rune Ofwerman(p), Jimmy Woode(b), Sture Kallin(d).

5:19 Left Alone	−1	(fl)	Enja 3055, Inner City IC-3007	
6:00 G.W.		(as)	−	−
5:26 God Bless the Child	−2	(bcl)	−	−
4:11 Miss Ann		(as)	−	−
Serene		(bcl)	Enja SPE-1	

−1: omit tp. −2: omit tp,p,b,d. CD issue on RH76947.

John Coltrane Quintet: Falconercentret, Copenhagen, 20 November 1961

John Coltrane(ss,ts), Eric Dolphy(as,bcl,fl), McCoy Tyner(p), Reggie Workman(b), Elvin Jones(d).

11:33 Delilah	(bcl)	Magnetic Records MRCD-116
13:13 Impressions	(as)	−
7:00 Naima	(bcl)	−
29:00 My Favorite Things	(fl)	−

116

same.   Koncerthuset, Stockholm, 23 November 1961

	11:30	Impressions	(as)	HPLP-1
	25:55	My Favorite Things	(fl)	–, Oppex-10, Jazz Bird 2006
	2:25	Naima (incomplete)	(bcl)	–
	8:57	Blue Train	(as)	HPLP-5, Charly CD117
	4:00	Naima	(bcl)	– –
	7:11	Impressions	(as)	– –
	20:48	My Favorite Things	(fl)	– –

Note: Again, there were 2 shows.

same.   TV, Baden-Baden, 26 November 1961

	7:30	Impressions	(as)	Video Artists VAI-69035
	11:06	My Favorite Things	(fl)	–

Note: audio portion issued on Jazz Connoisseur JC-112.

same.   Frankfurt, 27 November 1961

	17:00	Impressions	(as)	broadcast
	20:25	My Favorite Things	(fl)	–

same.   Stuttgart, 29 November 1961

	8:55	Impressions	(as)	private recording
	15:34	My Favorite Things	(fl)	–

Eric Dolphy Quartet: Munich, 1 December 1961

Eric Dolphy(bcl), McCoy Tyner(p), Reggie Workman(b), Mel Lewis(d).

	14:40	Softly as in a Morning Sunrise	(bcl)	Jazz Connoisseur 107,JA5234
	18:25	Oleo	(bcl)	Unique Jazz UJ-26
	24:00	Green Dolphin Street	(bcl)	Jazz Connoisseur 107
	12:08	The Way You Look Tonight	(bcl)	–

Note: All titles also on Natasha CD NI-4001, which gives location as Berlin.

John Coltrane Quintet: Berlin, 2 December 1961

John Coltrane(ts,ss), Eric Dolphy(as,fl), McCoy Tyner(p), Reggie Workman(b), Elvin Jones(d).

	12:31	Impressions	(as)	radio broadcast

Jimmy Garrison(b) for Workman.   Birdland, NYC, 10 February 1962

	18:41	My Favorite Things	(fl)	Ozone 10
	11:00	Mr. P.C.	(as)	–, Unique Jazz UJ-26
	10:39	Miles' Mode	(as)	– –

All titles also on Affinity Aff-79, Session 114, & Jazz Anthology 30JA5184. This was the last material to have surfaced with Dolphy and Coltrane together.

Pony Poindexter: NYC, 16 February 1962

Pony Poindexter(ss,as), Eric Dolphy, Sonny Red(as), Jimmy Heath, Clifford Jordan(ts), Pepper Adams(bar), Gildo Mahones(p), Ron Carter(b), Elvin Jones(d).

69687		B Frequency	(NS)	Epic 16035
69688-1	9:25	Lanyop	(as)	–
69688-2		Lanyop		CBS 38509

Gunther Schuller: Syracuse, N.Y., 10 March 1962

Note: According to the liner notes on ENJA's lp and CD issues of the album titled *Vintage Dolphy*, the performance of "Night Music" was from a concert at Syracuse University on 10 March 1962. However, this piece was also performed at the Carnegie Hall Concert of 14 March 1963 (see NOTE to that session). The reviews of that concert list this piece among those performed, and the ambience of the recording seems similar to the other titles made that day.

Benny Golson: NYC, c. April 1962

Bill Hardman(tp), Grachan Moncur III(tb), Eric Dolphy(as), Bill Evans(p), Ron Carter(b), Charlie Persip(d).

3:16	Groovin' High	(as)	Audio Fidelity LP2150/SD6150
2:44	Donna Lee	(as)	–
3:53	Quicksilver	(as)	–
3:43	Ornithology	(as)	–

omit Hardman.

3:00	If I Should Lose You	(as)	–

Note: Session arranged & conducted by Benny Golson. These performances were also issued on Audio Fidelity LP-1978/SD5978 with an orchestra overdubbed which was performing standard tunes based on the same chord patterns as follows:

> Groovin' High / Whispering
> Donna Lee / Indiana
> Quicksilver / Lover Come Back To Me
> Ornithology / How High the Moon
> If I Should Lose You / If I Should Lose You

Ed Summerlin: Church of the Epiphany, Washington, D.C., 3 June 1962

Don Ellis, Lou Glucken(tp), Slide Hampton, Dick Lieb(tb), Eric Dolphy(as), J.R. Monterose(ts), Barry Galbraith(g), Ron Carter(b), Charlie Persip(d), unidentified church organist & mixed choir, Ed Summerlin(cond).

            Jazz Vespers Service   TV broadcast

John Lewis and His Orchestra: New York, 5 October 1962

Harold Jones(fl), Eric Dolphy(alto-fl), Phil Woods(cl), William Arrowsmith(oboe), Don Stewart(basset-horn), Loren Glickman(bassoon), Gene Allen(bar), John Lewis(p), Jim Hall(g), Richard Davis(b), Connie Kay(d), Gary McFarland(cond).

6480		By My Side		Atlantic unissued
6481	7:11	Tillamook Two	(NS)	Atlantic LP/SD1425
6482	5:09	Another Encounter	(NS)	–

Eric Dolphy Quintet: Gaslight Inn, NYC, 7 October 1962

Edward Armour(tp), Eric Dolphy(as,bcl,fl), Herbie Hancock(p), Richard Davis(b), Edgar Bateman(d).

8:12	Miss Ann		(as)	Unique Jazz UJ10, Ingo 14
11:44	Left Alone	-1	(fl)	– –
7:54	I Got Rhythm	-2	(bcl)	Unique Jazz UJ26
4:38	Lady Be Good	-2	(NS)	(unissued)
11:32	G.W.		(as)	Unique Jazz UJ10
4:00	245 (incomplete)		(as)	– –

-1: Omit Armour. -2: Add Joe Carroll(v).

Charles Mingus Orchestra: Town Hall, NYC, 12 October 1962

Lonnie Hillyer, Snooky Young, Rolf Ericson, Ernie Royal, Eddie Armour, Clark Terry, Richard Williams(tp), Britt Woodman, Jimmy Cleveland, Willie Dennis, Quentin Jackson, Jimmy Knepper, Eddie Bert(tb), Don Butterfield(tu), Eric Dolphy(as,bcl,fl), Charlie Mariano, Charles McPherson(as), Dick Hafer(cl,fl,ts), Buddy Collette(fl,ts), Jerome Richardson(bar,fl,oboe,ss), Zoot Sims, Booker Ervin(ts), Pepper Adams(bar), Teddy Charles(vibes), Jaki Byard, Toshiko Mariano(p), Les Spann(g), Milt Hinton(b), Charles Mingus(b,narr), Osie Johnson, Danny Richmond(d).

	Osmosis (2 takes)			unissued
10:28	Epitaph I & II		(as)	United Artists UAJ14024
3:27	Freedom	−1	(NS)	
	Peggy's Blue Skylight			unissued
2:56	Clark in the Dark		(NS)	United Artists UAJ14024
	Portrait			unissued
3:00	Duke's Choice		(NS)	United Artists UAJ14024
	Don't Come Back			unissued
8:05	My Search		(NS)	United Artists UAJ14024
7:35	In a Mellotone(as)			

−1: "Freedom" features a Mingus narration and band vocal.

Note: "Epitaph" was edited into 2 parts for issue. The original issues mislabelled all titles as follows:

LABEL READS:			SHOULD READ:
Side A Track	1: "Clark in the Dark"	=	"My Search"
	2: "Epitaph I"	=	"In a Mellotone"
	3: "Epitaph II"	=	"Duke's Choice"
Side B Track	1: "Freedom"	=	"Clark in the Dark"
	2: "My Search"	=	"Epitaph I"
	3: "Don't Come Back"	=	"Freedom"
	4: "Finale"	=	"Epitaph II"

Eric Dolphy: New York City, c. 1962

Eric Dolphy(as,bcl,fl), with unknown (v),(p),(b),(d).

15:30	Jim Crow	(as,bcl,fl)	Blue Note BT85131,CDP48041

Orchestra U.S.A.:   New York, 4 February 1963

Louis Mucci, Herb Pomeroy, Nick Travis(tp), Mike Zwerin(tb), Robert Swisshelm, Bob Northern(frh), Harvey Philips(tu), Eric Dolphy(as,fl), Phil Woods(as,cl), Don Ashworth(bar,oboe), Robert DiDomenica(fl,piccolo), Wally Kane(fl,bassoon), Don Stewart(cl,basset-horn), Ray Shiner(oboe), Nathan Goldstein, Gerald Beal, Jerry Widoff, Gino Sambucco(vln), Julian Barber, Selwart Clark(vla), Joseph Tekula, Al Goldberg(cello), John Lewis(p), Jim Hall(g), Richard Davis(b), Connie Kay(d), Gary McFarland, Sticks Evans(perc), Gunther Schuller(cond).

5:20	Milesign	(as)	Colpix CLP448
3:36	Milano	(NS)	−
5:41	Grand Encounter	(NS)	−

same, except Philip West(oboe,English-horn) replaces Ashworth; Alfred Bruening(vln) replaces Widoff; Aaron Juvelier(vla) replaces Clark; and Michael Colgrass(perc) replaces McFarland.   New York, 27 February 1963

5:30	Natural Affection	(NS)	Colpix CLP448

| 5:18 | Donnie's Theme | (as) | – |
| 1:22 | The Star Spangled Banner | (NS) | – |

Freddie Hubbard and His Orchestra: New York, 8 March 1963

Freddie Hubbard, Edward Armour, Richard Williams(tp), Curtis Fuller, Melba Liston(tb), Bob Northern, Julius Watkins(frh), Eric Dolphy(as), Jerome Richardson(bar), Julius Held, Harry Cykman, Morris Stonzek, Arnold Eidus, Sol Shapiro, Charles McCracken, Gene Orloff, Harry Katzman, Harry Lookofsky, Paul Poliakin(strings), Cedar Walton(p), Reggie Workman(b), Philly Joe Jones(d), Wayne Shorter(cond).

Chocolate Shake	(NS)	Impulse A(S)38
Skylark	(NS)	–
I Got It Bad and That Ain't Good	(NS)	–

Note: Arrangements by Wayne Shorter.

Eric Dolphy Quartet: University of Illinois, 10 March 1963

Eric Dolphy(as,bcl,fl), Herbie Hancock(p), Richard Davis(b), J.C. Moses(d).

Softly as in a Morning Sunrise	unissued
South Street Exit	–
(unknown title)	–

Eric Dolphy(bcl).

God Bless the Child	–

add the University of Illinois Big Band, Cecil Bridgewater(tp).

Miles' Mode	–
(unknown title)	–

Note: Information from Uwe Reichardt's discography on Dolphy. As Dolphy was recording in New York on both 8 & 11 March, this must have been a rushed trip assuming the date is accurate.

Freddie Hubbard and His Orchestra: New York, 11 March 1963

Freddie Hubbard, Al DeRisi, Ernie Royal, Clark Terry(tp), Curtis Fuller, Melba Liston(tb), Bob Northern(frh), Robert Powell(tu), Eric Dolphy(as), Seldon Powell(ts), Charles Davis, Jerome Richardson(bar), Cedar Walton(p), Reggie Workman(b), Philly Joe Jones(d), Wayne Shorter(cond).

Carnival	(NS)	Impulse A(S)38
Thermo	(NS)	–
Aries (NS)		–

Note: Arrangements by Wayne Shorter.

Gunther Schuller: Carnegie Hall, NYC, 14 March 1963

Eric Dolphy(cl), Gloria Agostina(harp), Eddie Costa, Warren Chiasson(vibes), Richard Davis(b).

| 4:50 | Densities | (cl) | ENJA 5045-24, GM3005CD |

Eric Dolphy(bcl), Barry Galbraith(g), Chuck Israels, Art Davis(b), Sticks Evans(d).

| 3:50 | Night Music | (bcl) | ENJA 5045-24, GM3005CD |

Eric Dolphy(as), Jim Hall(g), Matthew Raimondi, Lewis Kaplan(vln), Samuel Rhodes(vla),Michael Rudiakov(cello), Richard Davis, Barre Phillips(b), Sticks Evans(d).

120

| 4:44 | Abstraction | (as) | ENJA 5045-24, GM3005CD |

Note: Although the above pieces were performed and reviewed at this concert, ENJA's liner notes cite "Night Music" as being from a Syracuse, NY, concert on 10 March 1962.

Eric Dolphy Quartet: Carnegie Hall, NYC, 18 April 1963

Eric Dolphy(as,bcl,fl), Edward Armour(tp), Richard Davis(b), J.C. Moses(d).

8:48	Half Note Triplets	(bcl)	ENJA 5045-24, GM3005CD
8:00	Ode to Charlie Parker	(fl)	–	–
6:20	Iron Man	(as)	–	–

Jam Session: same concert, 18 April 1963

Don Ellis, Nick Travis(tp), Jimmy Knepper(tb), Eric Dolphy, Phil Woods(as), Benny Golson(ts), Lalo Schifrin(p), Jim Hall(g), Barre Phillips(b), Charles Persip(d).

| 12:56 | Donna Lee | (as) | ENJA 5045-24,GM3005CD |

Teddy Charles and the All-Stars: New York, 26 April 1963

Eric Dolphy(bcl), Jerome Richardson(fl,ts), Zoot Sims(ts), Pepper Adams(bar), Teddy Charles(vibes), Hall Overton(p), Jimmy Raney(g), Teddy Kotick(b), Osie Johnson(d).

3:45	Scheherezade Blue	(NS)	United Artists UAI3365
2:21	Love for Three Oranges March	(NS)	–
3:37	Borodin Bossa Nova	(NS)	–

Freddie Hubbard Septet: New York, 2 May 1963

Freddie Hubbard(tp), Curtis Fuller(tb), Eric Dolphy(as,fl), Wayne Shorter(ts), Cedar Walton(p), Reggie Workman(b), Louis Hayes(d).

3:23	Clarence's Place	(as)	Impulse A(S)38
	Dedicated to You	(NS)	–
	Body and Soul	(NS)	–

Eric Dolphy: New York, late May – early June 1963

Woody Shaw(tp), Clifford Jordan(ss), Sonny Simmons(as), Prince Lasha(fl), Eric Dolphy(bcl), Garvin Bushell(bassoon), Bobby Hutcherson(vibes), Eddie Kahn, Richard Davis(b), J.C. Moses(d).

| 11:52 | Burning Spear | (bcl) | Douglas 785, CELCD5015 |

Eric Dolphy(bcl), Clifford Jordan(ss), Sonny Simmons(as), Prince Lasha(fl), Richard Davis(b), Charles Moffett(d).

| 9:05 | Music Matador | (bcl) | FM308, VJ2503, AJF-FS227 |

Woody Shaw(tp), Eric Dolphy(as,fl), Bobby Hutcherson(vibes), Eddie Kahn(b), J.C. Moses(d).

| 7:05 | Jitterbug Waltz | (fl) | FM308, VJ2503, AJF-FS227 |
| 9:09 | Iron Man | (as) | Douglas 785, CELCD5015 |

Richard Davis(b) for Kahn.

| 4:45 | Mandrake | (as) | – | – |

Eric Dolphy(bcl,fl), Richard Davis(b).

13:30	Alone Together	(bcl)	FM308, VJ2503
6:24	Come Sunday	(bcl)	Douglas 785, CELCD5015
8:03	Ode to C.P.	(fl)	– –

Eric Dolphy(as).

| 3:25 | Love Me | (as) | FM308, VJ2503 |

Note: Reverse of Archive of Jazz and Folk AJF-FS227 by Gene Ammons & Cannonball Adderly.

Charles Mingus Orchestra: New York, 20 September 1963

Eddie Preston, Richard Williams(tp), Britt Woodman(tb), Don Butterfield(tu), Eric Dolphy(as,bcl,fl), Dick Hafer(cl,fl,ts), Jerome Richardson(bar,fl,ss), Booker Ervin(ts), Jaki Byard(p), Charles Mingus(b,narr), Walter Perkins(d).

11756	6:19	Hora Decubitus	(as)	Impulse A-54
11757	5:37	Theme for Lester Young	(NS)	
11758	7:01	II B.S. (NS)		
11759		Freedom –1	(NS)	Impulse A-99
11760	4:02	Better Git Hit in Your Soul	(NS)	Impulse A-54
11761		Take the A Train		(unissued)
11762	4:40	Mood Indigo	(NS)	Impulse A-54

–1: band vocal; Mingus narrates.

Note: Better Git Hit in Your Soul was originally dated 20 January 1963 by Impulse liner notes to A(S)-54.

Gil Evans and His Orchestra: New York, c. September 1963

Jimmy Cleveland(tb), Gil Cohen, Don Corrado, Julius Watkins(frh), Eric Dolphy(fl,bcl), Steve Lacy(ss), Bob Tricarico(ts), Al Block(fl), Gil Evans(p), Barry Galbraith(g), Margaret Ross(harp), Paul Chambers, Richard Davis, Ben Tucker(b), Elvin Jones(d).

| 2:00 | Flute Song | (NS) | Verve V(6)8555 |

Gil Evans and His Orchestra: New York, c. September 1963

Johnny Coles, Ernie Royal, Louis Mucci(tp), Jimmy Cleveland, Tony Studd(tb), Jim Buffington, Bob Northern, Julius Watkins(frh), Eric Dolphy(as,bcl,fl), Steve Lacy(ss), Bob Tricarico(ts), Jerome Richardson(fl,bar), Gil Evans(p), Paul Chambers, Milt Hinton, Richard Davis(b), Osie Johnson(d).

| 3:30 | El Toreador | (NS) | Verve V(6)8555 |

John Coltrane Quintet: Philharmonic Hall, Lincoln Center, NYC,
                                             31 December 1963

John Coltrane(ss,ts), Eric Dolphy(as,fl,bcl), McCoy Tyner(p), Jimmy Garrison(b), Elvin Jones(d).

	My Favorite Things		unissued
	Alabama		–
	Impressions		–

Note: This concert, which also featured groups led by Cecil Taylor and Art Blakey, was known to have been recorded but the tapes may have been destroyed afterwards.

Sextet of the Orchestra U.S.A.:   New york, 10 January 1964

Nick Travis(tp), Mike Zwerin(btp), Eric Dolphy(as,bcl,fl), John Lewis(p), Richard Davis(b), Connie Kay(d).

6890	5:14	Alabama song	(bcl)	RCA LPM3498, 62852-RB(CD)
6891		Havana Song	(NS)	– –
6892	5:16	As You Make Your Bed	(as)	– –

New York Philharmonic Young People's Concert: NYC, 8 February 1964

Don Ellis(tp), Eric Dolphy(as), Benny Golson(ts), Richard Davis(b), Joe Cocuzzo(d), New York Philharmonic, Leonard Bernstein(narr), Gunther Schuller(cond).

13:15	Journey Into Jazz	(as)	TV Broadcast

Eric Dolphy Quintet: Englewood Cliffs, New Jersey, 25 February 1964

Freddie Hubbard(tp), Eric Dolphy(as,bcl,fl), Bobby Hutcherson(vibes), Richard Davis(b), Tony Williams(d).

8:21	Hat and Beard	(bcl)	Blue Note BLP4163,CDP48524
6:01	Something Sweet, Something Tender	(bcl)	– –
7:19	Gazzeloni	(fl)	– –
12:05	Out to Lunch	(as)	– –
8:19	Straight Up and Down	(as)	– –

Andrew Hill Sextet: Englewood Cliffs, New Jersey, 21 March 1964

Kenny Dorham(tp), Eric Dolphy(as,bcl,fl), Joe Henderson(ts), Andrew Hill(p), Richard Davis(b), Tony Williams(d).

12:14	Refuge (as)		Blue Note BLP4167, BN84167CD	
7:01	New Monestary	(as)	–	–
9:43	Spectrum	(as,bcl)	–	–
4:10	Flight 19	(NS)	–	–
3:46	Flight 19	(NS)	–	–
6:39	Dedication	(bcl)	–	–
7:00	Dedication	(bcl)	–	–

Charles Mingus Jazz Workshop: Town Hall, NYC, 4 April 1964

Johnny Coles(tp), Eric Dolphy(as,bcl,fl), Clifford Jordan(ts), Jaki Byard(p), Charles Mingus(b), Danny Richmond(d).

18:00	So Long Eric	(as)	JWS005, Fantasy JWS9
27:02	Meditations	(bcl,fl)	– –
	Orange Was the Color	unissued	

Note: "Meditations" issued in 2 parts as "Prayin' With Eric". CD issue on OJC042.

Gil Evans and His Orchestra: New York, 6 April 1964

Johnny Coles, Bernie Glow(tp), Jimmy Cleveland, Tony Studd(tb), Ray Alongo(frh), Bill Barber(tu), Steve Lacy(ss), Eric Dolphy(as,bcl,fl), Bob Tricarico(fl,ts), Garvin Bushell(fl), Gil Evans(p), Ron Carter, Paul Chambers(b), Elvin Jones(d).

10:25	Hotel Me	(NS)	Verve V(6)8555
6:13	Las Vegas Tango	(NS)	–

Charles Mingus Jazz Workshop: Concertgebouw, Amsterdam,
                                            10 April 1964

Johnny Coles(tp), Eric Dolphy(as,bcl,fl), Clifford Jordan(ts), Jaki Byard(p), Char-les Mingus(b,voice), Dannie Richmond(d,voice).

20:45	Parkeriana	(as)	Ulyssee Music AROC 50506
21:45	So Long Erlc	(as)	–
17:45	Orange Was the Color	(bcl)	Ulyssee Music AROC 50507
22:45	Meditations	(bcl,fl)	–
30:00	Fables of Faubus		Ulyssee Music AROC 50508

same.   University Aula, Oslo, 12 April 1964

21:30	So Long Eric	(as)	television recording	
15:00	Orange Was the Color	(NS)	–	Jazz Up Ju307
2:30	Parkeriana (false start)	(as)(NS)	–	–
12:00	Take the A Train	(bcl)	–	–
29:45	Fables of Faubus	(bcl)	–	–
23:30	Meditations	(bcl,fl)	radio broadcast	
21:46	Parkeriana	(as)	–	

Note: the unedited footage from the TV recording is in circulation among col-lectors.

same.   rehearsal, Stockholm, 13 April 1964

3:00	So Long Eric	(as)	Royal Jazz RJD518
:37	Meditations (false start)	(NS)	–
18:39	Meditations	(bcl,fl)	–
8:00	So Long Eric	(as)	–

same.   Koncerthuset, Stockholm, 13 April 1964

11:54	Peggy's Blue Skylight	(as)	Royal Jazz RJD518
12:04	When Irish Eyes...	(bcl)	–
19:40	Fables of Faubus	(NS)	–
	Orange Was the Color	–	

same.   Odd Fellow Palaet, Copenhagen, 14 April 1964

21:30	Meditations	(bcl,fl)	radio broadcast
13:55	Orange Was the Color	(bcl)	–
32:45	Fables of Faubus	(bcl)	–
16:47	So Long Eric	(as)–	

same.   Bremen, 16 April 1964

24:00	So Long Eric	(as)	Ingo 10
33:40	Fables of Faubus		Ingo 13
21:45	Parkeriana	(as)	Ingo 15
25:00	Meditations	(bcl,fl)	– , Unique Jazz UJ23

same.   Salle Wagram, Paris, 17 April 1964

23:30	So Long Eric	(as)	America 30AM003

Note: fades as Dolphy begins soloing

omit Coles   same concert

10:51	Orange Was the Color	(bcl)	radio broadcast
21:50	Parkeriana	(as)	–
23:08	Fables of Faubus	(bcl)	–
20:31	Meditations	(bcl,fl)	–
11:38	Peggy's Blue Skylight	(as)	–

Note: Johnny Coles developed a perforated gastric ulcer and collapsed before the performance of "Orange Was the Color" (possibly before the end of "So Long Eric" accounting for the fadeout) and missed the rest of the tour.

Charles Mingus Jazz Workshop: Paris, 18-19 April 1964

Eric Dolphy(as,fl,bcl); Clifford Jordan(ts); Jaki Byard(p); Charles Mingus(b,voice); Dannie Richmond(d,voice).

5:40	So Long Eric	(as)	America 30AM003
14:00	Orange Wa the Color	(bcl)	–
23:00	Parkeriana	(as)	America 30AM004
27:30	Meditations	(bcl,fl)	–
28:40	Fables of Faubus	(bcl)	America 30AH005

Eric Dolphy(fl), Charles Mingus(b).   same concert

I Can't Get Started   radio broadcast

Note: "So Long Eric" issued as "Goodbye Porkpie Hat" in 2 parts: Part 1 fades on Side A as Dolphy begins to solo; it is the version from the 17th. Side B begins with Dolphy's solo and is from the midnight April 18/19th concert.

same.   Liege, 19 April 1964

5:45	So Long Eric	(as)	TV broadcast
6:49	Peggy's Blue Skylight	(as)	–
24:27	Meditations	(bcl,fl)	–

same   Marseilles, 19 April 1964

So Long Eric		TV broadcast
Parkeriana		–
Meditations		–

Note: One of the above TV broadcasts is in circulation on video.

same   Bologna, 24 April 1964

unknown titles   radio broadcast

same   Wuppertal, 26 April 1964

37:10	Fables of Faubus	(bcl)	ENJA 3049,CD3049-45
4:58	I Can't Get Started –1	(fl)	– –
21:48	Meditations	(bcl,fl)	– –
16:20	Orange Was the Color	(bcl)	ENJA 3077,CD3077-38
11:17	Peggy's Blue Skylight	(as)	– –
22:47	So Long Eric	(as)	– –

–1:omit ts,p,d.

Note: "I Can't Get Started" listed as "Starting," as by Eric Dolphy; "Peggy's..." listed as "Charlemagne" on lp issue only.

same   Stuttgart, 28 April 1964

29:16	So Long Eric	(as)	Unique Jazz UJ-007
16:30	Orange Was the Color	(bcl)	–
3:00	These Foolish Things –1	(fl)	–
19:32	Peggy's Blue Skylight	(as)	Unique Jazz UJ-008
28:12	Meditations	(bcl,fl)	–
40:07	Fables of Faubus	(bcl)	Unique Jazz UJ-009

−1:omit ts,p,d.

Note: The Unique Jazz releases provide edited versions; the above timings refer to the original tapes.

Eric Dolphy Quartet: Paris, France, c.May-June 1964

Eric Dolphy(as), Kenny Drew(p), Guy Pedersen(b), Daniel Humair(d).

         Les   radio broadcast

Eric Dolphy Quartet: Cafe de Kroon, Eindhoven, Netherlands, 1 June 1964

Eric Dolphy(bcl), Misha Mengelberg(p), Jacques Schols(b), Han Bennink(d).

      17:52   Epistrophy   (bcl)   ICP015

Eric Dolphy Quartet: Hilversum, Netherlands, 2 June 1964

Eric Dolphy(as,bcl,fl), Misha Mengelberg(p), Jacques Schols(b), Han Bennink(d).

34717	11:15	Epistrophy	(bcl)	Limelight 82013/86013
34718	7:10	South Street Exit	(fl)	−
34719	4:50	The Madrig Speaks the Panther Walks	(as)	−
34720	5:25	Hypochristmutreefuzz	(bcl)	−
34721	11:20	You Don't Know What Love Is	(fl)	−
34722	5:25	Miss Ann	(as)	−

Note: CD issue on Fontana PO 822 226.

Eric Dolphy: Paris, France, 11 June 1964

Donald Byrd(tp), Eric Dolphy(as,bcl,fl), Nathan Davis(ts), Jacques Dieval(p), Jacques Hess(b), Franco Manzecchi(d).

5:39	Ode to Charlie Parker	−1,2	(fl)	West Wind 2063, Jazzway 1502
7:58	Serene	−2	(bcl)	West Wind 2016, −
10:05	245	−2,3	(as)	− −
6:10	G.W.	−4	(as)	− −
19:20	Springtime	−4	(bcl)	−, 2063
14:31	Naima	−3,4	(bcl)	− −

−1: omit Byrd; −2: omit Davis; −3: add Jacky Bambou(cga); −4: omit Dieval.

Note: Information on Dolphy's last recordings in Paris has been inconsistent. Donald Byrd recalled one, perhaps two sessions in a Paris radio station. Original information indicated the session or sessions were under Jacques Dieval's leadership, and that trumpet players Sonny Grey and Woody Shaw participated. Later information indicated Shaw and drummer Billy Brooks had not arrived in Paris in time to participate, while Uwe Reichardt's discography suggested Jean-Claude Fohrenbach(ts), Luigi Tristardo(b) and Jacques Thollot(d) may have participated in these sessions. Nathan Davis is quoted in "Paris – Pittsburgh: A Story in Jazz" by Gisela Albus, concerning the sessions with Jacques Dieval, and cites personnel as follows (p.713):

Jacques Dieval All-Stars: Paris, France, c. mid–June 1964

Donald Byrd, Sonny Grey(tp), Eric Dolphy, Nathan Davis, Jean-Claude Fohrenbach, Michel Roques(reeds), Jacques Dieval(p), Luigi Trussardi(b), Jacques Thollot(d).

       unknown titles   ORTF unissued

Davis goes on to state that Dolphy was recording "almost every day" with varying personnel in that period, including with a big band led by Sonny Grey, recording mostly originals with arrangements by Dolphy and Byrd. Performances listed as from 11 June 1964 may not all be from the same session or even all from that date.

Composer Credits

All tunes for which composer credits were readily available are listed alphabetically, followed by composer credit as listed on recordings, unless that source was known to be inaccurate.

Africa John Coltrane
African Lady Langston Hughes, Randy Weston
Afternoon in Paris John Lewis
Aggression Booker Little
Aisha McCoy Tyner
Alabama John Coltrane
Alabama Song Kurt Weill
All the Things You Could Be by Now If Sigmund Freud's
  Wife Was Your Mother Charles Mingus
Alone Together Howard Dietz, Arthur Swartz
Alto-Itis Oliver Nelson
Andante Luther Henderson
Another Encounter Gary McFarland
Aries Freddie Hubbard
As You Make Your Bed Kurt Weill

B Frequency Teo Macero
Bali H'ai Richard Rodgers
The Baron Eric Dolphy
Bee Vamp Booker Little
Bemoanable Lady Charles Mingus
The Best Things in Life Are Free Desilva
Better Git It in Your Soul Charles Mingus
Beyond the Blue Horizon Richard Whiting, Robin, Harling
Blue Monk Thelonious Monk
Blue Sands Buddy Collette
Blue Train John Coltrane
Blues in 6/8 Juan Amalbert, Carlos Ricci
Blues Minor John Coltrane

Body and Soul Green, Sour, Heyman, Eyton
Booker's Waltz Booker Little
Borodin Bossa Nova Alexander Borodin
Burning Spear Eric Dolphy
Butch and Butch Oliver Nelson

Caribe Gene Casey
Carnival Luiz Bonfa
Cascades Oliver Nelson
Chacha King Edvard Grieg
Chasin' the Trane John Coltrane
Chocolate Shake Duke Ellington, Paul F. Webster
Clarence's Place Freddie Hubbard
Close Your Eyes Bernice Petkere
Come Sunday Duke Ellington
Curtsy Ken McIntyre

Dahomey Dance John Coltrane
Dedicated to You S. Cohn, S. Chaplin, H. Zaret
Dedication Andrew Hill
Delilah Victor Young
Dianna Ken McIntyre
Do Nothing Till You Hear from Me Duke Ellington
Donna Lee Charlie Parker
Donnie's Theme John Lewis
Don's Delight Chico Hamilton, Howard McGhee
Don't Blame Me McHugh, Fields
The Drive Oliver Nelson
Duke's Choice Charles Mingus
Duquility Mal Waldron

Eclipse Charles Mingus
El Toreador Gil Evans
Epistrophy Kenny Clark, Thelonious Monk
Epitaph Charles Mingus
Ev'rything I've Got Richard Rodgers
Exactly Like You McHugh
Ezz-Thetic George Russell

Fables of Faubus Charles Mingus
Fair Weather Benny Golson
Far Cry Eric Dolphy
Far East Nat Pierce
Feathers Hale Smith

128

Fire Waltz Mal Waldron
First Bass Line Gene Casey
The First Take Ornette Coleman
Flight 19 Andrew Hill
Flute Song Gil Evans
Folk Forms No. 1 Charles Mingus
Folk Forms No. 2 Charles Mingus
Free Jazz Ornette Coleman
Freedom Charles Mingus

G. W. Eric Dolphy
Garvey's Ghost Max Roach
Gassin' the Wig Robert L. Ross
Gazzeloni Eric Dolphy
Gee, Baby, Ain't I Good to You Don Redman
Geo's Tune Ken McIntyre
Glad to Be Unhappy Richard Rodgers
God Bless the Child Billie Holiday, Herzog
Gongs East Chico Hamilton
Good Grief, Dennis Carson Smith
Grand Encounter Gary McFarland
Green Dolphin Street Bronislaw, Kaper
Greensleeves traditional
Groovin' High Dizzy Gillespie

Half-Mast Inhibition Charles Mingus
Hat and Beard Eric Dolphy
Havana Song Kurt Weill
Hazy Hues Booker Little
Head Shakin' Ken McIntyre
Hi-Fly Randy Weston
Hoe Down Oliver Nelson
Honesty Dave Baker
Hora Decubitus Charles Mingus
Hotel Me Miles Davis, Gil Evans
Hypochristmutreefuzz Misja Mengelberg

I Can't Get Started Ira Gershwin, Vernon Duke
I Don't Know Why F. G. Alhert
I Gave My Love a Cherry traditional
I Got it Bad and That Ain't Good Duke Ellington, Paul F. Webster
I Got Rhythm George and Ira Gershwin
I Let a Song Go Out of My Heart Duke Ellington
If I Should Lose You Ranger, Robin

I'll Remember April DePaul, Raye, Johnston
I'm Beginning to See the Light Don George, Johnny Hodges, Harry James,
    & Duke Ellington
I'm Gonna Wash That Man Right Out of My Hair Richard Rodgers
I'm in Love with a Wonderful Guy Richard Rodgers
Images Oliver Nelson
Impressions John Coltrane
In a Mellotone Duke Ellington
In a Sentimental Mood Duke Ellington
In the Blues Eric Dolphy
In the Red Abbey Lincoln, Max Roach, C. Bayen
India John Coltrane
Iron Man Eric Dolphy
It's Magic Cahn, Styne

Jaws Ernie Wilkins
Jitterbug Waltz Fats Waller
Journey into Jazz Gunther Schuller

Lady E Eric Dolphy
Lanyop Pony Poindexter
Las Vegas Tango Gil Evans
Laura John Mercer, Milt Raskin
Lautir Ken McIntyre
Left Alone Mal Waldron
Les Eric Dolphy
Like Someone in Love Van Heusen, Burke
Little Wig Joe Howard & Ralph Bass
Lock 'em Up Charles Mingus
Long Ago and Far Away Jerome Kern, George Gershwin
Love for Three Oranges March Sergei Prokofieff
Love Me Victor Young, Ned Washington
Lover Richard Rodgers
Lydiot George Russell

M. D. M. Charles Mingus
The Madrig Speaks, the Panther Walks Eric Dolphy
Mama Max Roach
Mama Lou Oliver Nelson
Mambo Ricci Juan Amalbert, Carlos Ricci
Man from South Africa Max Roach
Man of Words Booker Little
Mandrake Eric Dolphy
March On, March On Esmond Edwards

Meditations Charles Mingus
The Meetin' Oliver Nelson
Mendacity C. Bayen, Max Roach
Milano John Lewis
Miles' Mode John Coltrane
Milesign Gary McFarland
Mingus Fingus No. 2 Charles Mingus
Miss Ann Eric Dolphy
Miss Movement Eric Dolphy
Miss Toni Charles Greenlee
Modes Fred Katz
Mood Indigo Duke Ellington, Barney Bigard
Moods at Dusk Kenny Bright
Moods in Free Time Booker Little
More Than You Know Edward Elisen, William Rose, Vincent Youmans
Mr. P. C. John Coltrane
Mrs. Parker of K. C. Jaki Byard
Music Matador Prince Lasha, Huey Simmons
My Favorite Things Richard Rodgers, Oscar Hammerstein
My Search Charles Mingus
Mysterious Blues Charles Mingus

Naima John Coltrane
Nardis Miles Davis
Natural Affection John Lewis
Nature by Emerson Fred Katz
A New Day Booker Little
New Monastery Andrew Hill
Newport News Kenny Dorham
Night Float Gary McFarland
Night in Tunisia Dizzy Gillespie, Paparelli
Number Eight Eric Dolphy

Ode to Charlie Parker Jaki Byard
Ole John Coltrane
Oleo Sonny Rollins
111-44 Oliver Nelson
Orange Was the Color of Her Dress, Then Blue Silk Charles Mingus
Original Faubus Fables Charles Mingus
Original Untitled Ballad Billy Frazier
Ornothology Charlie Parker, Benny Harris
Osmosis Charles Mingus
Out There Eric Dolphy
Out to Lunch Eric Dolphy

Parkeriana Charles Mingus
Passion Flower Billy Strayhorn
Peggy's Blue Skylight Charles Mingus
Peggy's Discovery Charles Mingus, Melba Liston
Please Don't Come Back from the Moon Charles Mingus
Portrait Charles Mingus
Pottsville, USA Bill Potts
Praise for a Martyr Max Roach
Prayer for Passive Resistance Charles Mingus
The Prophet Eric Dolphy

Quicksilver Horace Silver
Quiet Please Booker Little

R & R Roy Eldridge, Ray Brown
Rally Ron Carter
Ralph's New Blues Milt Jackson
Refuge Andrew Hill
Retribution Abbey Lincoln, Julian Priester
'Round Midnight Thelonious Monk

Saucer Eyes Randy Nelson
Scheherezade Blue Rimsky-Korsakoff
Screamin' the Blues Oliver Nelson
Serene Eric Dolphy
17 West Eric Dolphy
She's Funny That Way Richard Whiting, Neil Moret
Six and Four Oliver Nelson
Sketch of Melba Randy Weston
Skylark Johnny Mercer, Hoagy Carmichael
So Long Eric Charles Mingus
Softly, as in a Morning Sunrise Romberg, Harms
Something Sweet, Something Tender Eric Dolphy
Something to Live For Duke Ellington, Billy Strayhorn
Sophisticated Lady Duke Ellington
South Street Exit Eric Dolphy
Speak Low Kurt Weill
Spectrum Andrew Hill
Spiritual John Coltrane
Spring Is Here Richard Rodgers
The Star Spangled Banner Francis Scott Key
Status Seeking Mal Waldron
Stolen Moments Oliver Nelson
Stormy Weather Harold Arlen, T. Koehler

Straight Ahead Abbey Lincoln, L. Baker, Mal Waldron
Straight Ahead Oliver Nelson
Straight Up and Down Eric Dolphy
Strange LaTouche, Fisher
Strength and Sanity Booker Little
Sunday Go Meetin' Gene Casey

'Taint Nobody's Bizness If I Do Grainger, Robbins
Take the A Train Billy Strayhorn
Teenie's Blues Oliver Nelson
Tender Warriors Max Roach
Tenderly Lawrence, Gross
Theme for Lester Young Charles Mingus
There is No Greater Love Jones
Thermo Freddie Hubbard
These Foolish Things Jack Strachey, Holt Marvel, Harry Link
They All Laughed George & Ira Gershwin
The Things We Did Last Summer S. Cahn, Jules Stein
Thirteen Mal Waldron
Thoughts George Russell
Three Seconds Oliver Nelson
Tillamook Two Gary McFarland
Trane Whistle Oliver Nelson
Tuesday at Two Gerald Wilson
II BS Charles Mingus
245 Eric Dolphy

Under Paris Skies traditional

Variants on a Theme of John Lewis (Django) Gunther Schuller
Variants on a Theme of Thelonious Monk (Criss Cross) Gunther Schuller
Vassarlean Charles Mingus

Walk Away Oliver Nelson
Warm Canto Mal Waldron
Warp and Woof Mal Waldron
The Way You Look Tonight Jerome Kern, Fields
We Diddit Mal Waldron
We Speak Booker Little
Weird Nightmare Charles Mingus
What Love Charles Mingus
When Lights Are Low Benny Carter, P. Maurice
When Malindy Sings Oscar Brown Jr.
Where I Live Gerald Wilson

Where or When Richard Rodgers
Whole Nelson Oliver Nelson
Woody'n You Dizzy Gillespie

Yearnin' Oliver Nelson
Yes Indeed Sy Oliver
You Are Too Beautiful Richard Rodgers
You Don't Know What Love Is G. DePaul, D. Raye
Yusef Isef Too Charles Mingus

Recordings by Eric Dolphy
of His Own Compositions:

TITLES:	RECORDING DATES:	COMMERCIAL ISSUES:
Baron, The	1960/August 16	NJLP8252, OJC023-2(CD)
Burning Spear	1963/May-June	Douglas 785
Dolphy-N	1960/November	Blue Note 85131, CDP48041
Far Cry (see Out There)		
G.W. (take 1)	1960/April 1	Prestige MPP2517
G.W. (take 2)	-	NJLP8236, OJC022-2(CD)
G.W.	1961/August 30	Enja 3007, IC-3017,R279636(CD)
G.W.	1961/November 19	Enja 3055, IC-3007
G.W.	1962/October 7	Unique Jazz UJ10
G.W.	1964/June 11	West Wind WW016, Jazzway 1502
Gazzeloni	1964/February 25	Blue Note 84163
Half Note Triplets	1963/April 18	Enja 5045-2, GM3005(CD)
Hat & Beard	1964/February 25	Blue Note 84163
In the Blues (3 takes)	1961/September 8	Prestige 7366, OJC416-2(CD)
Inner Flight (2 takes)	1960/November	Blue Note 85131, CDP48041
Iron Man	1963/April 18	Enja 5045-2, GM3005(CD)
Iron Man	1963/May-June	Douglas 785
Jim Crow	1962/ ?	Blue Note 85131, CDP48041
Lady E.	1959/May 20	Jazz Vault 111, Sesac 2901/2
Les	1960/April 1	NJLP8236, OJC022-2(CD)
Les (as Miss Ann)	1961/September 8	Prestige 7350, OJC414-2(CD)
Les	1961/September	Enja 3055, IC-3007
Les	1964/May-June	(unissued)

Mandrake (= Madrig...)	1963/May-June	Douglas 785
Madrig Speaks..., The	1964/June 2	Limelight 86013,Fontana 822226
Miss Ann	1960/December 21	NJLP8270, OJC400-2(CD)
Miss Ann (2 takes)	1961/September 6	(unissued)
Miss Ann	1961/September	
Miss Ann	1961/November 19	Enja 3055, IC-3007
Miss Ann	1962/October 7	Unique Jazz UJ10
Miss Ann	1964/June 2	Limelight 86013,Fontana 822226
Miss Movement	1959/February 4	Warner Bros.1344,Atlantic 4671

Number Eight (see *Potsa Lotsa*)

Out There (= *Far Cry*)	1960/August 15	NJLP8252, OJC023-2(CD)
Out There (as *Far Cry*)	1960/December 21	NJLP8270, OJC400-2(CD)
Out to Lunch	1964/February 25	Blue Note 84163
Potsa Lotsa (= #8)	1961/July 16	Prestige 7334, OJC353-2(CD)
Prophet, The	1961/July 16	NJLP8260, OJC133-2(CD)
Serene	1960/August 15	NJLP8252, OJC023-2(CD)
Serene	1960/December 21	Prestige MPP2517, OJC400-2(CD)
Serene	1961/September	Enja 3055, IC-3007
Serene	1961/November 19	Enja SPE-1
Serene	1964/June 11	West Wind WW016, Jazzway 1502
17 West	1960/August 15	NJLP8252, OJC023-2(CD)

Something Sweet, Something Tender
	1964/February 25	Blue Note 84163
South Street Exit	1963/March 10	(unissued)
South Street Exit	1964/June 2	Limelight 86013,Fontana 822226
Springtime	1964/June 11	West Wind WW016,2063
Straight Up & Down	1964/February 25	Blue Note 84163
Triple Mix	1960/November	Jazzway 1502
245 (take 1)	1960/April 1	Prestige MPP2517
245 (take 2)	-	NJLP8236, OJC022-2(CD)
245 (as *The Meeting*)	1961/August 30	Enja 3007, IC-3017,R279636(CD)
245	1961/September 4	Serene SER-03(CD)
245 (incomplete)	1962/October 7	Unique Jazz UJ10
245	1964/June 11	West Wind WW016

SOLO INDEX

(as)	*Geo's Tune* (1960/06/28)
(as)	*Groovin' High* (1962/04/?)
(as)	*Hazy Hues* (1961/04/04)
(as)	*Head Shakin'* (1960/06/28)
(as)	*Hoe-Down* (1961/02/23)
(as)	*Honesty* (1961/05/08)
(as)	*Hora Decubitus* (1963/09/20)
(as)	*Hot House* (1961/08/30)
(as)	*I'll Remember April* (1960/07/13)
(as)	*I'll Remember April* (1961/08/30)
(as)	*I'll Remember April* (1961/09/04)
(as)	*I'm Beginning to See the Light* (1958/04/?)
(as)	*If I Should Lose You* (1962/04/?)
(as)	*Impressions* (1961/11/01)
(as)	*Impressions* (1961/11/02)
(as)	*Impressions* (1961/11/18)
(as)	*Impressions* (1961/11/20)
(as)	*Impressions* (1961/11/23)
(as)	*Impressions* (1961/11/26)
(as)	*Impressions* (1961/11/27)
(as)	*Impressions* (1961/11/29)
(as)	*Impressions* (1961/12/02)
(as)	*In a Mellotone* (1962/10/12)
(as)	*In the Blues* (1961/09/08)
(as)	*Iron Man* (1963/05-06/?)
(as)	*Iron Man* (1963/04/18)
(as)	*Journey Into Jazz* (1964/02/08)
(as)	*Lanyop* (1962/02/16)
(as)	*Laura* (1961/09/04)
(as)	*Laura* (1961/09/08)
(as)	*Les* (1960/04/01)
(as)	*Les* (1961/09/08)
(as)	*Les* (1961/09/25)
(as)	*Little Wig* (1949/02/23)
(as)	*Lost in the Night* (1959/05/19)
(as)	*Love Me* (1963/05-06/?)
(as)	*Lydiot* (1961/05/08)
(as)	*Mama Lou* (1961/03/01)
(as)	*Mambo Ricci* (1960/08/19)
(as)	*Man From South Africa* (1961/08/09)
(as)	*Mandrake(= The Madrig Speaks...)* (1963/05-06/?)
(as)	*March On March On* (1960/05/27)
(as)	*Mendacity* (1961/08/01)
(as)	*Miles' Mode* (1962/02/10)
(as)	*Miles' Mode* (1961/11/01)
(as)	*Milesign* (1963/02/04)
(as)	*Miss Ann* (1960/12/21)
(as)	*Miss Ann* (1961/11/19)
(as)	*Miss Ann* (1961/09/?)
(as)	*Miss Ann* (1962/10/07)
(as)	*Miss Ann* (1964/06/02)
(as)	*Miss Movement* (1959/02/04)
(as)	*Modes* (1958/10/26)
(as)	*Moods in Free Time* (1961/04/04)

(as)	*More Than You Know* (1959/02/04)
(as)	*Mr. P. C.* (1962/02/10)
(as)	*Mysterious Blues* (1960/11/01)
(as)	*Nature by Emerson* (1958/12/29-30)
(as)	*New Monestary* (1964/03/21)
(as)	*Newport News* (1959/02/04)
(as)	*Night in Tunisia* (1960-61)
(as)	*Opening* (1959/05/19)
(as)	*Original Faubus Fables* (1960/10/20)
(as)	*Ornithology* (1962/04/?)
(as)	*Out of Nowhere* (1961/09/04)
(as)	*Out There(= Far Cry)* (1960/08/15)
(as)	*Out to Lunch* (1964/02/25)
(as)	*Parkeriana* (1964/04/10)
(as)	*Parkeriana* (1964/04/12)
(as)	*Parkeriana* (1964/04/16)
(as)	*Parkeriana* (1964/04/17)
(as)	*Parkeriana* (1964/04/18-19)
(as)	*Passion Flower* (1958/12/29-30)
(as)	*Peggy's Blue Skylight* (1964/04/13)
(as)	*Peggy's Blue Skylight* (1964/04/17)
(as)	*Peggy's Blue Skylight* (1964/04/20)
(as)	*Peggy's Blue Skylight* (1964/04/26)
(as)	*Peggy's Blue Skylight* (1964/04/28)
(as)	*Potsa Lotsa(= Number Eight)* (1961/07/16)
(as)	*Pottsville, U.S.A.* (1958/07/04)
(as)	*Pottsville, U.S.A.* (1958/10/26)
(as)	*Prayer for Passive Resistance* (1960/07/13)
(as)	*Quicksilver* (1962/04/?)
(as)	*Quiet Please* (1961/03/17)
(as)	*R & R* (1960/11/11)
(as)	*Refuge* (1964/03/21)
(as)	*'Round Midnight* (1961/05/08)
(as)	*Sippin' With Cisco* (1949/01/19)
(as)	*Six and Four* (1961/03/01)
(as)	*So Long Eric* (1964/04/04)
(as)	*So Long Eric* (1964/04/10)
(as)	*So Long Eric* (1964/04/12)
(as)	*So Long Eric* (1964/04/13)
(as)	*So Long Eric* (1964/04/14)
(as)	*So Long Eric* (1964/04/16)
(as)	*So Long Eric* (1964/04/17)
(as)	*So Long Eric* (1964/04/18-19)
(as)	*So Long Eric* (1964/04/20)
(as)	*So Long Eric* (1964/04/26)
(as)	*So Long Eric* (1964/04/28)
(as)	*Softly as in a Morning Sunrise* (1961/06/20)
(as)	*Status Seeking* (1961/06/27)
(as)	*Status Seeking* (1961/07/16)
(as)	*Stormy Weather* (1960/10/20)
(as)	*Straight Ahead* (1961/03/01)
(as)	*Straight Up & Down* (1964/02/25)
(as)	*Strange* (1958/10/27)
(as)	*'Tain't Nobody's Bizness...* (1960/11/01)

(as)	*Teenie's Blues* (1961/02/23)	
(as)	*Tenderly* (1960/12/21)	
(as)	*The Drive* (1960/05/27)	
(as)	*The Madrig Speaks the Panther Walks* (1964/06/02)	
(as)	*The Meetin'* (1960/05/27)	
(as)	*The Prophet* (1961/07/16)	
(as)	*The Way You Look Tonight* (1961/09/08)	
(as)	*They All Laughed* (1960/06/29)	
(as)	*Thirteen* (1961/06/27)	
(as)	*Three Seconds* (1960/05/27)	
(as)	*Tuesday at Two* (1958/12/29-30)	
(as)	*Under Paris Skies* (1958/10/26)	
(as)	*Warp & Woof* (1961/06/27)	
(as)	*We Diddit* (1961/06/27)	
(as)	*We Speak* (1961/03/17)	
(as)	*Wednesday Night Prayer Meeting* (1960/07/13)	
(as)	*Woody'n You* (1961/09/08)	
(as)	*Yearnin'* (1961/02/23)	
(as)	*245* (1960/04/01)	
(as)	*245* (1961/08/30)	
(as)	*245* (1961/09/04)	
(as)	*245* (1962/10/07)	
(as)	*245* (1964/06/11)	
(as)	*52nd Street Theme* (1961/09/04)	
(as)(NS)	*Andante* (1958/10/26)	
(as)(NS)	*In a Sentimental Mood* (1958/04/?)	
(as)(NS)	*Moods at Dusk* (1949/spring)	
(as)(NS)	*Truth* (1959/05/19)	
(as,bcl)	*MDM* (1960/10/20)	
(as,bcl)	*Spectrum* (1964/03/21)	
(as,bcl,fl)	*Jim Crow* (1962/?)	
(bcl)	*Aggression* (1961/07/16)	
(bcl)	*Alabama Song* (1964/01/10)	
(bcl)	*Alone Together* (1963/05-06/?)	
(bcl)	*Bee Vamp* (1961/07/16)	
(bcl)	*Booker's Waltz* (1961/07/16)	
(bcl)	*Burning Spear* (1963/05-06/?)	
(bcl)	*Come Sunday* (1963/05-06/?)	
(bcl)	*Dedication* (1964/03/21)	
(bcl)	*Delilah* (1961/11/20)	
(bcl)	*Dianna* (1960/06/28)	
(bcl)	*Epistrophy* (1964/06/01)	
(bcl)	*Epistrophy* (1964/06/02)	
(bcl)	*Fables of Faubus* (1964/04/10)	
(bcl)	*Fables of Faubus* (1964/04/12)	
(bcl)	*Fables of Faubus* (1964/04/14)	
(bcl)	*Fables of Faubus* (1964/04/16)	
(bcl)	*Fables of Faubus* (1964/04/17)	
(bcl)	*Fables of Faubus* (1964/04/18/19)	
(bcl)	*Fables of Faubus* (1964/04/26)	
(bcl)	*Fables of Faubus* (1964/04/28)	
(bcl)	*First Bass Line* (1960/08/19)	
(bcl)	*Free Jazz* (1960/12/21)	
(bcl)	*God Bless the Child* (1961/07/16)	

(bcl)	*God Bless the Child* (1961/08/30)
(bcl)	*God Bless the Child* (1961/09/08)
(bcl)	*God Bless the Child* (1961/11/19)
(bcl)	*Gongs East* (1958/12/29-30)
(bcl)	*Green Dolphin Street* (1960/04/01)
(bcl)	*Green Dolphin Street* (1961/09/?)
(bcl)	*Green Dolphin Street* (1961/12/01)
(bcl)	*Half-Note Triplets* (1963/04/18)
(bcl)	*Hat & Beard* (1964/02/25)
(bcl)	*Hypochristmutreefuzz* (1964/06/02)
(bcl)	*I Got Rhythm* (1962/10/07)
(bcl)	*I Got Rhythm* (1960-61)
(bcl)	*I Wish I Were in Love Again* (1960-61)
(bcl)	*Images* (1961/03/01)
(bcl)	*India* (1961/11/02)
(bcl)	*India* (1961/11/03)
(bcl)	*India* (1961/11/05)
(bcl)	*It's Magic* (1960/12/21)
(bcl)	*Miss Toni* (1960/04/01)
(bcl)	*Mrs Parker of K.C.(= Bird's Mother)* (1960/12/21)
(bcl)	*Music Matador* (1963/05-06/?)
(bcl)	*Naima* (1961/11/01)
(bcl)	*Naima* (1961/11/20)
(bcl)	*Naima* (1961/11/23)
(bcl)	*Naima* (1964/06/?)
(bcl)	*Nardis* (1961/05/08)
(bcl)	*Night Music* (1963/03/14)
(bcl)	*Oleo* (1961/09/08)
(bcl)	*Oleo* (1961/12/01)
(bcl)	*Orange Was the Color* (1964/04/10)
(bcl)	*Orange Was the Color* (1964/04/14)
(bcl)	*Orange Was the Color* (1964/04/17)
(bcl)	*Orange Was the Color* (1964/04/18-19)
(bcl)	*Orange Was the Color* (1964/04/26)
(bcl)	*Orange Was the Color* (1964/04/28)
(bcl)	*Rally* (1961/06/20)
(bcl)	*Ralph's New Blues* (1961/03/01)
(bcl)	*Screamin' the Blues* (1960/05/27)
(bcl)	*Serene* (1960/08/15)
(bcl)	*Serene* (1960/12/21)
(bcl)	*Serene* (1961/09/25)
(bcl)	*Serene* (1961/11/19)
(bcl)	*Serene* (1964/06/11)
(bcl)	*Softly as in a Morning Sunrise* (1961/12/01)
(bcl)	*Something Sweet Something Tender* (1964/02/25)
(bcl)	*Speak Low* (1958/10/27)
(bcl)	*Spiritual* (1961/11/01)
(bcl)	*Spiritual* (1961/11/02)
(bcl)	*Spiritual* (1961/11/03)
(bcl)	*Spiritual* (1961/11/05)
(bcl)	*Springtime* (1964/06/11)
(bcl)	*Take the A Train* (1964/04/12)
(bcl)	*Tender Warriors* (1961/08/03)
(bcl)	*The Baron* (1960/08/15)

(bcl)	*The First Take*	(1960/12/21)
(bcl)	*The Way You Look Tonight*	(1961/12/01)
(bcl)	*Thoughts*	(1961/05/08)
(bcl)	*What Is This Thing Called Love?*	(1961/09/04)
(bcl)	*What Love?*	(1960/07/13)
(bcl)	*What Love?*	(1960/10/20)
(bcl)	*When Irish Eyes are Shining*	(1964/04/13)
(bcl)	*When Lights are Low*	(1961/08/30)
(bcl)	*When Lights are Low*	(1961/09/04)
(bcl)	*When Lights are Low*	(1961/09/06)
(bcl)	*You're the Cutest One*	(1960-61)
(bcl)	*111-44*	(1961/03/01)
(bcl)(NS)	*Cawn Pawn*	(1959/05/20)
(bcl)(NS)	*Little Lost Bear*	(1959/05/19)
(bcl,fl)	*Meditations*	(1964/04/04)
(bcl,fl)	*Meditations*	(1964/04/10)
(bcl,fl)	*Meditations*	(1964/04/12)
(bcl,fl)	*Meditations*	(1964/04/13)
(bcl,fl)	*Meditations*	(1964/04/14)
(bcl,fl)	*Meditations*	(1964/04/16)
(bcl,fl)	*Meditations*	(1964/04/17)
(bcl,fl)	*Meditations*	(1964/04/18-19)
(bcl,fl)	*Meditations*	(1964/04/19)
(bcl,fl)	*Meditations*	(1964/04/26)
(bcl,fl)	*Meditations*	(1964/04/28)
(bcl,fl)	*Variants on a Theme of Monk*	(1960/12/20)
(cl)	*Densities*	(1963/03/14)
(cl)	*Eclipse*	(1960/08/15)
(cl)	*Warm Canto*	(1961/06/27)
(cl)(NS)	*Good Grief Dennis*	(1958/12/29-30)
(cl)(NS)	*I'm Gonna Wash That Man...*	(1958/07/04)
(cl)(NS)	*Long Ago & Far Away*	(1958/12/29-30)
(cl)(NS)	*The Morn1ng After*	(1958-59)
(cl,fl)(NS)	*I Gave My Love a Cherry*	(1958/12/29-30)
(fl)	*April Fool*	(1960/04/01)
(fl)	*April Rain*	(1960-61)
(fl)	*Bags' Groove*	(1961/09/04)
(fl)	*Beyond the Blue Horizon*	(1958/12/29-30)
(fl)	*Blue Sands*	(1958/07/04)
(fl)	*Cha-Cha King*	(1960-61)
(fl)	*Don's Delight*	(1958/10/26)
(fl)	*Don't Blame Me*	(1961/09/06)
(fl)	*Don't Blame Me*	(1961/09/25?)
(fl)	*Don't Blame Me*	(1961/09/?)
(fl)	*Fair Weather*	(1958/10/26)
(fl)	*Far East*	(1958/12/29-30)
(fl)	*Gazzeloni*	(1964/02/25)
(fl)	*Glad to Be Unhappy*	(1960/04/01)
(fl)	*Glad to Be Unhappy*	(1961/09/08)
(fl)	*Hi Fly*	(1961/08/30)
(fl)	*Hi Fly*	(1961/09/08)
(fl)	*I Can't Get Started*	(1964/04/26)
(fl)	*I'm in Love with a Wonderful Guy*	(1958/07/04)
(fl)	*Improvisations & Tukras*	(1960/07/08)

(fl)	*Inner Flight* (1960/11/?)	
(fl)	*Jitterbug Waltz* (1963/05-06/?)	
(fl)	*Lady E.* (1959/05/20)	
(fl)	*Lautir* (1960/06/28)	
(fl)	*Left Alone* (1960/12/21)	
(fl)	*Left Alone* (1961/11/19)	
(fl)	*Left Alone* (1962/10/07)	
(fl)	*Like Someone in Love* (1961/07/16)	
(fl)	*Lover* (1960-61)	
(fl)	*Mangolina* (1960-61)	
(fl)	*My Favorite Things* (1961/11/18)	
(fl)	*My Favorite Things* (1961/11/20)	
(fl)	*My Favorite Things* (1961/11/23)	
(fl)	*My Favorite Things* (1961/11/26)	
(fl)	*My Favorite Things* (1961/11/27)	
(fl)	*My Favorite Things* (1961/11/29)	
(fl)	*My Favorite Things* (1962/02/10)	
(fl)	*Ode to Charlie Parker* (1960/12/21)	
(fl)	*Ode to Charlie Parker* (1963/04/16)	
(fl)	*Ode to Charlie Parker* (1963/05-06?)	
(fl)	*Ode to Charlie Parker* (1964/06/?)	
(fl)	*Ole* (1961/05/25)	
(fl)	*Reincarnation of a Lovebird* (1960/10/20)	
(fl)	*Saucer Eyes* (1961/06/20)	
(fl)	*Sketch of Melba* (1960/08/15)	
(fl)	*Something to Live For* (1958/10/27)	
(fl)	*South Street Exit* (1964/06/02)	
(fl)	*Speak Low* (1960-61)	
(fl)	*Spring Is Here* (1960/08/19)	
(fl)	*Stolen Moments* (1961/02/23)	
(fl)	*Sunday Go Meetin'* (1960/08/19)	
(fl)	*These Foolish Things* (1964/04/28)	
(fl)	*To Her Ladyship* (1961/05/25)	
(fl)	*Triple Mix* (1960/11/?)	
(fl)	*Variants on a Theme of John Lewis* (1960/12/20)	
(fl)	*Where I Live* (1958/12/29-30)	
(fl)	*Yes Indeed* (1961/06/20)	
(fl)	*You Don't Know What Love Is* (1964/06/02)	
(fl)	*17 West* (1960/08/15)	
(fl)(NS)	*Ev'rything I've Got* (1956/10/27)	
(fl)(NS)	*Lord Randall*(intro.) (1958/07/04)	
(fl)(NS)	*Lullaby for Dreamers* (1959/05/19)	
(fl)(NS)	*Sleep* (1958-59)	
(fl)(NS)	*Theme for a Starlet* (1959/05/19)	
(NS)	*A New Day* (1961/03/17)	
(NS)	*Africa* (1961/05/23)	
(NS)	*Africa* (1961/06/07)	
(NS)	*African Lady* (1961/02/22)	
(NS)	*Aires* (1963/03/11)	
(NS)	*Another Encounter* (1962/10/05)	
(NS)	*B Frequency* (1962/02/16)	
(NS)	*Bali H'ai* (1961/04/?)	
(NS)	*Bernie's Tune* (1958/10/?)	
(NS)	*Better Get Hit in Your Soul* (1963/09/20)	

(NS)   *Blue Monk* (1961/02/22)
(NS)   *Blues a la Carte* (1949/spring)
(NS)   *Blues Minor* (1961/06/07)
(NS)   *Body & Soul* (1963/05/02)
(NS)   *Borodin Bossa Nova* (1963/04/26)
(NS)   *Carnival* (1963/03/11)
(NS)   *Cascades* (1961/02/23)
(NS)   *Chocolate Shake* (1963/03/08)
(NS)   *Clark in the Dark* (1962/10/12)
(NS)   *Dedicated to You* (1963/05/02)
(NS)   *Do Nothing... /I Let a Song Go...* (1960/05/25)
(NS)   *Don't Be Afraid* (1958/10/?)
(NS)   *Duke's Choice* (1962/10/12)
(NS)   *Duquility* (1961/06/27)
(NS)   *Eclipse* (1960/05/25)
(NS)   *El Toreador* (1963/09/?)
(NS)   *Fables of Faubus* (1964/04/13)
(NS)   *Fire Waltz* (1961/06/27)
(NS)   *Flight 19* (1964/03/21)
(NS)   *Flute Song* (1963/09/?)
(NS)   *Freedom* (1962/10/12)
(NS)   *Freedom* (1963/09/20)
(NS)   *Garvey's Ghost* (1961/08/01)
(NS)   *Gee Baby Ain't I Good to You* (1960/early)
(NS)   *Grand Encounter* (1963/02/04)
(NS)   *Greensleeves* (1961/05/23)
(NS)   *Half-Mast Inhibition* (1960/05/24)
(NS)   *Havana Song* (1964/01/10)
(NS)   *Honey Boy* (1960/08/30)
(NS)   *Hotel Me* (1964/04/06)
(NS)   *Howard's Idea* (1949/02/23)
(NS)   *Hunter's Hunters* (1949/spring)
(NS)   *I Don't Know Why* (1959/02/04)
(NS)   *I Got It Bad & That Ain't Good* (1963/03/08)
(NS)   *II B.S.* (1963/09/20)
(NS)   *In the Red* (1961/02/22)
(NS)   *It Tears Me All to Pieces* (1960/08/30)
(NS)   *Jaws* (1960/09/20)
(NS)   *Julie Is Her Name* (1958/10/?)
(NS)   *Just You Just Me* (1958/10/?)
(NS)   *Lady Be Good* (1962/10/07)
(NS)   *Las Vegas Tango* (1964/04/06)
(NS)   *Left Alone* (1961/02/22)
(NS)   *Lock 'em Up* (1960/11/11)
(NS)   *Love for 3 Oranges March* (1963/04/26)
(NS)   *Love is Laughing at Me* (1949/02/23)
(NS)   *Mama* (1961/08/03)
(NS)   *Man of Words* (1961/04/04)
(NS)   *Mess Around* (1960/early)
(NS)   *Milano* (1963/02/04)
(NS)   *Mingus Fingers,#2* (1960/05/24)
(NS)   *Mood Indigo* (1963/09/20)
(NS)   *My Search* (1962/10/12)
(NS)   *Natural Affection* (1963/02/27)

(NS)	*Night Float* (1960/09/09)
(NS)	*Orange Was the Color* (1964/04/12)
(NS)	*Pete's Beat* (1949/01/19)
(NS)	*Phantom Moon* (1949/02/23)
(NS)	*Praise for a Martyr* (1961/08/08)
(NS)	*Prayer for Passive Resistance* (1960/05/25)
(NS)	*Reincarnation of a Lovebird* (1960/11/11)
(NS)	*Retribution* (1961/02/22)
(NS)	*Sampson's Creep* (1949/spring)
(NS)	*Scheherazade Blue* (1963/04/26)
(NS)	*She's Funny That Way* (1959/02/04)
(NS)	*Skylark* (1963/03/08)
(NS)	*Slide Mr Trombone* (1958/10/?)
(NS)	*Someone I Love* (1958/10/?)
(NS)	*Song of the Underground Railroad* (1961/05/23)
(NS)	*Stolen Moments* (1960/09/20)
(NS)	*Straight Ahead* (1961/02/22)
(NS)	*Strength & Sanity* (1961/04/04)
(NS)	*Take the A Train/Exactly Like You* (1960/05/25)
(NS)	*Takin' Care of Business* (1960/08/30)
(NS)	*The Best Things in Life are Free* (1959/02/04)
(NS)	*The Damned Don't Cry* (1961/05/23)
(NS)	*The Masquerade is Over* (1958/10/?)
(NS)	*The Outskirts of Town* (1958/10/?)
(NS)	*The Star Spangled Banner* (1963/02/27)
(NS)	*The Things We Did Last Summer* (1961/04/?)
(NS)	*Theme for Lester Young* (1963/09/20)
(NS)	*There Is No Greater Love* (1960/early)
(NS)	*Thermo* (1963/03/11)
(NS)	*This is You* (1949/01/19)
(NS)	*This Little Girl of Mine* (1960/early)
(NS)	*Tillamook Two* (1962/10/05)
(NS)	*Trane Whistle* (1960/09/20)
(NS)	*Travelin' Light* (1958/10/?)
(NS)	*Until the Real Thing Comes Along* (1958/10/?)
(NS)	*Vassarlean* (1960/10/20)
(NS)	*Walk Away* (1960/09/20)
(NS)	*Weird Nightmare* (1960/05/25)
(NS)	*When Malindy Sings* (1961/02/22)
(NS)	*Where or When* (1959/02/04)
(NS)	*Whole Nelson* (1960/09/20)
(NS)	*You Are Too Beautiful* (1960/09/20)
(NS)	*245* (1961/09/?)

UNISSUED TITLES (for which solo notations cannot be determined)

(unissued)	*Alabama* (1963/12/31)
(unissued)	*Baby Don't You Cry* (1960/04/19)
(unissued)	*By My Side* (1962/10/05)
(unissued)	*Don't Cha Go Away Mad* (1960/04/19)
(unissued)	*God Bless the Child* (1963/03/10)
(unissued)	*I Can't Get Started* (1964/04/18-19)
(unissued)	*If You Could See Me Now* (1960/09/09)
(unissued)	*Impressions* (1963/12/31)

(unissued)	*India* (1961/11/01)
(unissued)	*Jazz Vespers Service* (1962/06/03)
(unissued)	*Les* (1964/05-06/?)
(unissued)	*Meditations* (1964/04/21)
(unissued)	*Miles' Mode* (1961/11/03)
(unissued)	*Miles' Mode* (1963/03/10)
(unissued)	*Minor Mode* (1949/01/19-02/23)
(unissued)	*Miss Ann* (1961/09/06)
(unissued)	*My Favorite Things* (1963/12/31)
(unissued)	*Naima* (1961/11/03)
(unissued)	*Orange Was the Color* (1964/04/04)
(unissued)	*Orange Was the Color* (1964/04/13)
(unissued)	*Osmosis* (1962/10/12)
(unissued)	*Parkeriana* (1964/04/21)
(unissued)	*Peggy's Blue Skylight* (1962/10/12)
(unissued)	*Please Don't Come Back from the Moon* (1962/10/12)
(unissued)	*Portrait* (1962/10/12)
(unissued)	*'Round Midnight* (1960/09/09)
(unissued)	*Shine On* (1960/04/19)
(unissued)	*So Long Eric* (1964/04/21)
(unissued)	*Softly as in a Morning Sunrise* (1963/03/10)
(unissued)	*Sophisticated Lady* (1958/04/?)
(unissued)	*South Street Exit* (1963/03/10)
(unissued)	*Take the A Train* (1963/09/20)
(unissued)	*The Way You Look Tonight* (1960/04/19)
(unissued)	*Yusef Isef Too* (1960/05/24)
(unissued)	(3 unknown titles) (1949/01/19-02/23)
(unissued)	(2 unknown titles) (1963/03/10)

TUNE INDEX

(bcl)	*Burning Spear* (1963/05-06/?)
(as)	*Butch & Butch* (1961/02/23)
(unissued)	*By My Side* (1962/10/05)
(as)	*Caribe* (1960/08/19)
(NS)	*Carnival* (1963/03/11)
(NS)	*Cascades* (1961/02/23)
(bcl)(NS)	*Cawn Pawn* (1959/05/20)
(fl)	*Cha-Cha King* (1960-61)
(as)	*Champs Elysee* (1959/05/19)
(as)	*Chasin' the Trane* (1961/11/01)
(as)	*Chasin' the Trane* (1961/11/02)
(NS)	*Chocolate Shake* (1963/03/08)
(as)	*Clarence's Place* (1963/05/02)
(NS)	*Clark in the Dark* (1962/10/12)
(as)	*Close Your Eyes* (1958/10/27)
(bcl)	*Come Sunday* (1963/05-06/?)
(as)	*Curtsey* (1960/06/28)
(as)	*Dahomey Dance* (1961/05/25)
(NS)	*Dedicated to You* (1963/05/02)
(bcl)	*Dedication* (1964/03/21)
(bcl)	*Delilah* (1961/11/20)
(cl)	*Densities* (1963/03/14)
(bcl)	*Dianna* (1960/06/28)
(NS)	*Do Nothing.../I Let a Song Go.. .*(1960/05/25)
(as)	*Dolphy-N* (1960/11/?)
(fl)	*Don's Delight* (1958/10/26)
(NS)	*Don't Be Afraid* (1958/10/?)
(fl)	*Don't Blame Me* (1961/09/06)
(fl)	*Don't Blame Me* (1961/09/25)
(fl)	*Don't Blame Me* (1961/09/?)
(unissued)	*Don't Cha Go Away Mad* (1960/04/19)
(as)	*Donna Lee* (1962/04/?)
(as)	*Donna Lee* (1963/04/18)
(as)	*Donnie's Theme* (1963/02/27)
(NS)	*Duke's Choice* (1962/10/12)
(NS)	*Duquility* (1961/06/27)
(NS)	*Eclipse* (1960/05/25)
(cl)	*Eclipse* (1960/08/15)
(NS)	*El Toreador* (1963/09/7)
(bcl)	*Epistrophy* (1964/06/01)
(bcl)	*Epistrophy* (1964/06/02)
(as)	*Epitaph* (1962/10/12)
(fl)(NS)	*Ev'rythin' I've Got* (1958/10/27)
(as)	*Ezz-thetic* (1961/05/08)
(bcl)	*Fables of Faubus* (1964/04/10)
(bcl)	*Fables of Faubus* (1964/04/12)
(NS)	*Fables of Faubus* (1964/04/13)
(bcl)	*Fables of Faubus* (1964/04/14)
(bcl)	*Fables of Faubus* (1964/04/16)
(bcl)	*Fables of Faubus* (1964/04/17)
(bcl)	*Fables of Faubus* (1964/04/18-19)
(bcl)	*Fables of Faubus* (1964/04/26)
(bcl)	*Fables of Faubus* (1964/04/28)
(fl)	*Fair Weather* (1958/10/26)

(as)	*Far Cry*(= *Out There*) (1960/12/21)	
(fl)	*Far East* (1958/12/29-30)	
(as)	*Fat Mouth* (1959/05/19)	
(as)	*Feathers* (1960/08/15)	
(NS)	*Fire Waltz* (1961/06/27)	
(as)	*Fire Waltz* (1961/07/16)	
(bcl)	*First Bass Line* (1960/08/19)	
(NS)	*Flight 19* (1964/03/21)	
(NS)	*Flute Song* (1963/09/?)	
(as)	*Folk Forms,#1* (1960/07/13)	
(as)	*Folk Forms,#1* (1960/10/20)	
(bcl)	*Free Jazz* (1960/12/21)	
(NS)	*Freedom* (1962/10/12)	
(NS)	*Freedom* (1963/09/20)	
(as)	*Frou Frou* (1959/05/19)	
(as)	*G.W.* (1960/04/01)	
(as)	*G.W.* (1961/08/30)	
(as)	*G.W.* (1961/11/19)	
(as)	*G.W.* (1962/10/07)	
(as)	*G.W.* (1964/06/11)	
(NS)	*Garvey s Ghost* (1961/06/01)	
(as)	*Gassin' the Wig* (1949/01/19)	
(fl)	*Gazzeloni* (1964/02/25)	
(NS)	*Gee Baby Ain't I Good to You* (1960/early)	
(as)	*Geo's Tune* (1960/06/28)	
(fl)	*Glad to Be Unhappy* (1960/04/01)	
(fl)	*Glad to Be Unhappy* (1961/09/08)	
(bcl)	*God Bless the Child* (1961/07/16)	
(bcl)	*God Bless the Child* (1961/08/30)	
(bcl)	*God Bless the Child* (1961/09/08)	
(bcl)	*God Bless the Child* (1961/11/19)	
(unissued)	*God Bless the Child* (1963/03/10)	
(bcl)	*Gongs East* (1958/12/29-30)	
(cl)(NS)	*Good Grief Dennis* (1958/12/29-30)	
(NS)	*Grand Encounter* (1963/02/04)	
(bcl)	*Green Dolphin Street* (1960/04/01)	
(bcl)	*Green Dolphin Street* (1961/09/?)	
(bcl)	*Green Dolphin Street* (1961/12/01)	
(NS)	*Greensleeves* (1961/05/23)	
(as)	*Groovin' High* (1962/04/?)	
(NS)	*Half-Mast Inhibition* (1960/05/24)	
(bcl)	*Half-Note Triplets* (1963/04/18)	
(bcl)	*Hat & Beard* (1964/02/25)	
(NS)	*Havana Song* (1964/01/10)	
(as)	*Hazy Hues* (1961/04/04)	
(as)	*Head Shakin'* (1960/06/28)	
(fl)	*Hi Fly* (1961/08/30)	
(fl)	*Hi Fly* (1961/09/08)	
(as)	*Hoe-Down* (1961/02/23)	
(as)	*Honesty* (1961/05/08)	
(NS)	*Honey Boy* (1960/08/30)	
(as)	*Hora Decubitus* (1963/09/20)	
(as)	*Hot House* (1961/08/30)	
(NS)	*Hotel Me* (1964/04/06)	

149

(NS)	*Howard's Idea*	(1949/02/23)
(NS)	*Hunter's Hunters*	(1949/spring)
(bcl)	*Hypochristmutreefuzz*	(1964/06/02)
(unissued)	*I Can't Get Started*	(1964/04/18-19)
(fl)	*I Can't Get Started*	(1964/04/26)
(NS)	*I Don't Know Why*	(1959/02/04)
(cl,fl)(NS)	*I Gave My Love a Cherry*	(1958/12/29-30)
(NS)	*I Got It Bad & That Ain't Good*	(1963/03/08)
(bcl)	*I Got Rhythm*	(1960-61)
(bcl)	*I Got Rhythm*	(1962/10/07)
(bcl)	*I Wish I Were In Love Again*	(1960-61)
(as)	*I'll Remember April*	(1960/07/13)
(as)	*I'll Remember April*	(1961/08/30)
(as)	*I'll Remember April*	(1961/09/04)
(as)	*I'm Beginning to See the Light*	(1958/04/?)
(cl)(NS)	*I'm Gonna Wash That Man...*	(1958/07/04)
(fl)	*I'm in Love with a Wonderful Guy*	(1958/07/04)
(as)	*If I Should Lose You*	(1962/04/7)
(unissued)	*If You Could See Me Now*	(1960/09/09)
(NS)	*II B.S.*	(1963/09/20)
(bcl)	*Images*	(1961/03/01)
(as)	*Impressions*	(1961/11/01)
(as)	*Impressions*	(1961/11/02)
(as)	*Impressions*	(1961/11/18)
(as)	*Impressions*	(1961/11/20)
(as)	*Impressions*	(1961/11/23)
(as)	*Impressions*	(1961/11/26)
(as)	*Impressions*	(1961/11/27)
(as)	*Impressions*	(1961/11/29)
(as)	*Impressions*	(1961/12/02)
(unissued)	*Impressions*	(1963/12/31)
(fl)	*Improvisations & Tukras*	(1960/07/08)
(as)	*In a Mellotone*	(1962/10/12)
(as)(NS)	*In a Sentimental Mood*	(1958/04/?)
(as)	*In the Blues*	(1961/09/08)
(NS)	*In the Red*	(1961/02/22)
(unissued)	*India*	(1961/11/01)
(bcl)	*India*	(1961/11/02)
(bcl)	*India*	(1961/11/03)
(bcl)	*India*	(1961/11/05)
(fl)	*Inner Flight*	(1960/11/7)
(as)	*Iron Man*	(1963/04/18)
(as)	*Iron Man*	(1963/05-06/?)
(NS)	*It Tears Me All to Pieces*	(1960/08/30)
(bcl)	*It's Magic*	(1960/12/21)
(NS)	*Jaws*	(1960/09/20)
(unissued)	*Jazz Vespers Service*	(1962/06/03)
(as,bcl,fl)	*Jim Crow*	(1962/?)
(fl)	*Jitterbug Waltz*	(1963/05-06/?)
(as)	*Journey Into Jazz*	(1964/02/08)
(NS)	*Julie Is Her Name*	(1958/10/?)
(NS)	*Just You Just Me*	(1958/10/?)
(NS)	*Lady Be Good*	(1962/10/07)
(fl)	*Lady E.*	(1959/05/20)

(as)	*Lanyop* (1962/02/16)
(NS)	*Las Vegas Tango* (1964/04/06)
(as)	*Laura* (1961/09/04)
(as)	*Laura* (1961/09/08)
(fl)	*Lautir* (1960/06/28)
(fl)	*Left Alone* (1960/12/21)
(NS)	*Left Alone* (1961/02/22)
(fl)	*Left Alone* (1961/11/19)
(fl)	*Left Alone* (1962/10/07)
(as)	*Les* (1960/04/01)
(as)	*Les* (1961/09/08)
(as)	*Les* (1961/09/25)
(unissued)	*Les* (1964/05-06/?)
(fl)	*Like Someone in Love* (1961/07/16)
(bcl)(NS)	*Little Lost Bear* (1959/05/19)
(as)	*Little Wig* (1949/02/23)
(NS)	*Lock 'em Up* (1960/11/11)
(cl)(NS)	*Long Ago & Far Away* (1958/12/29-30)
(fl)(NS)	*Lord Randall*(intro.) (1958/07/04)
(as)	*Lost in the Night* (1959/05/19)
(NS)	*Love for 3 Oranges March* (1963/04/26)
(NS)	*Love is Laughing at Me* (1949/02/23)
(as)	*Love Me* (1963/05-06/?)
(fl)	*Lover* (1960-61)
(fl)(NS)	*Lullaby for Dreamers* (1959/05/19)
(as)	*Lydiot* (1961/05/08)
(NS)	*Mama* (1961/08/03)
(as)	*Mama Lou* (1961/03/01)
(as)	*Mambo Ricci* (1960/08/19)
(as)	*Man From South Africa* (1961/08/09)
(NS)	*Man of Words* (1961/04/04)
(as)	*Mandrake*(= *The Madrig Speaks...*) (1963/05-06/?)
(fl)	*Mangolina* (1960-61)
(as)	*March On March On* (1960/05/27)
(as,bcl)	*MDM* (1960/10/20)
(bcl,fl)	*Meditations* (1964/04/04)
(bcl,fl)	*Meditations* (1964/04/10)
(bcl,fl)	*Meditations* (1964/04/12)
(bcl,fl)	*Meditations* (1964/04/13)
(bcl,fl)	*Meditations* (1964/04/14)
(bcl,fl)	*Meditations* (1964/04/16)
(bcl,fl)	*Meditations* (1964/04/17)
(bcl,fl)	*Meditations* (1964/04/18-19)
(bcl,fl)	*Meditations* (1964/04/20)
(unissued)	*Meditations* (1964/04/21)
(bcl,fl)	*Meditations* (1964/04/26)
(bcl,fl)	*Meditations* (1964/04/28)
(as)	*Mendacity* (1961/08/01)
(NS)	*Mess Around* (1960/early)
(NS)	*Milano* (1963/02/04)
(as)	*Miles' Mode* (1961/11/01)
(unissued)	*Miles' Mode* (1961/11/03)
(as)	*Miles' Mode* (1962/02/10)
(unissued)	*Miles' Mode* (1963/03/10)

(as)	*Milesign* (1963/02/04)
(NS)	*Mingus Fingers,#2* (1960/05/24)
(unissued)	*Minor Mode* (1949/01/19-02/23)
(as)	*Miss Ann* (1960/12/21)
(as)	*Miss Ann* (1961/09/?)
(unissued)	*Miss Ann* (1961/09/06)
(as)	*Miss Ann* (1961/11/19)
(as)	*Miss Ann* (1962/10/07)
(as)	*Miss Ann* (1964/06/02)
(as)	*Miss Movement* (l959/02/04)
(bcl)	*Miss Toni* (1960/04/01)
(as)	*Modes* (1958/10/26)
(NS)	*Mood Indigo* (1963/09/20)
(as)(NS)	*Moods at Dusk* (1949/spring)
(as)	*Moods in Free Time* (1961/04/04)
(as)	*More Than You Know* (1959/02/04)
(as)	*Mr P.C.* (1962/02/10)
(bcl)	*Mrs Parker of K.C.(= Bird's Mother)* (1960/12/21)
(bcl)	*Music Matador* (1963/05-06/?)
(fl)	*My Favorite Things* (1961/11/18)
(fl)	*My Favorite Things* (1961/11/20)
(fl)	*My Favorite Things* (1961/11/23)
(fl)	*My Favorite Things* (1961/11/26)
(fl)	*My Favorite Things* (1961/11/27)
(fl)	*My Favorite Things* (1961/11/29)
(fl)	*My Favorite Things* (1962/02/10)
(unissued)	*My Favorite Things* (1963/12/31)
(NS)	*My Search* (1962/10/12)
(as)	*Mysterious Blues* (1960/11/11)
(bcl)	*Naima* (1961/11/01)
(unissued)	*Naima* (1961/11/03)
(bcl)	*Naima* (1961/11/20)
(bcl)	*Naima* (1961/11/23)
(bcl)	*Naima* (1964/06/11)
(bcl)	*Nardis* (1961/05/08)
(NS)	*Natural Affection* (1963/02/27)
(as)	*Nature by Emerson* (1958/12/29-30)
(as)	*New Monestary* (1964/03/21)
(as)	*Newport News* (l959/02/04)
(NS)	*Night Float* (1960/09/09)
(as)	*Night In Tunisia* (1960-61)
(bcl)	*Night Music* (1963/03/14)
(fl)	*Ode to Charlie Parker* (1960/12/21)
(fl)	*Ode to Charlie Parker* (1963/04/18)
(fl)	*Ode to Charlie Parker* (1963/05-06/?)
(fl)	*Ode to Charlie Parker* (1964/06/11)
(fl)	*Ole* (1961/05/25)
(bcl)	*Oleo* (1961/09/08)
(bcl)	*Oleo* (1961/12/01)
(as)	*Opening* (1959/05/19)
(unissued)	*Orange Was the Color* (1964/04/04)
(bcl)	*Orange Was the Color* (1964/04/10)
(NS)	*Orange Was the Color* (1964/04/12)
(unissued)	*Orange Was the Color* (1964/04/13)

(bcl)	*Orange Was the Color* (1964/04/14)
(bcl)	*Orange Was the Color* (1964/04/17)
(bcl)	*Orange Was the Color* (1964/04/18-19)
(bcl)	*Orange Was the Color* (1964/04/26)
(bcl)	*Orange Was the Color* (1964/04/28)
(as)	*Original Faubus Fables* (1960/10/20)
(as)	*Ornithology* (1962/04/?)
(unissued)	*Osmosis* (1962/10/12)
(as)	*Out of Nowhere* (1961/09/04)
(as)	*Out There*(= *Far Cry*) (1960/08/15)
(as)	*Out to Lunch* (1964/02/25)
(as)	*Parkeriana* (1964/04/10)
(as)	*Parkeriana* (1964/04/12)
(as)	*Parkeriana* (1964/04/16)
(as)	*Parkeriana* (1964/04/17)
(as)	*Parkeriana* (1964/04/18-19)
(unissued)	*Parkeriana* (1964/04/21)
(as)	*Passion Flower* (1958/12/29-30)
(unissued)	*Peggy's Blue Skylight* (1962/10/12)
(as)	*Peggy's Blue Skylight* (1964/04/13)
(as)	*Peggy's Blue Skylight* (1964/04/17)
(as)	*Peggy's Blue Skylight* (1964/04/20)
(as)	*Peggy's Blue Skylight* (1964/04/26)
(as)	*Peggy's Blue Skylight* (1964/04/28)
(NS)	*Pete's Beat* (1949/01/19)
(NS)	*Phantom Moon* (1949/02/23)
(unissued)	*Please Don't Come Back From the Moon* (1962/10/12)
(unissued)	*Portrait* (1962/10/12)
(as)	*Potsa Lotsa*(= *Nunber Eight*) (1961/07/16)
(as)	*Pottsville U.S.A.* (1958/07/04)
(as)	*Pottsville U.S.A.* (1958/10/26)
(NS)	*Praise for a Martyr* (1961/08/08)
(as)	*Prayer for Passive Resistance* (1960/05/25)
(NS)	*Prayer for Passive Resistance* (1960/07/13)
(as)	*Quicksilver* (1962/04/?)
(as)	*Quiet Please* (1961/03/17)
(as)	*R & R* (1960/11/11)
(bcl)	*Rally* (1961/06/20)
(bcl)	*Ralph's New Blues* (1961/03/01)
(as)	*Refuge* (1964/03/21)
(fl)	*Reincarnation of a Lovebird* (1960/10/20)
(NS)	*Reincarnation of a Lovebird* (1960/11/11)
(NS)	*Retribution* (1961/02/22)
(unissued)	*'Round Midnight* (1960/09/09)
(as)	*'Round Midnight* (1961/05/08)
(NS)	*Sampson's Creep* (1949/spring)
(fl)	*Saucer Eyes* (1961/06/20)
(NS)	*Scheherezade Blue* (1963/04/26)
(bcl)	*Screamin' the Blues* (1960/05/27)
(bcl)	*Serene* (1960/08/15)
(bcl)	*Serene* (1960/12/21)
(bcl)	*Serene* (1961/09/25)
(bcl)	*Serene* (1961/11/19)
(bcl)	*Serene* (1964/06/11)

(NS)	*She's Funny That Way* (1959/02/04)
(unissued)	*Shine On* (1960/04/19)
(as)	*Sippin' With Cisco* (1949/01/19)
(as)	*Six and Four* (1961/03/01)
(fl)	*Sketch of Melba* (1960/08/15)
(NS)	*Skylark* (1963/03/08)
(fl)(NS)	*Sleep* (1958-59)
(NS)	*Slide, Mr. Trombone* (1958/10/?)
(as)	*So Long Eric* (1964/04/04)
(as)	*So Long Eric* (1964/04/10)
(as)	*So Long Eric* (1964/04/12)
(as)	*So Long Eric* (1964/04/13)
(as)	*So Long Eric* (1964/04/14)
(as)	*So Long Eric* (1964/04/16)
(as)	*So Long Eric* (1964/04/17)
(as)	*So Long Eric* (1964/04/18-19)
(as)	*So Long Eric* (1964/04/20)
(unissued)	*So Long Eric* (1964/04/21)
(as)	*So Long Eric* (1964/04/26)
(as)	*So Long Eric* (1964/04/28)
(as)	*Softly as in a Morning Sunrise* (1961/06/20)
(bcl)	*Softly as in a Morning Sunrise* (1961/12/01)
(unissued)	*Softly as in a Morning Sunrise* (1963/03/10)
(NS)	*Someone I Love* (1958/10/?)
(bcl)	*Something Sweet Something Tender* (1964/02/25)
(fl)	*Something to Live For* (1958/10/27)
(NS)	*Song of the Underground Railroad* (1961/05/23)
(unissued)	*Sophisticated Lady* (1958/04/?)
(un1ssued)	*South Street Exit* (1963/03/10)
(fl)	*South Street Exit* (1964/06/02)
(bcl)	*Speak Low* (1958/10/27)
(bcl)	*Speak Low* (1960-61)
(as,bcl)	*Spectrum* (1964/03/21)
(bcl)	*Spiritual* (1961/11/01)
(bcl)	*Spiritual* (1961/11/02)
(bcl)	*Spiritual* (1961/11/03)
(bcl)	*Spiritual* (1961/11/05)
(fl)	*Spring is Here* (1960/08/19)
(bcl)	*Springtime* (1964/06/11)
(as)	*Status Seeking* (1961/06/27)
(as)	*Status Seeking* (1961/07/16)
(NS)	*Stolen Moments* (1960/09/20)
(fl)	*Stolen Moments* (1961/02/23)
(as)	*Stormy Weather* (1960/10/20)
(NS)	*Straight Ahead* (1961/02/22)
(as)	*Straight Ahead* (1961/03/01)
(as)	*Straight Up & Down* (1964/02/25)
(as)	*Strange* (1958/10/27)
(NS)	*Strenth & Sanity* (1961/04/04)
(fl)	*Sunday Go Meetin'* (1960/08/19)
(as)	*'Tain't Nobody's Bizness...* (1960/11/01)
(NS)	*Take the A Train/Exactly Like You* (1960/05/25)
(unissued)	*Take the A Train* (1963/09/20)
(bcl)	*Take the A Train* (1964/04/12)

(NS)	*Takin' Care of Business* (1960/08/30)	
(as)	*Teenie's Blues* (1961/02/23)	
(bcl)	*Tender Warriors* (1961/08/03	
(as)	*Tenderly* (1960/12/21)	
(bcl)	*The Baron* (1960/08/15)	
(NS)	*The Best Things in Life are Free* (1959/02/04)	
(NS)	*The Damned Don't Cry* (1961/05/23)	
(as)	*The Drive* (1960/05/27)	
(bcl)	*The First Take* (1960/12/21)	
(as)	*The Madrig Speaks the Panther Walks* (1964/06/02)	
(NS)	*The Masquerade is Over* (1958/10/?)	
(as)	*The Meetin'* (1960/05/27)	
(cl)(NS)	*The Morning After* (1958-59)	
(NS)	*The Outskirts of Town* (1958/10/?)	
(as)	*The Prophet* (1961/07/16)	
(NS)	*The Star Spangled Banner* (1963/02/27)	
(NS)	*The Things We Did Last Summer* (1961/04/?)	
(unissued)	*The Way You Look Tonight* (1960/04/19)	
(as)	*The Way You Look Tonight* (1961/09/08)	
(bcl)	*The Way You Look Tonight* (1961/12/01)	
(fl)(NS)	*Theme for a Starlet* (1959/05/19)	
(NS)	*Theme for Lester Young* (1963/09/20)	
(NS)	*There Is No Greater Love* (1960/early)	
(NS)	*Thermo* (1963/03/11)	
(fl)	*These Foolish Things* (1964/04/28)	
(as)	*They All Laughed* (1960/06/28)	
(as)	*Thirteen* (1961/06/27)	
(NS)	*This is You* (1949/01/19)	
(NS)	*This Little Girl of Mine* (1960/early)	
(bcl)	*Thoughts* (1961/05/08)	
(as)	*Three Seconds* (1960/05/27)	
(NS)	*Tillamook Two* (1962/10/05)	
(fl)	*To Her Ladyship* (1961/05/25)	
(NS)	*Trane Whistle* (1960/09/20)	
(NS)	*Travelin' Light* (1958/10/?)	
(fl)	*Triple Mix* (1960/11/?)	
(as)(NS)	*Truth* (1959/05/19)	
(as)	*Tuesday at Two* (1958/12/29-30)	
(as)	*Under Paris Skies* (1958/10/26)	
(NS)	*Until the Real Thing Comes Along* (1958/10/?)	
(fl)	*Variants on a Theme of John Lewis* (1960/12/20)	
(bcl,fl)	*Variants on a Theme of Monk* (1960/12/20)	
(NS)	*Vassarlean* (1960/10/20)	
(NS)	*Walk Away* (1960/09/20)	
(cl)	*Warm Canto* (1961/06/27)	
(as)	*Warp & Woof* (1961/06/27)	
(as)	*We Diddit* (1961/06/27)	
(as)	*We Speak* (1961/03/17)	
(as)	*Wednesday Night Prayer Meeting* (1960/07/13)	
(NS)	*Weird Nightmare* (1960/05/25)	
(bcl)	*What Is This Thing Called Love?* (1961/09/04)	
(bcl)	*What Love?* (1960/07/13)	
(bcl)	*What Love?* (1960/10/20)	
(bcl)	*When Irish Eyes are Shinin'* (1964/04/13)	

(bcl)	*When Lights are Low* (1961/08/30)
(bcl)	*When Lights are Low* (1961/09/04)
(bcl)	*When Lights are Low* (1961/09/06)
(NS)	*When Malindy Sings* (1961/02/22)
(fl)	*Where I Live* (1958/12/29-30)
(NS)	*Where or When* (1959/02/04)
(NS)	*Whole Nelson* (1960/09/20)
(as)	*Woody'n You* (1961/09/08)
(as)	*Yearnin'* (1961/02/23)
(fl)	*Yes Indeed* (1961/06/20)
(NS)	*You Are Too Beautiful* (1960/09/20)
(fl)	*You Don't Know What Love Is* (1964/06/02)
(bcl)	*You're the Cutest One* (1960-61)
(unissued)	*Yusef Isef Too* (1960/05/24)
(bcl)	*111-44* (1961/03/01)
(fl)	*17 West* (1960/08/15)
(as)	*245* (1960/04/01)
(as)	*245* (1961/08/30)
(as)	*245* (1961/09/04)
(as)	*245* (1962/10/07)
(as)	*245* (1964/06/11)
(as)	*52nd Street Theme* (1961/09/04)

NAME INDEX

Name:	Instruments:	Dates:
Abdul-Malik, Achmed	(oud)	(1961/11/01)
	(oud)	(1961/11/02)
	(oud)	(1961/11/05)
Adams, Pepper	(bar)	(1962/02/16)
	(bar)	(1962/10/12)
	(bar)	(1963/04/26)
Agostina, Gloria	(harp)	(1963/03/14)
Alderson, Roger	(b)	(1949/01/l9)
	(b)	(1949/02/23)
Allen, Gene	(bar)	(1962/10/05)
Alongo, Ray	(frh)	(1964/04/06)
Amalbert, Juan	(cga)	(1960/08/19)
Anderson, Cat	(tp)	(1960/early)
Anderson, John	(tp)	(1958/10/?)
Andrews, Ernie	(v)	(1958/10/?)
Armour, Edward	(tp)	(1962/10/07)
	(tp)	(1962/10/12)
	(tp)	(1963/03/08)
	(tp)	(1963/04/18)
Arrowsmith, William	(oboe)	(1962/10/05)
Ashton, Bob	(bar)	(1960/09/20)
Ashworth, Don	(bar,oboe)	(1963/02/04)
Auer, Pepsi	(p)	(1961/08/30)
Axen, Bent	(p)	(1961/09/06)

	(p)	(1961/09/08)
	(p)	(1961/09/?)
Bailey, Benny	(tp)	(1960/11/01)
	(tp)	(1961/08/30)
Baker, Dave	(tb)	(1961/05/08)
Bambou, Jacky	(cga)	(1964/06/11)
Bank, Danny	(bar)	(1960/05/24)
Barber, Bill	(tu)	(1961/05/23)
	(tu)	(1961/06/06)
	(tu)	(1964/04/06)
Barber, Julian	(viola)	(1963/02/04)
	(viola)	(1963/02/27)
Barron, Bill	(ts)	(1960/05/24)
Barrow, George	(fl,ts)	(1960/09/20)
	(bar)	(1961/02/23)
Bateman, Edgar	(d)	(1962/10/07)
Beal, Gerald	(violin)	(1963/02/04)
	(violin)	(1963/02/27)
Belgrave, Marcus	(tp)	(1960/05/24)
Benjamin, Joe	(b)	(1961/06/27)
Bennink, Han	(d)	(1964/06/02)
Benton, Walter	(ts)	(1961/02/22)
Bernstein, Leonard	(narr)	(1964/02/03)
Bert, Eddie	(tb)	(1960/05/24)
	(tb)	(1962/10/12)
Bishop, Walter	(p)	(1960/06/28)
Blackwell, Ed	(d)	(1960/12/21)
	(d)	(1961/07/16)
Bley, Paul	(p)	(1960/05/25)
	(p)	(1960/11/11)
Block, Al	(fl)	(1963/09/?)
Bowman, Carl	(euphonium)	(1961/06/02)

Breuning, Alfred	(violin)	(1963/02/27)
Bridgewater, Cecil	(tp)	(1963/03/10)
Bright, Kenny	(tp)	(1949/spring)
Brown, Ruth	(v)	(1960/04/19)
	(v)	(1960/08/30)
Bryant, Bobby	(tp)	(1960/09/20)
Budimir, Dennis	(g)	(1958/10/26-27)
	(g)	(1958/12/29-30)
	(g)	(1959/02/04)
	(g)	(1959/05/19-20)
Buffington, Jim	(frh)	(1961/05/23)
	(frh)	(1963/09/?)
Bunick, Nico	(p)	(1960/10/20)
Burrell, Kenny	(g)	(1960/04/19)
	(g)	(1960/08/30)
Bushell, Garvin	(reeds)	(1961/05/23)
	(contrabassoon,oboe)	(1961/11/02)
	(contrabassoon,oboe)	(1961/11/05)
	(bassoon)	(1963/05-06/?)
	(fl)	(1964/04/06)
Butterfield, Don	(tu)	(1960/05/24)
	(tu)	(1962/10/12)
	(tu)	(1963/09/20)
Byard, Jaki	(p)	(1960/04/01)
	(p)	(1960/12/21)
	(p)	(1962/10/12)
	(p)	(1963/09/20)
	(p)	(1964/04/04)
	(p)	(1964/04/10)
	(p)	(1964/04/12)
	(p)	(1964/04/13)
	(p)	(1964/04/14)
	(p)	(1964/04/16)
	(p)	(1964/04/17)
	(p)	(1964/04/18-19)
	(p)	(1964/04/20)
	(p)	(1964/04/21)
	(p)	(1964/04/24)
	(p)	(1964/04/26)
	(p)	(1964/04/28)
Byrd, Donald	(tp)	(1964/06/11)
Calliman, Hadley	(ts)	(1949/spring)

Cameron, Jay	(bar)	(1960/04/19)
	(bar)	(1960/08/30)
Carlsson, Rune	(d)	(1961/09/04)
Carroll, Joe	(v)	(1962/10/07)
Carter, Ron	(cello)	(1960/08/15)
	(b)	(1960/11/?)
	(b)	(1960/12/21)
	(b)	(1961/04/04)
	(b,cello)	(1961/06/20)
	(cello)	(1961/06/27)
	(b)	(1962/02/16)
	(b)	(1962/04/?)
	(b)	(1962/06/03)
	(b)	(1964/04/06)
Casey, Gene	(p)	(1960/08/19)
Chambers, Paul	(b)	(1961/02/23)
	(b)	(1961/05/23)
	(b)	(1963/09/?)
	(b)	(1964/04/06)
Charles, Teddy	(vibes)	(1962/10/12)
	(vibes)	(1963/04/26)
Cherry, Don	(pocket-tp)	(1960/12/21)
Chiasson, Warren	(vibes)	(1963/03/14)
Cipriano, Gene	(as)	(1958/10/?)
Clark, Selwart	(viola)	(1963/02/04)
Cleveland, Jimmy	(tb)	(1960/09/20)
	(tb)	(1962/10/12)
	(tb)	(1963/09/?)
	(tb)	(1964/04/06)
Cocuzzo, Joe	(d)	(1964/02/08)
Cohen, Gil	(frh)	(1963/09/?)
Coker, Henry	(tb)	(1960/early)
Coleman, George	(ts)	(1960/04/19)
	(ts)	(1960/08/30)
Coleman, Ornette	(as)	(1960/12/20)
	(as)	(1960/12/21)

Coles, Johnny	(tp)	(1963/09/?)
	(tp)	(1964/04/04)
	(tp)	(1964/04/06)
	(tp)	(1964/04/10)
	(tp)	(1964/04/12)
	(tp)	(1964/04/13)
	(tp)	(1964/04/14)
	(tp)	(1964/04/16)
	(tp)	(1964/04/17)
Colgrass, Michael	(perc)	(1963/02/27)
Collette, Buddy	(ts)	(1959/02/04)
	(fl,ts)	(1962/10/12)
Collins, Burt	(tp)	(1960/04/19)
	(tp)	(1960/08/30)
Coltrane, John	(ss,ts)	(1961/05/23)
	(ss,ts)	(1961/05/25)
	(ts)	(1961/06/07)
	(ss,ts)	(1961/11/01)
	(ss,ts)	(1961/11/02)
	(ss,ts)	(1961/11/03)
	(ss,ts)	(1961/11/05)
	(ss,ts)	(1961/11/18)
	(ss,ts)	(1961/11/20)
	(ss,ts)	(1961/11/23)
	(ss,ts)	(1961/11/26)
	(ss,ts)	(1961/11/27)
	(ss,ts)	(1961/11/29)
	(ts)	(1961/12/02)
	(ss,ts)	(1962/02/10)
	(ss,ts)	(1963/12/31)
Comfort, Joe	(b)	(1958/10/?)
Corrado, Donald	(frh)	(1961/05/23)
	(frh)	(1961/06/07)
	(frh)	(1963/09/?)
Costa, Eddie	(vibes)	(1960/12/20)
	(vibes)	(1963/03/14)
Cousins, Lorraine	(v)	(1960/05/25)
Cram, Marshall	(btb)	(1958/10/?)
Curson, Ted	(tp)	(1960/05/24)
	(tp)	(1960/05/25)
	(tp)	(1960/07/13)
	(tp)	(1960/11/11)
	(tp)	(1961/10/20)
	(tp)	(1961/04/?)

Cykman, Harry	(violin)	(1963/03/08)
Davis, Art	(b)	(1961/02/22)
	(b)	(1961/03/17)
	(b)	(1961/05/25)
	(b)	(1961/06/07)
	(b)	(1961/08/01)
	(b)	(1961/08/03)
	(b)	(1961/08/08)
	(b)	(1961/08/09)
	(b)	(1963/03/14)
Davis, Charles	(bar)	(1963/03/11)
Davis, Eddie, Lockjaw	(ts)	(1960/09/20)
Davis, Nathan	(ts)	(1964/06/11)
Davis, Richard	(b)	(1961/07/16)
	(b)	(1962/10/05)
	(b)	(1962/10/07)
	(b)	(1963/02/04)
	(b)	(1963/02/27)
	(b)	(1963/03/10)
	(b)	(1963/03/14)
	(b)	(1963/04/18)
	(b)	(1963/05-06/?)
	(b)	(1963/09/?)
	(b)	(1964/01/10)
	(b)	(1964/02/08)
	(b)	(1964/02/25)
	(b)	(1964/03/21)
Davis, Sammy, Jr.	(v)	(1960/early)
Dennis, Willie	(tb)	(1962/10/12)
DeRisi, Al	(tp)	(1963/03/11)
Diaz, Felipe	(vibes)	(c.1960-61)
DiDomenica, Robert	(fl)	(1960/05/24)
	(fl)	(1960/12/20)
	(fl,picc)	(1963/02/04)
	(fl,p1cc)	(1963/02/27)
Dieval, Jacques	(p)	(1964/06/11)
Dorham, Kenny	(p)	(1960/11/01)
	(tp)	(1964/03/21)
Dotson, Hobart	(tp)	(1960/05/24)
Drew, Kenny	(p)	(1961/04/?)

Dunn, Clyde	(p)	(1964/05-06/?)
	(bar)	(1949/01/19)
	(bar)	(1949/02/23)
Duvivier, George	(b)	(1960/05/27)
	(b)	(1960/08/15)
	(b)	(1960/09/09)
	(b)	(1960/12/20)
	(b)	(1961/03/01)
	(b)	(1961/06/20)
Eidus, Arnold	(violin)	(1963/03/08)
Eldridge, Roy	(tp)	(1960/11/11)
Ellington, Bill	(b)	(1960/08/19)
Ellis, Don	(tp)	(1961/05/08)
	(tp)	(1962/06/03)
	(tp)	(1963/04/18)
	(tp)	(1964/02/08)
Elniff, Jorn	(d)	(1961/09/06)
	(d)	(1961/09/08)
Ericson, Ralph	(tp)	(1962/10/12)
Ervin, Booker	(ts)	(1960/05/25)
	(ts)	(1960/07/13)
	(ts)	(1960/10/20)
	(ts)	(1960/11/11)
	(ts)	(1961/06/27)
	(ts)	(1962/10/12)
	(ts)	(1963/09/20)
Eugenio, Carlos	(cowbell)	(1961/08/01)
	(cowbell)	(1961/04/03)
	(cowbell)	(1961/08/09)
Evans, Bill	(p)	(1960/12/20)
	(p)	(1961/02/23)
	(p)	(1962/04/?)
	(p)	(1963/09/?)
	(p)	(1964/04/06)
Evans, Sticks	(perc)	(1960/05/24)
	(d)	(1960/12/20)
	(perc)	(1963/02/27)
	(d)	(1963/03/14)
Farmer, Addison	(b)	(1949/spring)
Farmer, Art	(tp)	(1949/01/19)
	(tp)	(1949/02/23)

163

Farrell, Joe	(tp)	(1949/spring)
	(ts)	(1960/05/24)
	(ts)	(1960/05/25)
Flanagan, Tommy	(p)	(1960/04/19)
	(p)	(1960/08/30)
	(p)	(1960/11/11)
Fohrenbach, Jean-Claude	(ts)	(1964/06/?)
Foster, Frank	(ts)	(1960/early)
Fowlkes, Charles	(bar)	(1960/early)
Freeman, Russ	(p)	(1949/spring)
Friedman, Don	(p)	(1961/03/17)
	(p)	(1961/04/04)
Fuller, Curtis	(tb)	(1963/03/08)
	(tb)	(1963/03/11)
	(tb)	(1963/05/02)
Galbraith, Barry	(g)	(1962/06/03)
	(g)	(1963/03/14)
	(g)	(1963/09/?)
Garrison, Jimmy	(b)	(1961/04/?)
	(b)	(1961/11/01)
	(b)	(1961/11/02)
	(b)	(1961/11/03)
	(b)	(1961/11/05)
	(b)	(1962/02/10)
	(b)	(1963/12/31)
Gaylor, Hal	(b)	(1958/04/?)
	(b)	(1958/07/04)
Gershman, Nathan	(cello)	(1958/04/?)
	(cello)	(1958/07/04)
	(cello)	(1958/10/26-27)
	(cello)	(1958/12/29-30)
	(cello)	(1959/02/04)
	(cello)	(1959/05/19-20)
Giuffre, Jimmy	(bar)	(1960/09/09)
Glickman, Loren	(bassoon)	(1962/10/O5)
Glow, Bernie	(tp)	(1964/04/06)
Glucken, Leo	(tp)	(1962/06/03)
Goldberg, Alla	(cello)	(1963/02/04)
	(cello)	(1963/02/27)

Goldstein, Nathan	(violin) (violin)	(1963/02/04) (1963/02/27)
Golson, Benny	(ts) (ts) (ts)	(1960/09/09) (1963/04/18) (1964/02/08)
Gordon, Bob	(bar)	(1949/spring)
Gozzo, Conrad	(tp)	(1958/10/?)
Grant, Harold	(g,v)	(1949/spring)
Grant, Jewell	(bar)	(1958/10/?)
Green, Bill	(ts) (bar)	(1958/10/?) (1959/02/04)
Greene, Freddie	(g)	(1960/early)
Greenlea, Charles	(tb) (tb) (tb) (euphonium)	(1960/04/19) (1960/08/30) (1960/05/24) (1961/05/23)
Grey, Al	(tb)	(1960/early)
Grey, Sonny	(tp)	(1964/06/?)
Haden, Charlie	(b)	(1960/12/21)
Hafer, Dick	(cl,fl,ts) (cl,fl,ts)	(1962/10/12) (1963/09/20)
Hall, Jim	(g) (g) (g) (g) (g) (g) (g)	(1960/09/09) (1960/12/20) (1962/10/05) (1963/02/04) (1963/02/27) (1963/03/14) (1963/04/18)
Hamilton, Chico	(d) (d,v) (d,v) (d) (d,v) (d)	(1958/04/?) (1958/07/04) (1958/10/26-27) (1958/12/29-30) (1959/02/04) (1959/05/19-20)
Hampton, Slide	(tb) (tb)	(1960/05/24) (1962/06/03)
Hancock, Herbie	(p) (p)	(1962/10/07) (1963/03/10)
Hanna, Roland	(p)	(1960/05/24)

	(p)	(1960/05/25)
Hardman, Bill	(tp)	(1962/04/?)
Harrison, Joe	(p)	(1949/01/19)
	(p)	(1949/02/23)
Hawkins, Coleman	(ts)	(1961/02/22)
Hayes, Louis	(d)	(1963/05/02)
Haynes, Roy	(d)	(1960/04/01)
	(d)	(1960/05/27)
	(d)	(1960/08/15)
	(d)	(1960/09/20)
	(d)	(1960/12/21)
	(d)	(1961/02/23)
	(d)	(1961/03/01)
	(d)	(1961/04/?)
	(d)	(1961/11/02)
Heath, Jimmy	(ts)	(1962/02/16)
Held, Julius	(strings)	(1963/03/08)
Henderson, Joe	(ts)	(1964/03/21)
Hess, Jacques	(b)	(1964/06/11)
Higgins, Billy	(d)	(1960/12/21)
Hill, Andrew	(p)	(1964/03/21)
Hillyer, Lonnie	(tp)	(1960/10/20)
	(tp)	(1960/11/11)
	(tp)	(1962/10/12)
Hinton, Milt	(b)	(1962/10/12)
	(b)	(1963/09/?)
Horn, Paul	(as)	(1959/02/04)
Horton, Danny	(tb)	(1949/01/19)
	(tb)	(1949/02/23)
	(tb)	(1949/spring)
Howard, Joe	(ts)	(1949/01/19)
	(ts)	(1949/02/23)
	(ts)	(1949/spring)
Hubbard, Freddie	(tp)	(1960/04/01)
	(tp)	(1960/12/21)
	(tp)	(1961/02/23)
	(tp)	(1961/05/23)

	(tp)	(1961/05/25)
	(tp)	(1963/03/08)
	(tp)	(1963/03/11)
	(tp)	(1963/05/02)
	(tp)	(1964/02/25)
Humair, Daniel	(d)	(1964/05-06/?)
Hunt, Joe	(d)	(1961/05/08)
Hutcherson, Bobby	(vibes)	(1963/0-06/?)
	(vibes)	(1964/02/25)
Israels, Chuck	(b)	(1961/09/08)
	(b)	(1963/03/14)
Jackson, Quentin	(tb)	(1962/10/12)
Jenkins, Arthur	(p)	(c.1960-61)
Johansson, Rony	(p)	(1961/09/04)
Johnson Osie	(d)	(1962/10/12)
	(d)	(1963/04/26)
	(d)	(1963/09/?)
Johnson, Plas	(ts)	(1958/10/?)
Jones, Ed	(b)	(1960/early)
Jones Elvin	(d)	(1961/05/23)
	(d)	(1961/05/25)
	(d)	(1961/06/07)
	(d)	(1961/11/01)
	(d)	(1961/11/02)
	(d)	(1961/11/03)
	(d)	(1961/11/05)
	(d)	(1961/11/18)
	(d)	(1961/11/20)
	(d)	(1961/11/23)
	(d)	(1961/11/26)
	(d)	(1961/11/27)
	(d)	(1961/11/29)
	(d)	(1961/12/02)
	(d)	(1962/02/10)
	(d)	(1962/02/16)
	(d)	(1963/09/?)
	(d)	(1963/12/31)
	(d)	(1964/04/06)
Jones, Harold	(fl)	(1962/10/05)
Jones, Jo	(d)	(1960/11/01)
	(d)	(1960/11/11)

Jones, Philly Joe	(d)	(1963/03/08)
	(d)	(1963/03/11)
Jones, Sam	(b)	(1960/06/28)
Jones, Thad	(tp)	(1960/early)
Jordan, Clifford	(ts)	(1961/08/01)
	(ts)	(1961/08/03)
	(ts)	(1961/08/08)
	(ts)	(1961/08/09)
	(ts)	(1962/02/16)
	(ss)	(1963/05-06/?)
	(ts)	(1964/04/04)
	(ts)	(1964/04/10)
	(ts)	(1964/04/12)
	(ts)	(1964/04/13)
	(ts)	(1964/04/14)
	(ts)	(1964/04/16)
	(ts)	(1964/04/17)
	(ts)	(1964/04/18-19)
	(ts)	(1964/04/20)
	(ts)	(1964/04/21)
	(ts)	(1964/04/24)
	(ts)	(1964/04/26)
	(ts)	(1964/04/28)
Jorgensen, Knud	(p)	(1961/09/?)
Juvelier, Aaron	(viola)	(1963/02/27)
Kahn, Eddie	(b)	(1963/05-06/?)
Kallin, Sture	(d)	(1961/09/?)
	(d)	(1961/11/19)
Kane, Wally	(fl,bassoon)	(1963/02/04)
	(fl,bassoon)	(1963/02/27)
Kaplan, Lewis	(violin) (1963/03/14)	
Katzman, Harry	(strings)	(1963/03/08)
Kay, Connie	(d)	(1960/09/09)
	(d)	(1962/10/05)
	(d)	(1963/02/04)
	(d)	(1963/02/27)
	(d)	(1964/01/10)
Kidd, Alvey	(cga)	(1949/01/19)
	(cga)	(1949/02/23)
	(cga)	(1949/spring)
Knepper, Jimny	(tb)	(1949/01/19)

	(tb)	(1949/02/23)
	(tb)	(1949/spring)
	(tb)	(1960/05/24)
	(tb)	(1960/05/25)
	(tb)	(1960/10/20)
	(tb)	(1960/11/11)
	(tb)	(1962/10/12)
	(tb)	(1963/04/18)
Kotick, Teddy	(b)	(1963/04/26)
Kyner, Sonny, Red	(as)	(1962/02/16)
Lacy, Steve	(ss)	(1963/09/?)
	(ss)	(1964/04/06)
LaFaro, Scott	(b)	(1960/12/20)
	(b)	(1960/12/21)
Lalli, Gina	(tabla,v)	(1960/07/08)
LaPorta, John	(as,cl)	(1960/05/24)
Lasha, Prince	(fl)	(1963/05-06/?)
Lateef, Yusef	(fl,ts)	(1960/05/24)
	(ts)	(1960/05/25)
Lewis, John	(p)	(1960/09/09)
	(p)	(1962/10/05)
	(p)	(1963/02/04)
	(p)	(1963/02/27)
	(p)	(1964/01/10)
Lewis, Mel	(d)	(1961/12/01)
Libove, Charles	(violin)	(1960/12/20)
Lieb, Dick	(tb)	(1962/06/03)
Lincoln, Abbey	(v)	(1960/11/01)
	(v)	(1961/02/22)
	(v)	(1961/08/01)
Lindgren, Kurt	(b)	(1961/09/04)
Liston, Melba	(tb)	(1960/09/20)
	(tb)	(1963/03/08)
	(tb)	(1963/03/11)
Little, Booker	(tp)	(1960/12/21)
	(tp)	(1961/02/22)
	(tp)	(1961/03/17)
	(tp)	(1961/04/04)

	(tp)	(1961/05/23)
	(tp)	(1961/06/07)
	(tp)	(1961/07/16)
	(tp)	(1961/08/01)
	(tp)	(1961/08/03)
	(tp)	(1961/08/08)
	(tp)	(1961/08/09)
Lookofsky, Harry	(violin)	(1963/03/08)
Lopez, Tommy	(cga)	(c.1960-61)
Mahones, Gildo	(p)	(1962/02/16)
Maini, Joe	(as)	(1949/spring)
Manzecchi, Franco	(d)	(1964/06/11)
Mariano, Charlie	(as)	(1960/04/19)
	(as)	(1960/08/30)
	(as)	(1962/10/12)
Mariano, Toshiko	(p)	(1962/10/12)
Marshall, Wendell	(b)	(1960/09/20)
Mason, Roger	(tamboura)	(1960/07/08)
McCracken, Charles	(cello)	(1960/05/24)
	(cello)	(1963/03/08)
McFall, Reuben	(tp)	(1949/spring)
McFarland, Gary	(cond)	(1962/10/05)
	(perc)	(1963/02/04)
McIntyre, Ken	(as,fl)	(1960/06/28)
McKinney, Bernard	(tb)	(1960/04/19)
	(tb)	(1960/08/30)
McPherson, Charles	(as)	(1960/10/20)
	(as)	(1960/11/11)
	(as)	(1962/10/12)
Mengelberg, Misha	(p)	(1964/06/01-02)
Metlock, James	(tp)	(1949/01/19)
	(tp)	(1940/02/23)
Mingus, Charles	(b)	(1960/05/24)
	(b)	(1960/05/25)
	(b,p)	(1960/07/13)
	(b,vcl)	(1960/10/20)
	(b)	(1960/11/11)

170

	(b,narr)	(1962/10/12)
	(b,narr)	(1963/09/20)
	(b)	(1964/04/04)
	(b,voice)	(1964/04/10)
	(b,voice)	(1964/04/12)
	(b,voice)	(1964/04/13)
	(b,voice)	(1964/04/14)
	(b,voice)	(1964/04/16)
	(b,voice)	(1964/04/17)
	(b,voice)	(1964/04/18-19)
	(b)	(1964/04/20)
	(b)	(1964/04/21)
	(b,voice)	(1964/04/24)
	(b,voice)	(1964/04/26)
	(b,voice)	(1964/04/28)
Mitchell, Billy	(ts)	(1960/early)
Moffett, Charles	(d)	(1963/05-06/?)
Moncur, Grachan,III	(tb)	(1962/04/?)
Monterose, J.R.	(ts)	(1962/06/03)
Moore, Danny	(tp)	(1960/04/19)
	(tp)	(1960/08/30)
Morrison, John, Peck	(b)	(1960/11/01)
Moseholm, Erik	(b)	(1961/09/06)
	(b)	(1961/09/08)
	(b)	(1961/09/?)
Moses, J.C.	(d)	(1963/03/10)
	(d)	(1963/04/18)
	(d)	(1963/05-06/?)
Mucci, Louis	(tp)	(1963/02/04)
	(tp)	(1963/02/27)
	(tp)	(1963/09/?)
Nasser, Jamil	(b)	(1961/08/30)
Nelson, Oliver	(as,ts)	(1960/05/27)
	(as)	(1960/09/20)
	(as,ts)	(1961/02/23)
	(as,cl,ts)	(1961/03/01)
Newman, Bob	(ts)	(1960/04/19)
	(ts)	(1960/08/30)
Newman, Joe	(tp)	(1960/early)
Northern, Bob	(frh)	(1961/05/23)
	(frh)	(1961/06/07)
	(frh)	(1963/02/04)

	(frh)	(1963/02/27)
	(frh)	(1963/03/08)
	(frh)	(1963/03/11)
	(frh)	(1963/09/?)
Ofwerman, Rene	(p)	(1961/11/19)
Oliver, Sy	(cond)	(1960/early)
Orloff, Gene	(strings)	(1963/03/08)
Overton, Hall	(p)	(1963/04/26)
Palmer, Earl	(d)	(1958/10,?)
Patrick, Pat	(bar)	(1961/05/23)
	(bar)	(1961/06/07)
Payne, Sonny	(d)	(1960/early)
Pedersen, Guy	(b)	(1964/05-06/?)
Pena, Ralph	(b)	(1959/05/19-20)
Perkins, Walter	(d)	(1963/09/20)
Persip, Charlie	(d)	(1961/06/20)
	(d)	(1961/06/27)
	(d)	(1962/04/?)
	(d)	(1962/06/03)
	(d)	(1963/04/18)
Philips, Harvey	(tu)	(1963/02/04)
	(tu)	(1963/02/27)
Phillips, Barre	(b)	(1963/03/14)
	(b)	(1963/04/18)
Pisano, John	(g)	(1958/04/?)
	(g)	(1958/07/04)
Poindexter, Pony	(as)	(1962/02/16)
Poliakin, Paul	(strings)	(1963/03/08)
Pomeroy, Herb	(tp)	(1960/09/09)
	(tp)	(1963/02/04)
	(tp)	(1963/02/27)
Porcino, Al	(tp)	(1958/10/?)
Porter, Roy	(d)	(1949/01/19)
	(d)	(1949/02/23)
	(d)	(1949/spring)

172

Powell, Benny	(tb)	(1960/early)
Powell, Bud	(p)	(1960/07/13)
Powell, Robert	(tu)	(1963/03/11)
Powell, Seldon	(ts)	(1963/03/11)
Preston, Eddie	(tp)	(1949/01/19)
	(tp)	(1949/02/23)
	(tp)	(1963/09/20)
Priester, Julian	(tb)	(1960/04/19)
	(tb)	(1960/08/30)
	(tb)	(1961/02/22)
	(tb)	(1961/03/17)
	(tb)	(1961/04/04)
	(euphonium)	(1961/05/23)
	(tb)	(1961/08/01)
	(tb)	(1961/08/03)
	(tb)	(1961/08/08)
	(tb)	(1961/08/09)
Pring, Bob	(tb)	(1958/10/?)
Raimondi, Matthew	(violin)	(1963/03/14)
Ramirez, Louis	(timbales) (c.1960-61)	
Ramos, Manuel	(d,timbales)	(1960/08/19)
Raney, Jimmy	(g)	(1963/04/26)
Rhodes, George	(p)	(1960/early)
Rhodes, Samuel	(violin)	(1963/03/14)
Richardson, Jerome	(fl,ts)	(1960/09/20)
	(bar,fl,oboe,ss)	(1962/10/12)
	(bar)	(1963/03/08)
	(bar)	(1963/03/11)
	(fl,ts)	(1963/04/26)
	(bar,fl,ss)	(1963/09/20)
	(bar,fl)	(1963/09/?)
Richmond, Danny	(d)	(1960/05/24)
	(d)	(l960/05/25)
	(d)	(1960/07/13)
	(d,voice)	(1960/10/20)
	(d)	(1960/11/11)
	(d)	(1962/10/12)
	(d)	(1964/04/04)
	(d,voice)	(1964/04/10)
	(d,voice)	(1964/04/12)

	(d,voice)	(1964/04/13)
	(d,voice)	(1964/04/14)
	(d,voice)	(1964/04/16)
	(d,voice)	(1964/04/17)
	(d,voice)	(1964/04/18-19)
	(d)	(1964/04/20)
	(d)	(1964/04/21)
	(d,voice)	(1964/04/24)
	(d,voice)	(1964/04/26)
	(d,voice)	(1964/04/28)
Roach, Max	(perc)	(1960/05/24)
	(d)	(1961/02/22)
	(d)	(1961/03/17)
	(d)	(1961/04/04)
	(d)	(1961/08/01)
	(d)	(1961/08/03)
	(d)	(1961/08/08)
	(d)	(1961/08/09)
Robinson, Leroy	(as)	(1949/01/19)
	(as)	(1949/02/23)
Rodriguez, Bobby	(b)	(c.1960-61)
Ross, Margaret	(harp)	(1963/09/?)
Ross, Robert	(tp)	(1949/01/19)
	(tp)	(1949/02/23)
	(tp)	(1949/spring)
Royal, Ernie	(tp)	(1960/04/19)
	(tp)	(1960/08/20)
	(tp)	(1962/10/12)
	(tp)	(1963/03/11)
	(tp)	(1963/09/?)
Royal, Marshall	(as)	(1960/early)
Rudiakov, Michael	(cello)	(1963/03/14)
Russell, George	(p)	(1961/05/08)
Ruther, Wyatt	(b)	(1958/10/26-27)
	(b)	(1958/12/29-30)
	(b)	(1959/02/04)
	(b)	(1959/05/19)
Sambucco, Gino	(violin)	(1963/02/04)
	(violin)	(1963/02/27)
Sanders, Roger	(cga)	(1961/02/22)
Schiffrin, Lalo	(p)	(1963/04/18)

Schiopffe, William	(d)	(1961/09/?)
Schols, Jacques	(b)	(1964/06/01-02)
Schuller, Gunther	(cond) (frh) (cond) (cond) (cond) (cond)	(1960/05/24) (1960/09/09) (1960/12/20) (1963/02/04) (1963/02/27) (1964/02/08)
Scott, George	(perc)	(1960/05/24)
Shapiro, Sol	(violin)	(1963/03/08)
Shaw, Woody	(tp)	(1963/05-06/?)
Shiner, Ray	(oboe) (oboe)	(1963/02/04) (1963/02/27)
Shorter, Wayne	(cond) (cond) (ts)	(1963/03/08) (1963/03/11) (1963/05/02)
Shulman, Harry	(oboe)	(1960/05/24)
Simmons, Sonny	(as)	(1963/05-06/?)
Simons, Charles	(vibes)	(1960/08/19)
Sims, Pete	(d) (d)	(1960/04/19) (1960/08/30)
Sims, Zoot	(ts) (ts)	(1962/10/12) (1963/04/26)
Smith, Buster	(d)	(1961/08/30)
Solomon, Clifford	(ts) (ts)	(1949/01/19) (1949/02/23)
Spann, Les	(g)	(1962/10/12)
Sparks, Paul	(v) (v)	(1949/01/19) (1949/02/23)
Stewart, Don	(basset-horn) (cl,basset-horn) (cl,basset-horn)	(1962/10/05) (1963/02/04) (1963/02/27)
Stonzek, Morris	(violin)	(1963/03/08)
Studd, Tony	(tb)	(1963/09/?)

	(tb)	(1964/04/06)
Sulieman, Idries	(tp)	(1961/11/19)
Summerlin, Ed	(cond)	(1962/06/03)
Swallow, Steve	(b)	(1961/05/08)
Swisshelm, Bob	(frh)	(1961/05/23)
	(frh)	(1961/06/07)
	(frh)	(1963/02/04)
	(frh)	(1963/02/27)
Taylor, Art	(d)	(1960/05/28)
Tekula, Joseph	(cello)	(1960/12/20)
	(cello)	(1963/02/04)
	(cello)	(1963/02/27)
Terry, Clark	(tp)	(1960/05/24)
	(tp)	(1960/10/20)
	(tp)	(1962/10/12)
	(tp)	(1963/03/11)
Thollot, Jacques	(d)	(1964/06/?)
Totah, Knoby	(b)	(1960/04/19)
	(b)	(1960/08/30)
Travis, Nick	(tp)	(1963/02/04)
	(tp)	(1963/02/27)
	(tp)	(1963/04/18)
	(tp)	(1964/01/10)
Tricarico, Bob	(ts)	(1963/09/?)
	(fl,ts)	(1964/04/06)
Tristardo, Luigi	(b)	(1964/06/?)
Tucker, Ben	(b)	(1963/09/?)
Tucker, George	(b)	(1960/04/01)
Tyner, McCoy	(p)	(1961/05/23)
	(p)	(1961/05/25)
	(p)	(1961/06/07)
	(p)	(1961/11/01)
	(p)	(1961/11/02)
	(p)	(1961/11/03)
	(p)	(1961/11/05)
	(p)	(1961/11/18)
	(p)	(1961/11/20)
	(p)	(1961/11/23)
	(p)	(1961/11/26)

	(p)	(1961/11/27)
	(p)	(1961/11/29)
	(p)	(1961/12/01)
	(p)	(1961/12/02)
	(p)	(1962/02/10)
	(p)	(1963/12/31)
Valeler, Carlos	(cga)	(1961/08/01)
	(cga)	(1961/08/03)
	(cga)	(1961/08/09)
Vamos, Roland	(violin)	(1960/12/20)
Waldron, Mal	(p)	(1961/02/22)
	(p)	(1961/06/20)
	(p)	(1961/06/27)
	(p)	(1961/07/16)
	(p)	(1961/08/01)
	(p)	(1961/08/03)
	(p)	(1961/08/08)
	(p)	(1961/08/09)
Walton, Cedar	(p)	(1963/03/08)
	(p)	(1963/03/11)
	(p)	(1963/05/02)
Watkins, Julius	(frh)	(1961/05/23)
	(frh)	(1961/06/07)
	(frh)	(1963/03/08)
	(frh)	(1963/09/?)
Wells, Dave	(tb)	(1958/10/?)
West, Philip	(oboe,Eh)	(1963/02/27)
White, Benny	(g)	(1949/01/19)
	(g)	(1949/02/23)
Whitley, Robert	(cga)	(1961/02/22)
Widoff, Jerry	(violin)	(1963/02/04)
Wiggins, Gerald	(p)	(1958/10/?)
Wiginton, William	(tb)	(1949/01/19)
	(tb)	(1949/02/23)
	(tb)	(1949/spring)
Williams, Richard	(tp)	(1960/04/19)
	(tp)	(1960/05/24)
	(tp)	(1960/05/27)
	(tp)	(1960/08/30)
	(tp)	(1960/09/20)
	(tp)	(1962/10/12)

	(tp)	(1963/03/08)
	(tp)	(1963/09/20)
Williams, Tony	(d)	(1964/02/25)
	(d)	(1964/03/21)
Woode, Jimmy	(b)	(1961/09/?)
	(b)	(1961/11/19)
Woodman, Britt	(tb)	(1960/10/20)
	(tb)	(1961/06/07)
	(tb)	(1962/10/12)
	(tb)	(1963/09/20)
Woods, Phil	(cl)	(1962/10/05)
	(as,cl)	(1963/02/04)
	(as,cl)	(1963/02/27)
	(as)	(1963/04/18)
Workman, Reggie	(b)	(1961/05/23)
	(b)	(1961/05/25)
	(b)	(1961/06/07)
	(b)	(1961/11/01)
	(b)	(1961/11/02)
	(b)	(1961/11/03)
	(b)	(1961/11/05)
	(b)	(1961/11/18)
	(b)	(1961/11/20)
	(b)	(1961/11/23)
	(b)	(1961/11/26)
	(b)	(1961/11/27)
	(b)	(1961/11/29)
	(b)	(1961/12/01)
	(b)	(1961/12/02)
	(b)	(1963/03/08)
	(b)	(1963/03/11)
	(b)	(1963/05/02)
Wyands, Richard	(p)	(1960/05/27)
	(p)	(1960/09/20)
	(p)	(1961/03/01)
Young, Snooky	(tp)	(1960/early)
	(tp)	(1962/10/12)
Zaratzian, Harry	(viola)	(1960/12/20)
Zwerin, Mike	(tb)	(1963/02/04)
	(tb)	(1963/02/27)
	(b-tp)	(1964/01/10)

Bibliography

ARTICLES ABOUT ERIC DOLPHY

Avakian, George. "A Gentle Gentleman of a Man," *Jazz*, October 1964,
     p. 14.
Cooke, Jack. "Eric Dolphy," *Jazz Monthly*, January 1966, pp. 25–30.
Coss, Bill. "Caught in the Act: Eric Dolphy-Ree Dragonette," *Down Beat*,
     17 January 1963, pp. 42–43.
DeMichael, Don. "John Coltrane and Eric Dolphy Answer the Jazz Critics,"
     Down Beat, 12 April 1962, pp. 20–30.
Feather, Leonard. *The Encyclopedia of Jazz in the Sixties* (New York: Hori-
     zon Press, 1966), pp. 108–9.
Heckman, Don. "The Value of Eric Dolphy," *Down Beat*, 8 October 1964,
     p. 17.
"In Tribute: Eric Dolphy 1928–1964," *Down Beat*, 27 August 1964, p. 10.
"Reed Man Eric Dolphy Dies in Berlin," *Down Beat*, 13 August 1964, p. 8.
Robinson, Stanley G. "The Modern Touch," in *The Los Angeles Sentinel*,
     9 July 1964, p. 6B.
Williams, Martin. "Introducing Eric Dolphy," *The Jazz Review*, July 1960,
     p. 16.
———. "Introducing Eric Dolphy," in *Jazz Panorama* (New York: Collier
     Books, 1964), pp. 281–3 (reprints the above).

ADDITIONAL REFERENCES USED IN THE TEXT

"Ad Lib," *Down Beat*, 5 January 1961, pp. 10, 46; 27 September 1962,
     p. 10; 9 April 1964, p. 44.
Balliett, Whitney. *Such Sweet Thunder* (New York: Bobbs-Merrill, 1966),
     pp. 63–4, 96.
"Chords and Discords: Mingus Replies," *Down Beat*, 17 January 1963,
     p. 8.
Coss, Bill. "Caught in the Act: a Report of a Most Remarkable Event,"
     Down Beat, 6 December 1962, p. 40.
———. "John Lewis and the Orchestra," *Down Beat*, 14 February 1963,
     p. 20.
DeMichael, Don. "The Monterey Festival," *Down Beat*, 9 November 1961,
     p. 12–14.
Feather, Leonard. *The Encyclopedia of Jazz in the Sixties*, New York: Hori-
     zon Press, 1966.
Heckman, Don. "Caught in the Act: Gunther Schuller," *Down Beat*, 9 May
     1963, p. 34.
———. "Ron Carter," *Down Beat*, 9 April 1964, pp. 18–19.

Hoefer, George. "Caught in the Act: Gunther Schuller," *Down Beat*, 1 September 1960, p. 44.

"In Between, the Adventure," *Down Beat*, 13 April 1961, p. 15.

"International Jazz Critics Poll," *Down Beat*, 3 August 1961, pp. 16–24, 44–62.

Jones, Leroi. "Ted Curson," *Down Beat*, 30 August 1962, pp. 20, 37.

———. "Caught in the Act: John Coltrane-Cecil Taylor-Art Blakey," *Down Beat*, 27 February 1964, p. 34.

Lees, Gene. "Trouble at Newport," *Down Beat*, 18 August 1960, pp. 20–23, 44.

———. "View of the Third Stream," *Down Beat*, 13 February 1964, pp. 16–17.

Mingus, Charles. *Beneath the Underdog*, New York: Alfred A. Knopf, 1971.

"Mingus Sharply Criticized for Tour Behavior," *Down Beat*, 18 June 1964, p. 10.

"Mingus in Europe, Part II—or Get It Straight," *Down Beat*, 16 July 1964, p. 11.

Morgenstern, Dan. "Richard Davis: the Complete Musician," *Down Beat*, 2 June 1966, pp. 16–17.

"Music: Flute Fever," *Time*, 11 March 1966, p. 49.

Spellman, A. B. *Four Lives in the Bebop Business* (New York: Pantheon, 1966), p. 15.

Thiele, Bob. "Mingus Ho-Hum," *Jazz*, October 1964, pp. 20–21.

Tynan, John. "Take 5," *Down Beat*, 23 November 1961, p. 40.

Welding, Pete. "Report From Washington: First International Jazz Festival," *Down Beat*, 19 July 1962, pp. 20–21, 60.

———. "Caught in the Act: Gunther Schuller," *Down Beat*, 20 December 1962, p. 39.

Williams, Martin. "Caught in the Act: Sonny Rollins-John Lewis," *Down Beat*, 5 July 1962, p. 38.

———. "Two Reviews of 'Third Stream' Music; II. Full Face (1960)," in *Jazz Panorama* (New York: Collier Books, 1964), pp. 302–5.

Other titles of interest

ASCENSION
John Coltrane and his Quest
Eric Nisenson
298 pp.
80644-4 $13.95

**BIRD: The Legend
of Charlie Parker**
Edited by Robert Reisner
256 pp., 50 photos
80069-1 $13.95

**BIRD LIVES!
The High Life and Hard Times of
Charlie (Yardbird) Parker**
Ross Russell
431 pp., 32 photos
80679-7 $15.95

**CHASIN' THE TRANE
The Music and Mystique
of John Coltrane**
J. C. Thomas
256 pp., 16 pp. of photos
80043-8 $10.95

CHUCK STEWART'S JAZZ FILES
Photographs by Charles Stewart
Text by Paul Carter Harrison
144 pp., 215 photos
80442-5 $17.95

JAZZ PEOPLE
Valerie Wilmer
167 pp., 14 photos
80434-4 $11.95

**JAZZ SPOKEN HERE
Conversations with 22 Musicians**
Wayne Enstice and Paul Rubin
330 pp., 22 photos
80545-6 $14.95

THE JAZZ WORD
Edited by Dom Cerulli,
Burt Korall, and
Mort L. Nasatir
248 pp., 7 photos
80288-0 $9.95

JOHN COLTRANE
Bill Cole
278 pp., 25 photos
80530-8 $13.95

**KEITH JARRETT
The Man and His Music**
Ian Carr
264 pp., 20 illus.
80478-6 $13.95

**MILES DAVIS
The Early Years**
Bill Cole
256 pp. 80554-5 $13.95